RAIN/DRIZZLE/FOG

CINEMAS OFF CENTRE SERIES

Malek Khouri, general editor

The Cinemas Off Centre series highlights bodies of cinematic work that, for various reasons, have been ignored, marginalized, overlooked, and/or obscured within traditional and dominant canons of film and cinema studies. The series presents cutting edge research that provokes and inspires new explorations of past, present, and emerging cinematic trends by individuals and groups of filmmakers from around the world.

EDITED BY DARRELL VARGA

RAIN/DRIZZLE/FOG
FILM AND TELEVISION IN ATLANTIC CANADA

UNIVERSITY OF
CALGARY
PRESS

CINEMAS OFF CENTRE SERIES · No. 2

University of Calgary Press
2500 University Drive NW
Calgary, Alberta
Canada T2N 1N4
www.uofcpress.com

LIBRARY AND ARCHIVES CANADA CATALOGUING IN PUBLICATION

Rain, drizzle, fog : film and television in Atlantic Canada / edited by Darrell Varga.

(Cinemas off centre series; 1912-3094; 2)
Includes bibliographical references and index.
ISBN 978-1-55238-248-6

1. Motion pictures–Atlantic Provinces–History and criticism. 2. Television programs–Atlantic Provinces–History. 3. Motion pictures producers and directors–Atlantic Provinces–History.
I. Varga, Darrell, 1966- II. Series.
PN1993.5.C3R34 2008   791.4309715   C2008-906202-7

The University of Calgary Press acknowledges the support of the Alberta Foundation for the Arts for our publications. We acknowledge the financial support of the Government of Canada through the Book Publishing Industry Development Program (BPIDP) for our publishing activities. We acknowledge the financial support of the Canada Council for the Arts for our publishing program.

This book has been published with the help of a grant from the Canadian Federation for the Humanities and Social Sciences, through the Aid to Scholarly Publications Programme, using funds provided by the Social Sciences and Humanities Research Council of Canada.

Printed and bound in Canada by Marquis Printing Inc.
∞ This book is printed on FSC Silva Edition paper

Cover design, page design and typesetting by Melina Cusano

Table of Contents

Acknowledgments

This book has been published with the help of a grant from the Canadian Federation for the Humanities and Social Sciences, through the Aid to Scholarly Publications Program, using funds provided by the Social Sciences and Humanities Research Council of Canada. I would like to thank my friend and colleague Malek Khouri for inviting this book into the Cinema Off Centre series. It has been a pleasure to work with the University of Calgary Press staff, especially editor Peter Enman, as well as senior editor John King, and Karen Buttner. Thanks to Stephen Rife for work on the index. Two anonymous manuscript reviewers provided sharp insights that have greatly assisted in the development of this book. I am grateful for their professional efforts and of course with shortcomings remaining the responsibility of the authors and of myself as editor. I am very appreciative of the research opportunities afforded to me as Canada Research Chair at NSCAD University. During the time of this book's making I have had the great pleasure to meet and interview many filmmakers throughout Atlantic Canada. That research forms an integral part of a second manuscript on Atlantic Canadian cinema currently in development. Here I would like to especially acknowledge two filmmakers whose work I admire and who have provided me with assistance, insight, and good humour: Bill MacGillivray and Mike Jones. Rosemary House has been generous in responding to my inquiries and has the best film title, here borrowed for this book. Ron Foley MacDonald has been a great source of information on filmmaking in the region. Several of the chapters in this book began as conference papers presented at the Film Studies Association of Canada annual conference. The many images illustrating this book have been generously provided by: Rosemary House, Victoria King, Anne Troake, Domino Films, AFCOOP, CFAT, Mongrel Media, Maroon Films, Lee-Anne Poole at Emotion Pictures, Picture Plant, Gordon Pinsent's agent Penny Noble, Steve Gravestock at The Toronto International Film Festival Group, Barrie Dunn and Graeme Hopkins at TPB Productions, The National Film Board of Canada, Nova Scotia Archives and Records Management, and the CBC Still Photo Collection.

INTRODUCTION:

"NOTHING EVER HAPPENS DOWN THERE"[1]

DARRELL VARGA

This book is a critical introduction to film and television production in Atlantic Canada. We do not claim to account for the entire production history of the region; rather, the various chapters offer analysis of some important aspects of this work in relation to the geographic, political, and social construction of place and with respect to film and television policy. My title is borrowed from the excellent documentary *Rain, Drizzle, and Fog* (NFB, 1998), a passionate portrait of the city of St. John's directed by Rosemary House.[2] The film integrates the history and geography of St. John's, Newfoundland, with the processes of culture through which geographic space is transformed into lived place. This story is told through prominent Newfoundland artists, including the writers Ed Riche and Des Walsh, musician Anita Best, and performers Andy Jones, Mary Walsh, and Bryan Hennessey. Together, their work can be characterized as being both strongly rooted in the history of Newfoundland and engaged with the conditions of contemporary society. A big part of this interrelation is the presence of the Catholic Church, and Andy Jones points out that for his generation the church had a hand in all of the arts, from architecture and music through to the intense performance of the Mass. This institutional performance of morality is set against the fact of grinding poverty and class divisions, the challenge of the fishery, and the recurrence of disaster – drownings, shipwrecks, fire – a narrative occasionally interrupted in the film by the recurring bad news of the weather.

Shooting *Rain, Drizzle, and Fog* from Signal Hill in St. John's. Courtesy
of Rosemary House, photo by Justin Hall.

The artist-commentators reflect on the near impossibility of surviving these
geographic and economic conditions in what the filmmaker describes as
the city that was never meant to be – when St. John's was established as a
British fishing port in 1497, it was a criminal offence to set up a permanent

residence. The film's expression of St. John's culture is shaped by this understanding of history. Culture performs the narrative and gives it value even if it is at odds with the historical record, as historians Margaret Conrad and James Hiller explain: "There is an old and handy myth that the British government opposed settlement in Newfoundland and made it illegal. The truth is more complex. Until the 1660s the government supported settlement. Thereafter, British policy reflected the assumption that Newfoundland was an industry, not a colony, and settlement was largely ignored."[3] Given the harsh environment and lack of infrastructure, ignoring settlement runs close to making it illegal. Creative expression is a product of these conditions and also exceeds the fixed terrain of geography. The film punctuates its commentary with portrait-like shots of people on the streets of St. John's, thus articulating a matter-of-fact sense of community and presence found in the complex landscape of the body. This relation to the quotidian is central to the ethos of contemporary filmmaking in Atlantic Canada, especially in Newfoundland. This point is better understood if we consider that the group of performers in *Rain, Drizzle, and Fog* are of the first generation to professionally perform, in the province and elsewhere, work that is explicitly rooted in this place.[4] That this expression of culture and community is both rooted in and exceeds geography is finally expressed in the film's closing song, *The St. John's Waltz*, performed by Newfoundland musician Ron Hynes and with the various characters of the film coming together in the venerable pub The Ship Inn – gathering place for the city's art community. It is a song that expresses the melancholic romance of land and sea, but also situates these terms against the blood of nationhood: "For country or for king/Or for money or fame but there are no names/On the graves where men lie sleeping." It is the role of culture in the relation between place, nation, and lived reality evoked in this song that informs all the chapters in this collection. Our collective effort is to understand identity not as a national imaginary, but as something produced in the lived experience of place.

The question of Canadian national identity was fundamentally transformed in 1967 when historian Ramsey Cook proposed an understanding of the country through "limited identities" related to class, ethnicity, and region in place of an overarching national character.[5] Here, the historian is legitimizing the already-existing regional ethos, but his intervention long precedes the strain of identity politics that came to characterize debates over the relationship between culture and politics dominant in the 1980s. It is also at odds with the rise of nationalism associated with the country's centennial celebrations and the later institution of various federal programs such as multiculturalism policies and official bilingualism, not to mention the establishment of the Canadian Film Development Corporation (in 1968), which were meant to entrench at the level of policy a common understanding of Canadian identity. At the same time, and contrary to Cook's thesis, many Canadian critics and scholars working in the nascent field of film studies were driven by a heartfelt cultural nationalism, striving to articulate a concept of national cinema co-extensive with the various New Wave and other national cinema movements emergent in various parts of the world, as a bulwark against the dominance of Hollywood cinema and strongly influenced by the unifying national cultural narrative of Margaret Atwood's seminal book *Survival*.[6] The idea of "limited identities" is set against the prevailing approach to the writing of Canadian history leading up to the 1970s, a sentiment best expressed by historian Frank Underhill in the phrase I re-appropriate for the title of this introduction. Underhill regarded activity, whether cultural, political, or economic, in "the regions" as unimportant except insofar as that activity relates to the centre. In fact, it is the colonial disposition toward the regions (and toward the then new scholarship in social, feminist, and labour history) that motivated regional historians to undertake serious research on aspects of society and political economy specific to place.

We now have an established moving picture industry in this country with a handful of auteurs, yet Hollywood remains a substantial presence. As Toby Miller and others has argued, Hollywood is no longer a geographic locale (though it certainly is that), but is a sensibility both for cinema and for economic relations – a sensibility formed through conditions of production, financing, distribution, and the division of labour. Miller's book *Global Hollywood* argues that to understand a national cinema today, we need to think about more than just the film itself because a national cinema is equally defined by the array of tax breaks, subsidies, discounted labour costs, and other policy and economic structures through which film activity comes into being.[7] In Atlantic Canada, and in other Canadian regions, the presence of offshore (largely American) productions shooting on location provides employment and strongly influences the development of technical infrastructure, but it also provides the economic cover for the ideological determination of cinema culture and the place of cinema within the broader social and economic terrain.

In Nova Scotia, for instance, the provincial film office (Film Nova Scotia, formerly called The Nova Scotia Film Development Corporation) understands its role, in the words of C.E.O. Ann MacKenzie, as "being located in economic development and tourism, both as an economic story and a cultural story."[8] Similarly, the slogan for the New Brunswick provincial film office at the time of this writing is "Call us Chameleon," in promotion of the region as location for productions originating elsewhere.[9] The marketing of the region as stand-in for elsewhere is, on the one hand, an outcome of the global flow of capital, but it is also produced through policies and regulations that are specific to the territory and nation-state. The movies are then both of, and not of, a given locale. This book navigates this problem as well as the complex relation between the concept of national cinema and regional specificity, and the relation between film as global industry and the tricky idea of cinema as art form.

In general, this book privileges independent author-driven productions; however, we acknowledge that the context of production in this country is shaped by the significant overlap of film and television, and we avoid considering work in these media as entirely distinct practices. Likewise, we acknowledge the complexity of the concept of authorship and by no means use it as an essentialist device. The contributors to this book approach the concept of region not simply as a function of geography but also as an idea that is produced through conditions of economy, social organization, and politics, among other factors.[10] The book complements existing scholarship on Canada's west coast film scene, notably Mike Gasher's *Hollywood North* and Serra Tinic's *On Location: Canada's Television Industry in a Global Market*. However, the east and west coast regions of this country differ considerably, not least in their respective relation to Hollywood. We seek to understand the idea of place through the apparatus of cinema as something that is always in process rather than as a quaint object hidden in the national cabinet of curiosities. As Tinic says: "Nation-states do not emanate monolithic, unified identities that are easily translatable into media narratives. Rather, every nation [and region] contains competing cultural definitions of collective identity – regional, transnational, ethnic, linguistic – vying for inclusion and representation on the national stage."[11] The approach throughout this collection is to understand film and video production not simply as closed texts but also as a social technology through which concepts of place and space, or of margin and centre, are produced and negotiated.

This book begins with a trio of essays providing the historical context for contemporary filmmaking in the region. Colin Howell and Peter Twohig articulate the *Acadiensis* perspective, which emerged among a group of regional historians in the 1970s to counter the blatant stereotyping and the central Canada bias in Canadian history.[12] Here, the concept of region is not an essentialist outcome of geography, but is understood as a borderland produced though material conditions and political and economic forces both from within and from outside. They discuss the persistence of anti-modernist stereotypes in National Film Board films, especially those made before 1990, but also inflected differently in more recent productions. In particular, the authors seek to measure the degree to which this nationalist institution reflects the changing cultural and intellectual environment in which the concept of region is produced, whereby earlier taken-for-granted assumptions are now inflected in the dialectical relationship between locality and global capitalism. Howell and Twohig demonstrate the degree to which region, or place, continues to matter in the expression of culture and society in its specificity and in relation to the broader forces of modernity.

This specificity is important to our understanding of the presence of Acadian cinema. As Pierre Véronneau points out, these films imagine place by making use of stereotypical images of Acadia, but also take on the concepts of borders and border crossing – thus emphasizing the act of wandering as central to the Acadian experience in North America. Acadian cinema revolves around the interventions of the National Film Board, and its study illuminates the contradictions of this nationalist agency in relation to the concept of regionalism. The contradictions are likewise evident with the introduction of the *Challenge for Change* program, discussed in chapters by Tracy Zhang and Jerry White, as well as in the more recent shift toward private-sector co-productions, a consequence of NFB budget cutbacks. As in Howell and Twohig's chapter, these studies reveal the contradictory presence of the NFB in the region. While the Board established an office in Moncton, Véronneau indicates the less than sympathetic stance initially taken by the NFB's Montreal head office toward this regional outpost. However, by the late 1980s there is an integration of the more accomplished Acadian filmmakers in the nationalist mandate of the NFB by allowing them to work on projects with a subject matter that is not exclusively Acadian. By 2000 the crisis of funding within the Board eventually gives cause for it to support co-productions and the establishment of the provincial film development office: New Brunswick Film, helping to open up the region to more commercially oriented production and inviting tensions over the concept of what is an Acadian film.

Location and regionality are a measure not just of production activity but also of consumption. Greg Canning's research on exhibition practices in the small town of Truro, Nova Scotia, is set against dominant assumptions of early movie-going patterns that have been established through studies in large urban centres, notably New York City. Canning makes the point that this emphasis distorts our understanding of the vast majority of North Americans who lived in rural areas at the time, and needs to be measured against the specificity of life in Atlantic Canada. Here, we come to understand the degree to which the movies are integrated into modern life, as well as the degree of autonomy exercised by theatre owners over both the programming and the concept of entertainment within the moral economy of the town. The small-town theatre quickly became an important centre of community life, but was overwhelmingly dominated by imported foreign productions. Of particular note is the local resistance to the transformation of cinema that occurs around 1908 in the United States, away from non-fiction programs alongside vaudeville fare and toward the dominance of narrative fiction film. These earlier forms manage to hang on for much longer in small-town Nova Scotia, and the theatre environment is itself rather vaudevillian, with such extraordinary audience lures as live chickens and a baby giveaway!

The ensuing three chapters on film in Newfoundland take up in various ways the relation between place and labour through an examination of films on the seal hunt, on the resettlement of outport communities, and the Fogo Islands. Noreen Golfman's chapter on films dealing with the controversial annual seal hunt investigates the relation between image making and the question of who has a right to speak of a place and a people – developing the argument through a contrast of celebrity-driven anti-sealing campaigns set against regionally specific voices. Malek Khouri discusses the overlooked Gordon Pinsent film *John and the Missus* (1987) about the Newfoundland government's resettlement program of the 1950s and early 1960s, when entire remote outport communities were abandoned and their citizens moved to more centralized areas, on the premise that the move was necessary to provide essential services and employment opportunities. This radical transformation of space encouraged significant response on the part of artists, as indicated in this preface to the Maritime History Archive: "Captured in film, poetry, visual art and music, the response to resettlement was an important political thread in the province's cultural renaissance in the 1970s."[13] There was a high degree of coercion in facilitating this relocation through financial assistance to otherwise impoverished families, and the policy of the Department of Welfare, in 1963, made the strategy explicit: "No assistance may be granted to an individual unless the head of the household of every family living in an isolated community signs a petition agreeing to move."[14]

This event is an extremely important one in the history of the province; it is at once a signifier of modernity and a brutal disregard for local culture undertaken at the same time as the province is constructed as an ideal pastoral destination for tourists, as James Overton notes: "If underdevelopment in Newfoundland provides the context for attempts to use tourism as an economic development strategy, it also provides the 'raw material' for a certain kind of tourist development."[15] The resettlement program is consistent with the ideological common-sense logic of modern capitalism. Khouri's chapter situates *John and the Missus* within this historical context and in relation to its period of production, the mid-1980s and the ascent of neo-conservatism, along with the displacement of the local for the sake of investor rights in the form of the Free Trade Agreement with the U.S. (which began negotiations in 1986). The Pinsent film expresses regionally based dissent while marginalizing collective social protest, and in this way perpetuates the dehistorical production of the antimodernist narrative of local culture in a narrative that, however compelling and well-crafted, posits the late-capitalist concept of progress as inevitable.[16]

The concept of belonging is important to national and regional identity, but is likewise produced through stereotypes and exclusions. Jerry White examines these concerns through analysis of NFB's Newfoundland Project (The Fogo Island films), providing a broad analysis of these films as important to the idea of community building, but also as sophisticated non-narrative works that substantially contribute to the evolution of observational cinema within and outside of the NFB. A comparison with the modernist impulse of the Glenn Gould radio documentary *The Latecomers* (1969) is one of the pleasures of this chapter. These films provide a complex negotiation between the documentary impulse, aesthetic concerns, and the rise of Canadian nationalism. White makes the point that to consider the films only as minor case studies of media use in regionally based community politics is to miss the broader implications of these works in cinema history as well as to undermine their politics.[17] That these films have been marginalized as unimportant in the national and cinematic narrative speaks as much to the processes of exclusion that shape culture and nationalism as to the place of the region within the nation-state.

The region and centre relation is similarly measured in television production. A useful starting point is the viewer outrage directed at the CBC for its cancellation of the highly popular Maritime music show *Don Messer's Jubilee* in 1969. The twenty-one thousand impassioned letters of protest sent to the CBC and to members of Parliament are symptomatic of social anxieties over the nation's urbanization and the rise of what has come to be known as multiculturalism. Though the cancellation of *Jubilee* has been a landmark public relations disaster for the CBC, the discourse around the show and its cancellation informs the persistent use of the region on the part of the national broadcaster as spatial signifier of nostalgia and authenticity. This antimodernism is turned on its head in more contemporary television, notably in the highly popular series *Trailer Park Boys* and the short-lived and less well-known *Gullage's*. While there is a generalized assumption that the local is effaced in globalization, in works of culture we also observe the local deployed as signifier of authenticity, as object of trade in the international market for media exotica. The taken-for-granted universal humanism of regional television narratives serves as a mask for the marked anti-humanism of globalization. John McCullough discusses how both shows use the concept of the local as capital in the marketplace of Global Hollywood and as a measure of "popularity" through which the limit of regional specificity in the global media marketplace is produced.

The "local" is more often the currency of independent film and video activity, and so it is necessary to consider the claims to space made by indie filmmakers. Tracy Zhang maps the economic and ideological relationship between state agencies such as the NFB and the Canada Council with the rise of grassroots production co-operatives in Halifax: the Atlantic Film-maker's Co-operative (AFCOOP) and the Centre for Art Tapes (CFAT). Zhang makes use of interviews with founding members of these organizations in order to chart the history of film and video production in the region and, as in Véronneau's chapter, illustrate the tension between region and centre. The financial support for film and video co-operatives, like support for the *Challenge for Change* program, is on the one hand a democratization of media access but it is also a process of governmentality whereby the grassroots are integrated within the mainstream.[18] While grassroots media organizations represent a key break from centralized control over production, their funding structure and relationship to other state institutions provide a different form of influence. Again, as with Véronneau's discussion of Acadian cinema, the specificity of local history sheds light on the functioning of national cultural organizations, illuminating aspects of the history of the NFB and the Canada Council in ways that are absent in nationalist-centred narratives.

One filmmaker who has successfully crossed over from the co-op scene to the commercial industry is Thom Fitzgerald, director of such films as *The Hanging Garden* (1997), *The Event* (2003), *Three Needles* (2005) and other titles.[19] Bruce Barber's analysis of Fitzgerald's first feature *The Movie of the Week* (1990), made while the director was a student at the NSCAD University in Halifax, draws attention to themes and ideas that become important in his later and more well-known work. It also provides an opportunity to examine the history of film activity at NSCAD and the influence of this art school on the development of the regional film community.[20] A later graduate of this institution, in photography, is Andrea Dorfman, whose debut feature, *Parsley Days*, is located in the working-class neighbourhood of north-end Halifax – a space rooted in local history but also in the contemporary vitality of place and creativity. In this way, according to Andrew Burke, the film parallels the expression of the contemporary vernacular found in the architecture practice of Nova Scotian Brian Mackay-Lyons and connects with the aesthetic preoccupations of regional artists and filmmakers such as William D. MacGillivray, Lulu Keating, and Thom Fitzgerald. Burke suggests that Dorfman's film provides an important way out from under the suffocating weight of what he calls "Heritage Cinema," the practice of mining a nostalgic idealization of place. The most well-known "heritage" example would be the *Anne of Green Gables* TV franchise produced by Toronto-based Sullivan Entertainment beginning in 1985. As Patsy Kotsopoulos points out elsewhere, the big business of Anne tourism on Prince Edward Island is matched on screen by a "deregionalization, creating a regionless romance appropriate for a geographically dispersed viewership."[21] In contrast, in the indie films of Fitzgerald and Dorfman the specificity of the region is not erased; instead, what is evoked is a sense of history that is present but that we are no longer in thrall to.

In my discussion of a series of fiction films all dealing with the figure of the artist, I map an important era in Atlantic-based and Canadian film – the shift from art house to commercial movie culture. In this temporal span, the ideal of a Canadian cinema as being cast separately from the market-driven dominant cinema was discarded by both policy design and financial imperative. In this context, art cinema is increasingly expected to be marketable in an international context. By taking up the subject of art and the place of the artist in local culture, these films (*Life Classes*, Dir: William D. MacGillivray, 1987; *Candy Mountain*, Dir: Robert Frank and Rudy Wurlitzer, 1987; *New Waterford Girl*, Dir: Allan Moyle, 1999; and *Congratulations*, Dir: Mike Jones, 2000) deal with the concept of creativity in relation to the social production of place. Nowhere in these films is place simply idealized as the romantic locale for creation; instead, both place and artist are conditioned by economic and social relations, yet the spark of creativity allows us to see the relation between space and place in new and productive ways.

This book concludes with filmmaker Sylvia Hamilton's reflections on the making of her film *Portia White: Think On Me* (2000), about the Nova Scotia–born classical singer. Portia White had an international concert profile in the 1940s and '50s, celebrated by critics and audiences alike, but since her death in 1968 there has been no print or film biography. Indeed, her story is one of many unwritten histories, both of important Black Canadians and of the formation of the film and television industry in this country (among her many accomplishments, White was a sought-after vocal coach for performers during the nascent days of television in 1950s Toronto). Hamilton's chapter is distinguished from the others in this book by its focus on her personal engagement with her film's subject and reflection on her working method, including fragments of interviews and journal entries, some of which take the form of the filmmaker's own letters to Portia White, offering a privileged glimpse into this filmmaker's process. The author's personal reflections are situated with a discussion of the historical, social, and economic context – the systemic racism experienced by White, the function of language in relation to power, but also the communities out of which the filmmaker and her subject emerge, and the important function of film in sustaining community and facilitating dialogue and critical engagement.

Hamilton demonstrates the vital relationship between the local and global, the situatedness of the subject and the broader structure of culture and history in which subject and the process of representation exists. In this way, her work demonstrates the limits of the category Atlantic Canadian cinema, a term that collapses together work from many diverse places. We also learn how the specificity of place opens up understanding of both the structural forces giving shape to experience and the function of culture in (to follow Raymond Williams) articulating a structure of feeling.[22] Feeling is never just an expression of creative vision, but also self-consciously refers to the conditions of production. Likewise, culture is never simply given, but is produced in no small part by the whole constellation of determinants which produce and give shape to space, place, and meaning.

NOTES

1   This quote, referring to the history of Atlantic Canada, was made in 1964 by influential Canadian historian Frank Underhill, in a discussion on the continued, and in his view legitimate, central Canadian emphasis in Canadian history. Frank Underhill, *The Image of Confederation* (Toronto: CBC, 1964), 63.

2   See also *Hard Rock and Water*, directed by Barbara Doran (2005) as the political-economic complement to *Rain, Drizzle and Fog* – both films feature performer Mary Walsh, among others.

3   Margaret R. Conrad and James Hiller, *Atlantic Canada: A Region in the Making* (Toronto: Oxford University Press, 2001), 71.

4   In my discussion of Mike Jones's film *Congratulations* and the early performances of Codco, I refer to the stereotypes found in central Canada related to Newfoundland. This issue also is taken up in Noreen Golfman's chapter on representations of the seal hunt.

5   Ramsey Cook, "Canadian Centennial Celebrations," *International Journal* 22 (1967): 663. Cook's statement is discussed in relation to the development of regional history and the concept of borderlands in Stephen J. Hornsby and John G. Reid, eds., *New England and the Maritime Provinces: Connections and Comparisons* (Montreal and Kingston: McGill-Queen's University Press, 2005), 8.

6   Atwood's book, subtitled *A Thematic Guide to Canadian Literature*, was originally published in 1972 (Toronto: McClelland and Stewart) and follows on the work of Northrop Frye to articulate a unity of themes important to Canadian culture. For a concise overview of dominant approaches in Canadian film scholarship, see Will Straw, "Canadian Cinema," in John Hill and Pamela Church Gibson, eds., *Oxford Guide to Film Studies* (Oxford University Press, 1998), 523–26.

7   Toby Miller et al., *Global Hollywood* (London: BFI, 2001).

8   Ann Mackenzie, NSFDC statement to Standing Committee on Canadian Heritage, Halifax, 23 February 1999, accessed online 12 March 2007: http://cmte.parl.gc.ca/Content/HOC/committee/361/cher/evidence/ev1039263/cherev72-e.htm.

9   The slogan is used in campaigns aimed at attracting foreign producers to shoot in the province, and is found on the website http://www.nbfilm.com.

10 The absence of commentary on film from New Brunswick and Prince Edward Island is acknowledged. This, along with critical commentary on a host of other important films from the region, is the subject of a second manuscript currently in development. The present collection is the first substantial work of critical analysis on Atlantic Canadian cinema, and is presented as a starting point for dialogue rather than the final word.

11 Serra Tinic, *On Location: Canada's Television Industry in a Global Market* (Toronto: University of Toronto Press, 2005), viii.

12 The name refers to the important history journal *Acadiensis*, established in 1971 at the University of New Brunswick. David Frank, a member of this group, describes the name as taken from a magazine originally published from 1901 to 1908 to promote culture and unity within the region: "The name was an invented one, derived from the historical and scientific name for the territory of 'Acadia' – a geographic region including the present-day Maritime Provinces and adjacent areas to the north around the Gulf of St. Lawrence and to the south in northern New England." In "Acadiensis, 1901 and 1999," *Canadian Review of American Studies* 30(3) (2000): accessed 6 February 2007: http://www.utpjournals.com/product/cras/303/Frank.html.

13   "'No Great Future': Government Sponsored Resettlement in Newfoundland and Labrador since Confederation," Memorial University Maritime History Archive: http://www.mun.ca/mha/resettlement/rs_intro.php.

14   Ibid., "Annual Report for the Year ended March 31, 1963."

15   For an overview of the invention of folk tradition in service of the tourism economy, see James Overton, *Making a World of Difference: Essays on Tourism, Culture and Development in Newfoundland* (St. John's: Memorial University, 1996), 105 and passim.

16   As detailed in the case of Nova Scotia by Ian Mckay, *The Quest of the Folk: Antimodernism and Cultural Selection in Twentieth-Century Nova Scotia* (Montreal and Kingston: McGill-Queen's University Press, 1994).

17   Technological innovations (the then new developments in portable sound and camera equipment) were an important part of this process. White cites Janine Marchessault, "Reflections on the Dispossessed: Video and the 'Challenge for Change' Experiment," *Screen* 36(2) (Summer 1995): 131–46. See also Marchessault, "Amateur Video and the Challenge for Change," in Marchessault, ed., *Mirror Machine: Video and Identity* (Toronto: YYZ, 1995): 13–25.

18   On the concept of govenmentality (borrowed from Foucault) in relation to the development of Canadian film policy, see Michael Dorland, *So Close to the State/s: The Emergence of Canadian Feature Film Policy* (Toronto: University of Toronto Press, 1998).

19   For a discussion of *The Hanging Garden* in relation to concepts of class, sexual identity, and regionality, see Malek Khouri, "Other-ing the Worker in Canadian 'Gay Cinema': Thom Fitzgerald's *The Hanging Garden*, in Darrell Varga and Malek Khouri, eds., *Working on Screen: Representations of the Working Class in Canadian Cinema* (Toronto: University of Toronto Press, 2006), 134–47. See also Andrew Burke's critique of Khouri's analysis in his contribution to the present collection.

20   For an overview of the impact of this art school, see Bruce Barber, ed., *Conceptual Art: The NSCAD Connection 1967–1973* (Halifax: Anna Leonowens Gallery/NSCAD University, 2001). In former NSCAD president Gary Neill Kennedy's essay in Barber's collection, "NSCAD and the Sixties," he points out that it was commonplace, on the part of nationalist commentators, to refer to the college as an "American outpost" in spite of the presence of important Canadian artists Joyce Wieland and Greg Curnoe, who are especially concerned with nationalism (24).

21   Patsy Aspasia Kotsopoulos, "L.M. Montgomery on Television: The Romance and Industry of the Adaptation Process," in *Canadian Cultural Poesis: Essays on Canadian Culture*, ed. Garry Sherbert, Annie Gérin, and Sheila Petty (Waterloo, ON: Wilfrid Laurier University Press, 2006), 272.

22   The concept comes from Williams in *The Long Revolution* (London, UK: Chatto and Windus, 1961). Here, he attempts to describe the totality of culture in relation to material conditions, moral judgment, and the idea of the individual in a social context.

A REGION ON FILM: METROPOLITANISM, PLACE, AND MEANING IN NFB FILMS

COLIN HOWELL AND PETER L. TWOHIG

This chapter probes the work of filmmakers primarily associated with the National Film Board as they tell stories about Canada to Canadians and construct understandings of both the nation and the Atlantic region in turn. For historians like ourselves, film represents a significant and special resource, incorporating important historical information and analysis into powerful "visual texts." NFB productions, therefore, not only fulfill the organization's broad mandate enshrined in the National Film Act (1950) to "interpret Canada to Canadians and to other nations," but are themselves important historical documents constructed in particular historical contexts. The powerful messages these films convey, moreover, can either challenge or reinforce hegemonic notions of "common sense." For example, as Malek Khouri points out with reference to the NFB's sympathetic treatments of the working class in the 1930s, there is a significant tradition within the NFB of challenging conventional understandings.[1] By contrast, films dealing with Atlantic Canada tended before 1990 to reinforce antimodernist assumptions about regional backwardness and simplicity at the very time a generation of regional historians was trying to put these notions to rest.

Drawing upon the anthropological work of Levi-Strauss, Thomas Schatz has argued that commercial filmmaking is, at its core, a process of constructing contemporary myths.[2] For historians, the shifting lens of filmmakers over time presents an opportunity to reflect on, interrogate, and explicate malleable meanings of region. We argue here that despite the past and present complexities of Atlantic Canada, the overriding message of films produced before 1990 was of a region dogged by tradition, ground down by capitalist rapacity, and never quite able – or willing – to achieve the benefits of modernity. Commonplace stereotypes of regional conservatism, entrepreneurial ineptitude, and the nostalgic veneration of the "authentic" and "innocent" lives of the Atlantic Canadian "folk" were reinforced in documentary films with especially powerful effect. The enduring motif is of a tradition-bound region attached to the sea and soil, struggling to find a place within a federation that has failed to live up to its promises, and in a world where modernity has passed it by. As Jane Gaines has written, "technologically recorded images stand to most people … as hard evidence of the existence of the real world."[3] In that regard the influence of the NFB on prevailing assumptions about Atlantic Canada's place in Confederation was for many years decidedly conservative and unhelpful.

Over the past decade or so this derisive characterization has been employed less frequently. While antimodernist images continue to surface on film, they are increasingly absorbed into an investigation of the region's connection to the world beyond its borders and/or to themes and issues that have universal resonances. Filmmakers such as Michael Donovan and television and movie productions like the *Trailer Park Boys*, for example, present what may appear at first glance as stereotypical and derisive images of regional backwardness, but at the same time they give us a textured and human portrait of those living on the social margin, wherever that might be. Moreover, given the fact that films of this sort are constructed in the most modern of contexts – characterized by high production costs, international distribution networks, and a sensitivity to market conditions outside the region – the arbitrary distinctions between Atlantic Canada and the wider world that are implicit in the regional stereotype have begun to erode. The breaking down of received presumptions about region, moreover, reflects two of the prevailing intellectual currents of contemporary life: the growing interest in boundary crossing and borderlands in an increasingly globalized world,[4] and the postcolonial assault on arbitrary distinctions involving the inside and the outside, the intrinsic and extrinsic, the self and the other. For filmmakers and historians alike, the "common sense" of our own time complicates the very meaning of region itself and demands more self-conscious attention to the complexities of all forms of cultural production, including art, photography, and film.[5]

The imagining of the Atlantic region in more recent films aptly illustrates shifting notions of place and identity. Freed from the emphasis on tradition that fettered earlier films, we can pose some questions about the broad history of filmmaking relating to Atlantic Canada. What is the legacy of NFB representations of Atlantic Canada over the past half-century and what are the dominant images of region that films have promulgated? (These questions can also be raised with respect to the Canadian Broadcasting Corporation's representation of the region, and indeed that institution is involved in some of the productions cited in this chapter. The CBC's complex involvement in the production of the region is also taken up in Jen Vanderburgh's chapter on the *Don Messer's Jubilee* as well as in John McCullough's analysis of *Gullage's* and *Trailer Park Boys* elsewhere in this book.) If, as we contend, films are an important resource for exploring changing and hegemonic representations of region over time, how have recent films responded to new insights in the meaning of Atlantic Canada as an interpretive space? And finally, how might filmmakers and historians alike probe the changing perceptions of space and place, region and nation, and address the interaction between local identities and the global forces associated with late-modern capitalist culture?

In responding to questions of this sort our chapter seeks to bridge the oft-cited gulf between analyses of cultural forms such as film and the social and material conditions and differences that shape regional identity in Atlantic Canada. Indeed, one of our objectives is to bring historians and moving image researchers into a more constructive dialogue than has hitherto existed.[6] Our approach relies upon a technique widely used by historians, i.e., constructing exhaustive historiographical (in this case filmographical) overviews of a particular issue. Of course, it is impossible to explore the full variety of films that portray Atlantic Canada. As a result we select films that provide a framework or scaffolding for understanding, comparing, and assessing changing notions of the region. By elucidating the approaches deployed in an admittedly broad – one might even say encyclopaedic selection of NFB films – we present insights into the nature and changing representations of the region and its place within the Canadian federation. In particular, we stress that the messages associated with NFB films before 1990 have changed over the past twenty years. Rather than emphasizing the exceptionalism of the Atlantic region, as earlier films did, or emphasizing the hope or promise of modernism, recent films have achieved a balance between place and other themes.

Film, Atlantic Canada, and the Myth of Exceptionalism: 1945-90

Although the notion of the Maritimes as a distinctive community, fundamentally different in character from other places, was well established by the 1920s and '30s, Newfoundland's postwar entry into Confederation required the re-imagining of the Maritime region as "Atlantic Canada."[7] For many policy makers and cultural producers, including those associated with the NFB, the inclusion of Newfoundland and Labrador within the broader narrative of region and nation building was an important priority. Still, the concept of region, and how region connected to the nation, continued to provide an uncontested framework for interpretation. So did discussions of modernity and traditionalism which, in the absence of more thoughtful approaches, have abounded in films pertaining to the eastern provinces. An early example of this can be found in the film *Newfoundland: Atlantic Province* (1949), which celebrated Newfoundland's entry into Confederation. Filled with pageantry, it opens with formal ceremonies on Parliament Hill. Prime Minister Louis St. Laurent is captured saying that the people of Newfoundland "will not lose your identity, of which you are so proud," while the narration highlights how "the dream of Confederation has always included … Newfoundland and Labrador." A shared identity involving both Newfoundland and Canada is the important theme of the early part of the film.

But this is also a film that celebrates the modernist hope. It presents images of busy St. John's harbour and asserts Newfoundland's strategic position "midway between New York and London," a point undoubtedly underscored by the experience of World War II and the growing importance of transatlantic air travel. History is invoked as well, reminding the viewing audience that the first transatlantic air crossing began in Newfoundland. When the film was produced in 1949, nearly half a million travellers went through the Gander airport, and three thousand people worked there. Newfoundland's place in the global world of air travel is nicely captured through airline announcements in different languages and images of airline employees from around the world. Other aspects of Newfoundland's modernity are emphasized, including its housing stock, the pulp and paper mill in Cornerbrook, the enormous hydroelectric power potential, and the mineral wealth of Labrador, which is simultaneously considered to be "bleak and barren."

As a counterpoint to images of modernity, the film emphasizes that the "real wealth" of Newfoundland could not be found in mineral resources, forestry products, or the fishery, but with the people. Finally we meet the Greeley family, who are sending their young daughter Hazel off to school. Fred Greeley is an inshore fisher and Bertha is using a wash tub to clean clothes by hand. And there is an image of the Newfoundland dog. It is January and Mr. Greeley launches his boat to go fishing. "It is a hard life but she [Bertha] knows he is doing it for her and for her daughter Hazel," says the film. The film cuts to a classroom scene where the children are told that Newfoundland will soon join Canada and the students are asked to say something about their new country. And when the teacher asks what Newfoundland could send to Canada, Hazel Greeley answers, "fish." As the strains of "Lots o' fish in Bonavista Harbour" begin at this point, we see a large schooner, and are told that half the population is dependent upon fishing for their livelihood. The technology of fishing, its harshness and danger, is contrasted with the "highly mechanized" fish plants and the "rigid inspection" of the fish, and the search for "new and bigger markets" for the products of the sea, all of which serve to emphasize modernity's inevitable promise.

The movie ends with a comparison of Newfoundland and Canada, emphasizing their shared history and path forward, a path that is about economic development, trade, and intensified resource exploitation. It is impossible to watch this film now, as students are apt to do, without a deep sense of irony. The industrial development schemes of the Smallwood government, the environmental consequences of intensified fishing, and the impact of resource development on the Innu, in particular, all emerge as topics from this film. But the film's real purpose was to introduce Newfoundland to other Canadians and to celebrate the idea of Canada, now complete. As such, it excludes detail on the bitter disputes within Newfoundland over the idea and terms of Confederation.

Of course, postwar optimism faded as regional economic development sputtered during the 1950s. Furthermore, as the Canadian state turned its attention to issues of 'regional disparity,' the Atlantic region itself became problematized, at once pitied and derided as an economic laggard and as a dependent community where little of consequence ever happened.[8] Such derisive attitudes linger today, even when they are given a different but equally patronizing spin. Take, for example, the following entry for Nova Scotia in the online *Canadian Encyclopedia*: "Once regarded as the boondocks, Nova

Scotia is seen increasingly as a place where the good life can be lived even with a per capita income that is below the national average. Nova Scotians generally insist that material development does no harm to the pleasant living they now enjoy."[9] So here is Nova Scotia: poor but happy, a place which is not concerned with the latest creature comforts, nor corrupted by the crass commercialism of North American society. But when, precisely, was the province considered to be the 'boondocks' and by whom? While the entry is for Nova Scotia, moreover, this representation is easily extended by many Canadians to encompass the entire Atlantic region.

Historians, geographers, economists, and sociologists of the first *Acadiensis* generation (1970–90) denounced such blatant stereotyping of the region. E.R. Forbes challenged such a view when he called upon historians to "provide a historical perspective which would help [Maritimers] understand their plight in a modern world." For scholars outside the region, Forbes concluded, "it is still easier to make a token reference to the stereotype, toss in a few anecdotes about quaint Maritime customs and then shift the discussion back to the 'important' regions."[10] Yet the stereotype endured. Phil Buckner, John Reid, and other *Acadiensis*-generation scholars remained perplexed that scholars elsewhere seemed resistant to including the results of their work in a revised national narrative.[11] In their mind the inattention of nationalist historians to the complexity of Atlantic Canadian history seemed an impediment to full partnership and equitable advantage in Confederation for the region. Furthermore, as regional scholars investigated Atlantic Canada's post-Confederation history they explored broad processes of metropolitan and hinterland interaction, core and periphery relationships, capitalist development and underdevelopment models, and industrialization and deindustrialization. In so doing they proclaimed a region quite different from the one imagined by those who looked upon it from afar as a defeated and defeatist culture unable to escape its past.

While the work of the *Acadiensis* generation derived from a collective conviction that a regional narrative could be constructed free of derisive stereotyping, the work of filmmakers on the region during these years was far less coherent or integrated. As a result, an assessment of the impact of the NFB on the region's image is complicated by the vast number of films produced and the varied subject matter that they address. Different filmmakers, of course, have different angles of vision. NFB films packaged as the "Atlantic Canada Series" present a number of disconnected images that try to capture the diversity of life in the Atlantic Region, touching on such varied subjects as politics in Prince Edward Island, the progress of a supertanker through the Strait of Canso, the life of a cemetery caretaker in Saint John, New Brunswick, the biography of Nova Scotian entrepreneur Charlie McCullough, the relationship of old and new farm families in New Brunswick, and contemporary Acadian politics and culture and the issue of bilingualism in Moncton.

A number of films dramatized regional issues by emphasizing the contribution of individuals to regional transformation, social justice and economic reform. These productions, among them *Moses Coady* (1976); *I Like to See the Wheels Turn* (1981); *Robichaud* (1990); and Barbara Doran's *A Little Fellow from Gambo: The Joey Smallwood Story* (1970), addressed the commonplace preoccupation of the 1970s and '80s with issues of entrepreneurial lethargy, social conservatism, and the difficulties political leaders had in overcoming a resistance to change. At one and the same time these productions celebrated those few dynamic personalities that demonstrated an ability to rise above the commonplace, and reinforced the widespread images of a dysfunctional region.

I Like to See the Wheels Turn chronicled the life of Kenneth Colin (K.C.) Irving, whose traditional Presbyterian and capitalist veneration of hard work, abstinence from alcohol, and family values are presented as an affirmation of his Maritime roots, and a foundation upon which the mighty Irving business empire was constructed. Of course, for those convinced that the economic problems of the Atlantic region were largely a product of deficient entrepreneurial acumen, Irving at one and the same time reinforced those attitudes and stood as an example of what could be done if one tried hard enough to succeed. Ironically, Irving's personal success implied regional failure. Diane Francis, editor of the *Financial Post* and author of *Controlling Interest: Who Owns Canada*, for example, blamed Canada's economic disabilities – and particularly those of Atlantic Canada – on the concentration of wealth and economic power in the hands of a few powerful families. These "family fiefdoms" she suggested, "resulted in a new form of economic feudalism nowhere more evident than in New Brunswick's private sector, apart from a few notable competitors like the wealthy Irvings and McCains."[12] Francis's preoccupation with the issue of entrepreneurship allowed her little appreciation of the structural characteristics of a regional economy which would allow for the prominence of these families at the same time as it impeded the growth of a productive industrial sector. In a pipe dream radio interview with Peter Gzowski, Francis even plumped for the immigration to the Maritimes of well-heeled businessmen from Hong Kong who could drag the soporific region into the new awakening of global competitiveness.

By contrast, the NFB's 1976 film *Moses Coady* suggested that the region could generate is own saviours. Director Kent Martin chronicled the quasi-feudal conditions confronting farmers and fishermen in interwar northeastern Nova Scotia, and the program of self-help, popular education, and co-operation that Coady and others at Saint Francis Xavier University in Antigonish offered in response. A self-styled champion of small producers as they took on the corporations, fish merchants, and aristocratic bureaucrats, Coady, with his fiery oratory and Catholic reform principles, helped spawn a plethora of marketing co-ops, co-op buying clubs, consumer co-ops, producer-owned canning factories, and credit unions that provided loans for farm machinery, fishing boats, and new homes. The film concludes that Coady and the Antigonish Movement helped confront defeatism and helped mobilize a population experiencing the worst of times during the Depression. Although there is much truth in this, there is little acknowledgement in the film of the larger political and ideological landscape of the interwar years, which included the political program of Maritime Rights and the radical working-class responses to class warfare in the coalfields. Furthermore, by focusing on Coady, the film diverted attention from the issue of how the movement failed over time to achieve his broader vision of the co-operative commonwealth. As Stephen Dutcher suggests in a recent study, it is important to understand the diverse nature of co-operative action in the region. He calls for an analysis "that is considerably more complex than a focus on the pre-war social movement nature of the Antigonish Movement," and that addresses the profound social and economic changes that continued to take place during and after the Second World War.[13]

Other films, such as *12000 Men* (1978), *"They Didn't Starve Us Out": Industrial Cape Breton in the 1920s* (1991) and *Potatoes* (1976), focused less on uncommon individuals who pushed a relatively passive citizenry in the direction of modernity, and more on how workers and primary producers have responded to the process of capitalist development and underdevelopment. The first two of these films addresses the struggles of workers and their families in industrial Cape Breton as they confronted the coal and steel operators and the penetration of the region by modern industrial capitalism at the end of the nineteenth century. In what is now a well-known story, these films chronicle the bitter strikes of 1909 and the early 1920s, the imprisonment of the miner's spokesman J.B. MacLachlan, for seditious libel in 1923, the death of miner William Davis that grew out of labour's war against Besco and its deplorable treatment of its workers. Although the title *12000 Men* is unfortunate, given the important role played by miners' wives, and despite questionable use of photographs and film clips from Britain and the United States, the film is more powerful and less Whiggish in tone than *They Didn't Starve Us Out*.

Gary Toole's *Potatoes* (1976) is a smart and compelling look at how New Brunswick potato producers have experienced the intrusion of modern machine technology into their operations. Although mechanization has meant more efficient farm production and increased output, the enormous capital outlays on machinery have created a situation where more is produced with less return. Furthermore, as frozen food production has meant a decline in the fresh potato market, many farmers contract with McCain's for a prearranged stable price. Stability has nonetheless meant a loss of traditional independence, and the film notes the increasing willingness of potato producers to join together under the banner of the National Farmer's Union. Taken together, the message of the film is similar to that of *12000 Men*. Although the struggles of primary producers and working people to protect themselves from the deleterious effects of capitalist development on their lives are acknowledged, whatever victories working people in the region achieve are seen as likely to be partial ones at best. This conclusion is somewhat different from that presented in *They Didn't Starve Us Out*, which emphasizes the success of the miners in bringing Besco down and providing inspiration to workers elsewhere in Canada.

However different the approaches taken in these films – some biographical and nostalgic, others analytical and theoretical – collectively they proclaimed the Atlantic region as a spatial, cultural, and political category whose essential characteristics could and should be identified and/or debated. Notwithstanding the heterogeneous nature of these films, moreover, it is hard to escape the conclusion that they did more to reinforce an antimodernist perspective than challenge it. The folkish construction of the Maritimes – reminiscent in many ways of the discovery of Appalachia in the United States – remained an enduring theme in the documentary rendering of this region's history before 1990. In general, the films of the NFB glorified the region's pre-Confederation past, and especially the "golden age" of sail. In the classic film of this genre, *Empty Harbours Empty Dreams* (1976), the Maritimes in 1867 is depicted as a community thriving from her attachment to the sea. With Confederation, that prosperity was lost and the Maritimes entered a subsequent century-long period of decline. While the prosperity of the nineteenth-century wooden shipbuilding industry and the international shipping trades are thus vividly presented, the images of the twentieth century are those of lonely seagulls standing vigil over empty fishing boats in empty harbours. It is worth noting, moreover, that the notion of "empty harbours" not only reinforced the idea of a region whose glory years were behind it, but served those wishing to develop the east coast fishery as a technologically modernized offshore industry at the expense of the small-boat or inshore fishermen at a crucial time in the struggle against over-fishing. However romanticized the lives of those who struggled to survive on the soil or at sea, the message seemed to be the same for them as for the region as a whole: time had passed both by.

Over the years, numerous NFB productions exalted innocent lives of "honest toil" threatened by the relentless yet necessary forces of modernization. Of course, filmmakers were not alone in this. As Ian McKay has told us, the "quest of the folk" had been a particularly powerful preoccupation of regional cultural producers for decades.[14] Central to this romantic portrait was a belief in the special attachment to and character-building influence of those who made their living from the sea. Films such as *The Sea Got in Your Blood* (1965), *The Baymen* (1965), and *A Rosewood Dream* (1970) celebrated the nobility of those "born to the sea" and lamented the younger generation's flight to urban occupations. At the same time they ignored the structural realities resting beneath capitalist exploitation of natural resources and the class inequalities that arose from it. Rather than a sense of injustice, what emerges from films of this type, and from *Change by Degrees* (1975), in which a young Sambro fisherman takes a 360-degree look at his village from his rooftop in order to preserve "the last remnants of a way of life," is a wistful lament about inevitable lost innocence.

In *The Islanders* (1974) this nostalgia is offered as a substitute for more rigorous historical analysis. As one central Canadian commentator described it, the film, based on memories of the days of sailing ships and a time when Prince Edward Islanders had to "carve their homesteads out of an imposing forest wilderness," tells a "personal history of a people ..., the kind of history that doesn't appear in the history texts." It is a film filled with pastoral images, where people moved to the rhythm of hard work and the heritage of fishing and, especially, of farming. Individuals "worked the land which meant you worked for yourself." Small family farms are at the centre of this film, a beautiful patchwork of rurality which is small enough for children to walk to school. The smallness of Charlottetown is also emphasized, and still photographs emphasize mud streets and board sidewalks. But when? The images are not dated and we are not told of change over time. Nor is Charlottetown compared with other regional centres such as Fredericton, Saint John, St. John's, or Halifax. We are left with a sense of difference and distinctiveness. Even the "friendly little railway" which came in the early 1870s is different since "It couldn't take you away." Here is a film celebrating the culture of the Cradle of Confederation and, viewed today, the film seems decidedly old-fashioned to students looking for a sharper critical edge or an entry point into critical discussions.

The same can be said for other NFB films that celebrated those who worked the land or maintained traditional crafts. *The Chairmaker and the Boys* (1958) told the story of Ernest Hart, a Margaree Valley carpenter, blacksmith, and handyman, and his relationship with his grandson. Fifteen years later, *Margaree People* (1974) reiterated this message of a traditional culture facing destruction, in what the NFB catalogue calls "a nostalgic study of a passing way of life." And, in *Don't Knock the Ox* (1970), NFB crews attended the International Ox Pull at Bridgewater, Nova Scotia, to shoot "a holdover from the pioneer past when oxen cleared the land and tilled the soil." But one older film provides an opportunity for students to dig more deeply into the process of cultural selection that has secured a primacy of place for this nostalgic imagery. The short black and white film *Songs of Nova Scotia* (1958) introduces us to the career of folklorist Helen Creighton. Creighton is unquestionably the representative *par excellence* of folk imagery in the region. Not only is there a good deal of scholarship about her, but her many books remain required reading for people inside and outside the region. Framed alongside readings in cultural studies, this film can become an entry point for students to discuss a wide range of topics, from rough culture to tourism. They can also begin to contemplate the extent to which the 'quest of the folk' required a veneration of regional simplicity and the artistry of the simple life.

It is just that "innocence" that is exalted in *Maud Lewis: A World Without Shadows* (1976), a short film that explores Nova Scotia's famous folk artist, with many images of her art. Made before Lewis became known beyond a limited artistic community in the region, this is a documentary bound in a specific image of the artist, and one who was decidedly local. Lewis rarely ventured far from her Marshalltown home, just outside Digby,

Nova Scotia, and local scenes informed much of her art. It is striking how this is a narrative of triumph. Lewis, viewers conclude, managed to achieve distinction despite the limited mobility in her arms and despite her poverty, and created evocative images of rural life. The narrative arc of this film emphasizes simplicity, of her materials, of her colours (never mixing the Tinsol paint, but instead using it straight out of the tube), and of her material conditions, living in her 10x9 house without electricity or running water.

Recent Film and the Reconstruction of Atlantic Canada

Indeed, Lewis's modest house and its representation in the film stand in contrast to rural housing depicted in *A Ballad of South Mountain* (1987), directed by Hubert Schuurman and produced by Shelagh Mackenzie and Rex Tasker. This film follows the lives of two rural families, the Groves and the Browns, and explores rural poverty in Nova Scotia's Annapolis Valley. The opening frames of the film show images of the farm, milking cows, and harvesting, the pastoral setting of the Annapolis Valley and its wealth. This is contrasted with images of South Mountain and of the people who live there, people who have lost their traditional place in the economy. The people there can no longer survive through hunting and trapping. Seemingly, they are being left behind by the modern world, but Schuurman does not romanticize this.

The arc of the film follows the families as they are moving to new houses provided through the efforts of an interfaith church group. The opening of the film, though set in Nova Scotia's Annapolis Valley, reminds the viewer that the community could be anywhere. In this way, the local is not at the centre of this representation, which intends instead to highlight the general question of rural poverty, regardless of setting. It is important to note that the film was made before the stories of sexual abuse of children became well known, sensationalized through the media and popular accounts such as David Cruise and Alison Griffiths' *On South Mountain: The Dark Secrets of the Goler Clan*.[15] There is, however, no notion of romance attached to the inadequate housing endured by the Groves and the Browns, unlike the portrayal in *A World Without Shadows*.

This hard-headed realism is evident as well in the well-known NFB film *Remember Africville* (1991). The late Shelagh Mackenzie's film documents a forum held at Mount Saint Vincent University in 1989 which offered powerful testimonials about Africville from multiple perspectives. MacKenzie intercut archival still photographs and historic footage with this forum, resulting in a powerful documentary of an important story. Speakers at the forum, such as Irving Carvery, highlighted the consequences of the destruction of Africville and a profound sense of loss. Others, including Gus Wedderburn, highlighted the poverty that characterized some of the residents. In a powerful moment from the forum, Wedderburn repeats several times that he "did not see the flowers," implicitly impugning any temptation to romanticize the community and the problems it faced. Of course, as the film so aptly documents, the roots of Africville's 'problems' did not rest solely with the residents of the community but rather with a city unwilling to supply water, sewer, paved roads or other amenities. In this way, the city of Halifax constructed the material conditions that later became the justification for its ultimate destruction.

Remember Africville is an engaging community study. Following the film, discussions usually turn first to questions of racism, which is an obvious and important theme of the film. Viewers are often horrified to realize the extent of racism in Halifax and frequently use the film as a vehicle to consider race relations in their own experience, whether they are from the region or not. The film, however, does not explore other analytical paths very fully. But any discussion of Africville does create an opportunity to address questions of public housing and other aspects of the welfare state, questions of 'urban renewal' and other stories of community destruction or relocation, including the destruction of outport communities in Newfoundland or the efforts to 'centralize' Aboriginal communities, to name only two examples.

A final analytical tack may be to raise questions about history and memory, another important aspect of MacKenzie's film. Why, students are asked, does the experience of Africville continue to resonate with former residents and their descendants? The discussion is always a productive one and creates an opportunity to consider the destruction of other communities, such as the working-class community of Greenbank, a small, predominantly white community of 30–40 houses, known locally as Tar Paper Alley or, more recently, as the "white Africville." The residents of Greenbank lived there until 1956, when the land was sold and ultimately redeveloped as a container pier. *Remember Africville* is a film that is accessible, powerful, and beautifully crafted and, from a university teacher's point of view, an important vehicle to explore many themes that resonate with communities throughout the Atlantic Region and beyond. Taken together, *Remember*

Africville and *A Ballad of South Mountain* represent an important point of transition in the imagining of region on film.

Turning to recent films, we can pose some questions. Are new films freed from either the burden of explaining Atlantic Canada as an assumed geography, one that is clearly delimited from other parts of Canada and North America because of its history, culture, or place within the broader processes of capitalism? Do the new representations of the Atlantic region blend, as many postmodern films do, seriousness and farce or trenchant criticism of a specific setting with the imperative to situate that setting within a broader context? This is to say, what is the relation between shifting notions of Atlantic Canada as an interpretive unit of analysis and its representation in films of the later 1980s, 1990s and those of the new century? It is, of course, beyond the scope of this paper to explore the full variety of films and other media that portray Atlantic Canada. Instead, we intend to select only a few illustrative films and to raise questions about the relationship between film and changing notions of region. It is our hope that such an exercise in raising questions may stimulate further research into film and the Atlantic region, as a way of exploring cultural representation, as well as processes of cultural selection and production.

The new representations of region, rather than exploring particular moments of the past or the folkish qualities of Atlantic Canada, instead shifted through the 1990s to explore a different set of questions. Ian McKay and others have highlighted a similar shift in focus the scholarship of the region.[16] In many ways, research has moved from region as an assumption, geographically rooted and fixed, to one in which region is decidedly more fluid and continually held up to critical scrutiny. At the same time, reinterpreting the Atlantic region not only as a geographic place but as an analytical space will fulfill McKay's hope that studies of the "Atlantic Region will likely play a central role in ... reshaping our understanding of the Canadian experience." For this to occur, region has to remain a central element in our interpretive frameworks. But in recent films, region has receded to such an extent that the narratives presented seem unconnected to other interpretive frameworks. Has the pendulum swung too far, away from representations of an assumed and distinctive place to one in which any story can simply be written upon the canvas of the Atlantic region?

Three recent films illustrate the region as canvas. *Brother 2 Brother* (2004) was directed by Russell Wyse as one of the films of the Reel Diversity competition, a partnership among the CBC, NFB, Vision TV, and the Writers Guild of Canada. This film follows 21-year-old Corey Lucas, an African Nova Scotian growing up in the "Jellybean Square" housing project of north-end Dartmouth. The film focuses on a retreat held by the Brothers Reaching Out Society (BROS) and is an exploration of the social marginalization of young black men, but the struggle of this young man could be situated anywhere. Rosemary House's film *Hospital City* (2006) was filmed in the Health Sciences Centre in St. John's, Newfoundland.[18] It is a fascinating exploration of hospital workers – the cooks, cleaners, laboratory staff, nurses, and others who are the lifeblood of the modern hospital complex. However, with the exception of the distinctive accents and occasional establishing shots of St. John's, this documentary could have been filmed in any hospital in North America. This is to say that there is very little in the film that links the narrative arc to the social setting.

And finally, *Cottonland* (2006) is the stunning collaboration between Nance Ackerman and Eddie Buchanan, a film that explores the illegal use of the prescription painkiller OxyContin in the Cape Breton community of Glace Bay. OxyContin has displaced heroin as the street drug of choice in cities such as Edmonton, Toronto, Quebec City, Fredericton, and Saint John, according to a study published in the *Canadian Medical Association Journal*.[17] What is distinctive about *Cottonland* is that, while it is very much an analysis of the cost of personal dependency, it situates both addiction and dependency in the broader social and economic conditions of Glace Bay. While the film emphasizes the local context, it also succeeds in placing that context in an analytical frame that permits comparison with other communities. In this way, setting is both a crucial element in the film and a launching point for comparison with other communities, including the neighbouring Mi'kmaq community of Membertou and other coal mining communities enduring their own OxyContin epidemic, notably the Appalachian communities from which the vernacular term for OxyContin, "Hillbilly Heroin," was derived.

Cottonland is successful, in part, because it achieves a balance between local and regional questions, and more universal concerns, including those of economic decline, addiction, and the limited capacity of social service institutions. The degree to which the local and the regional emerges in a given film is a function of a variety of factors. As discussed elsewhere in this book, the influence of broadcasters and funding agencies is one important factor, but those forces exist alongside the interests of individual filmmakers. *Cottonland* is fully financed by the National Film Board, but

Thomas Ogley in *Cottonland*. Photo by director Nance Ackerman, courtesy of National Film Board of Canada.

this arrangement, the norm for the NFB until budget cutbacks of the 1990s, is increasingly difficult for filmmakers to obtain, and this does contribute to the erosion of a uniform house style. Unlike either *Brother 2 Brother* or *Hospital City*, where setting recedes almost entirely from view, place matters in *Cottonland*. It matters in critical ways, not in the essentialist or reductionist rendering of earlier notions of region, which avoid critical or even analytical positions. Instead, in *Cottonland*, region (or place) becomes a unit of analysis, something that must be fully conceptualized and considered. Even issues considered to be deeply personal, such as those of dependency and addiction, are placed within an interpretive framework that forces the viewer to consider multiple layers and explanations, including those of economic hardship and community decline, neither of which is unique to Glace Bay.

Conclusion: Region Proclaimed, Region Deconstructed

This chapter has tried to demonstrate the stubbornness of the myth of the conservative Maritimes, and to assess the ways in which filmmakers and historians have perpetuated and challenged these assumptions. Over the years historians within Atlantic Canada have bemoaned stereotypes about the quaint, traditional, and folkish character of a region unable to fully accommodate itself to modernity. The deconstruction of these stereotypes, moreover, led scholars and filmmakers to reflect upon how images of region are at once externally and internally constructed, and to understand imagined regions and their borders as permeable rather than fixed categories. In turn, a growing preoccupation with the crossing of spatial and intellectual boundaries and the multiplicity of subject identities spawned in the contemporary globalized world has meant that the very notion of region has lost some of its force as a metaphorical category and framework for analysis. But it is our firm belief that place or region continues to matter. What is required are new ways of seeing or imagining region that transcend the nostalgic romanticism of the folk and the dualistic constructions of traditionalism and modernity, and at the same time understand region as more than mere neutral space upon which universal themes or particular subjective experiences parade. Our study of films about Atlantic Canada and of regional historiography suggests a possible trajectory from region proclaimed to region deconstructed, and hopefully to a reconstructed sense

Glace Bay, Nova Scotia, in the film *Cottonland*. Photo by director Nance Ackerman, courtesy of National Film Board of Canada.

of region in the future. During the 1970s and '80s filmmakers and historians both unselfconsciously proclaimed the Atlantic Region as an entity that required study and analysis, and in their own ways produced claims about the region's character. Stereotypical assumptions about regional conservatism were both maintained and challenged. Whatever one's presumptions about the region, its importance was asserted and maintained.

By the mid-1980s and early 1990s, however, there was a growing reluctance to make sweeping claims about the region. As post-colonial theorists questioned the inclusiveness of older narratives about nation and empire, they were also inclined to be suspicious of regional narratives such as those developed by the first *Acadiensis* generation. Given the propensity of post-colonial deconstructionists to question the value of more holistic analysis, and the conceit of synthesis, there was a clear tendency to reduce the idea of region as a unit of interpretive analysis and to present it simply as a geographical space within which particular circumstances and subjective experiences could be explored. Just as recent issues of *Acadiensis* seem to lack a shared social and political purpose and tend instead toward self-contained pieces of research, films in the 1990s interpreted the region as a space where issues of universal significance could be articulated. It does seem, however, that the region reduced may have been a necessary step in understanding its fluid borders, and the need to explore more carefully the continually shifting boundaries and interconnections between local, regional, national, imperial, and global experiences.[19] Today, a willingness to reconstruct region with an appreciation of multiple layers of experience and meaning, and to probe more deeply the importance of place as an analytical space, is re-emerging. In our view, it is about time!

NOTES

1   Malek Khouri, *Filming Politics: Communism and the Portrayal of the Working Class at the National Film Board of Canada, 1939–46* (Calgary: University of Calgary Press, 2007).

2   Thomas Schatz, *Hollywood Genres: Formulas, Film-Making and the Studio System* (Philadelphia: Temple University Press, 1981).

3   Jane M. Gaines, "Appleshop Documentaries: Inventing and Preserving Appalachia," *Jump Cut*, no. 34 (1989), 54.

4   William H. New, *Borderlands: How We Talk About Canada* (Vancouver: UBC Press, 1998).

5   Lianne McTavish, "Beyond the Margins: Re-Framing Canadian Art History," *Acadiensis* 30(1) (Autumn 2000): 104–17; Jacques Derrida, *The Truth in Painting*, trans. Geoff Bennington and Ian McLeod (Chicago: University of Chicago Press, 1987); Homi K. Bhaba, *The Location of Culture* (London: Routledge, 1990); and Edward W. Said, *Culture and Imperialism* (New York: Knopf, 1993).

6   In his recent review of Gene Walz, ed., *Canada's Best Features; Critical Essays on 15 Canadian Films* (Amsterdam and New York: Rodopi, 2002), David Frank notes that "none of the chapters are contributed by historians, who are also typically absent from journals in the field. Frank continues by noting the types of questions that are of concern to historians, and how attention to these concerns might enrich the field of film studies. *Canadian Historical Review* 85(4) (December 2004): 878.

7   James K. Hiller, "Newfoundland Confronts Canada, 1867–1949," in E.R. Forbes and D.A. Muise, *The Atlantic Provinces in Confederation* (Toronto: University of Toronto Press 1993).

8   See, e.g., Roy E. George, *A Leader and a Laggard: Manufacturing Industry in Nova Scotia, Quebec and Ontario* (Toronto: University of Toronto Press, 1970).

9   www.thecanadianencyclopedia.com, visited 7 December 2006.

10   E.R. Forbes, "In Search of a Post-Confederation Maritime Historiography, 1900–1967," *Acadiensis* 7(1) (Autumn 1978): 21. See also E.R. Forbes, *Challenging the Regional Stereotype. Essays on the Twentieth Century Maritimes* (Fredericton, NB: Acadiensis Press, 1989).

11   John G. Reid, "Towards the Elusive Synthesis: The Atlantic Provinces in Recent General Treatments of Canadian History," *Acadiensis* 16(2) (Spring 1987): 121; Phillip A. Buckner, "'Limited Identities' and Canadian Historical Scholarship: An Atlantic Provinces Perspective," *Journal of Canadian Studies* 23(1 & 2) (Spring/Summer 1988).

12   Diane Francis, *Controlling Interest: Who Owns Canada?* (Toronto: MacMillan of Canada, 1986).

13   Stephen Dutcher, "'Looking Towards the Promised Land': Modernity, Antimodernism and Co-operative Wholesaling in the Maritime Provinces, 1945–1961," *Acadiensis* 34(2) (Spring 2005): 46–73. The quote is from p. 48.

14   Ian McKay, *The Quest of the Folk: Antimodernism and the Politics of Cultural Selection in Twentieth-Century Nova Scotia* (Montreal and Kingston: McGill-Queens University Press, 1994).

15   David Cruise and Alison Griffiths, *On South Mountain: The Dark Secrets of the Goler Clan* (Toronto: Penguin, 1997).

16   Ian McKay, "A Note on 'Region' in Writing the History of Atlantic Canada," *Acadiensis* 29(2) (Spring 2000): 89–101; Colin Howell, "Development, Deconstruction and Region," *Acadiensis* 29(1) (Autumn 2000): 3–23.

17   Benedikt Fischer, Jürgen Rehm, Jayadeep Patra, and Michelle Firestone Cruz, "Changes in Illicit Opioid Use Across Canada," *Canadian Medical Association Journal* 175(11) (November 21, 2006): 1385–87.

18   *Hospital City* is not exclusively funded by
     the NFB, but the filmmaker has asserted
     that this has had no influence on the film.
     She explains that the film is about the
     apparatus of a large urban hospital and
     that she had no intention of emphasizing
     the particular place (St. John's) and yet
     she finds the specificity of the voice of
     her subjects to be unmistakably of the
     region. Personal e-mail correspondence
     between Rosemary House and Darrell
     Varga, 15 January 2008.

19   Stephen J. Hornsby and John G. Reid,
     *New England and the Maritime Prov-
     inces: Connections and Comparisons*
     (Montreal: McGill-Queen's University
     Press, 2005). The new focus on border-
     land connections, evident in the work
     of John Reid, Elizabeth Mancke, and
     others, has led to an understanding of
     region, colony, empire, and nation as
     processes of interaction rather than as
     fixed entities.

2

A JOURNEY THROUGH ACADIAN CINEMA

PIERRE VÉRONNEAU
TRANSLATED BY SHANA MCGUIRE

Contemporary Acadian cinema is now over thirty years old, but its origins can be traced back to the very early days of cinema itself with the first Canadian-made feature-length film, *Évangeline* (1913), a film which has disappeared and for which only photographs remain. There is also a long history of non-Acadian filmmakers coming to the Maritimes to shoot footage of Acadia. The National Film Board of Canada has sent Quebecois production teams to the area, resulting in the films *Voix d'Acadie* by Roger Blais (1952) and *Chéticamp* by Raymond Garceau (1962). A lone Acadian, Léonard Forest, is recruited in 1953, yet when the NFB decides to shoot a new film, *Les Aboiteaux (The Dikes)*, in the Acadian region, they turn to a Quebecois, Roger Blais. Blais, however, knows little about the area and the NFB must hire Forest for the research and writing of the project. The scale of *Les Aboiteaux* is surprising: touted as a real "super-production," it is maintained that almost a hundred extras participated in this fictional-documentary. For the first time, Acadians have star billing on the silver screen. The release of the film in 1955 convinces those in charge at the NFB of Forest's capabilities. The following year, Forest is able to shoot a new docudrama, this time in Nova Scotia, *Pêcheurs de Pomcoup (Fisherman of Pubnico*, 1956). In focusing on what is considered to be the oldest Acadian community in Nova Scotia, the film also tells of a long fidelity to the sea which has had an impact on both the personality and history of the town. This is the first, but nonetheless ephemeral, Acadian production. Several parameters which come to dominate Acadian film production for many years are already apparent: filming essentially local subjects; turning toward the sea as an element of their specificity; and reflecting the survival of traditions.

In 1967, the Canadian government creates the interdepartmental program "Challenge for Change," which includes a sector devoted to the cinema. Filmmakers who become involved in this venture aim to use film as a tool for bringing about social change and to experiment with new methods of distribution. This provides a perfect occasion for Forest to propose a feature documentary, *Les Acadiens de la Dispersion* (1967), accompanied by a satellite film, *Acadie libre* (1966–69). Signalling the advent of the deportation theme in Acadian cinema, this film transports the spectator from the Acadian region in the Maritimes to Louisiana, while covering topics such as survival, culture, and the future. Detecting in the Acadian nationalist movement an echo of their own nationalism, several Quebecois filmmakers will, for their part, make two films in Acadia: *Éloge du chiac* (Michel Brault, 1969) and *L'Acadie, l'Acadie?!?* (M. Brault and Pierre Perrault, 1971). Despite the many merits of these films, they nonetheless portray a Quebecois perspective on Acadian reality – a practice which has not yet disappeared.[1]

Finding in "Challenge for Change" a structure which allows for the expression of Acadian concerns, Forest naturally becomes a local leader of the program. Wanting to establish a link between film projects and the popular milieu, an idea in keeping with the program's philosophy which claims to want people to express themselves, to take control and find solutions to their own circumstances, he is particularly interested in encouraging the involvement of the general public. One such example is *La Noce est pas finie* (1971), a film directed by Forest with the help of a group of people from New Brunswick whose lives and problems he details in the film. This collective project thus becomes the first Acadian feature fiction film. Next, Forest makes *Un soleil pas comme ailleurs* (*A Sun Like Nowhere Else*, 1972), a film which testifies to the cultural and political awakening of the Acadians of northeastern New Brunswick. He consequently becomes more and more convinced of the necessity of creating a production studio in the Acadian region which would promote the existence of regional cultural expression.[2] The NFB is not in a rush to act but will eventually be forced into action by the government. In the spring of 1972 Ottawa decides to establish a national film policy that proposes in particular the regionalization of NFB activities within specific studios.

Regionalization at the NFB

In 1974, in an effort to conform to the new government policy as well as to meet Francophone expectations, the French Production Branch creates three production centres outside Quebec in order to allow Francophones from these areas access to cinematographic expression. In Acadia, this initiative proves difficult and conflict ensues between them and the head office in Montreal. Acadians are, however, very clear about their objectives: in particular, they want films and filmmakers to be better rooted in the realities of the region; that experienced filmmakers be more accessible and available to those who might need their advice; and that it become easier to find local artists who might be given the opportunity to make their region known to the rest of the country. In other words, they want the NFB to respect their cultural identity while at the same time allowing regional identities to be communicated through their own creative means.

The local spirit remains steadfast. The first projects accepted form a disparate yet eloquent collection: a Super 8mm short film on the *Acadian Frolic* (Monique Légère & Normand LeBlanc); a feature length fiction in 1/2-inch video, *Opération sans boussole*, that Michel Blanchard shoots in the Magdalen Islands; and a 16mm film on an evening poetry reading at the University of Moncton, *La Nuit du 8* (1975). We remain in an educational setting in *Une simple journée* (Charles Thériault, 1975), a fictional documentary describing a day in the life of a typical Dieppe student.

In 1977, NFB French Production outside Quebec is given an autonomous budget which allows Acadian filmmakers to go forward with their projects. One worth mentioning is *Abandounée* (Anna Girouard, 1976), the first fictional film, in the strict sense if the term, undertaken by Acadians in the region. The film deals with the life of a family and their village during the Great Depression, an event which provides the backdrop for showing the underdevelopment of Acadian culture. The documentary *Y'a du bois dans ma cour* (Luc Albert), filmed in 1976, offers a close look at New Brunswick's forestry industry. There is also the feature-length fictional video, *La Bringue* (François Godin). Claude Renaud finally makes a fictional short, *La Confession* (1977), a film that probes the ways in which a woman deals with the burden of morality and religion in her daily life. Like *Abandounée*, it attempts to exorcise a stifling past. The quality of this film, the best up to this point, is a sign of interesting work to follow. To ensure that all Acadian regions are represented, the studio also accepts a project from the Nova Scotian Phil Comeau, once again a fictional piece. *La Cabane* (1977) tells the story of a group of young people from Baie Ste-Marie who, in their quest for identity, rebel against the uncertainties of the future. Comeau continues the momentum with *Les Gossipeuses* (*The Gossips*, 1978), an ambitious satirical comedy filmed in Baie Ste-Marie. The film takes on questions of matriarchy, religion, and the arrival of a foreigner into their closed-off universe. C. Renaud has a repeat success with *Souvenir d'un écolier* (1979), a film that tackles the issue of the burdensome religious presence felt in Acadian culture. The story takes place during the 1950s, a period that Renaud accurately reconstructs; he has quite a strong command of the film as a whole. Still within the realm of fiction, Robert Haché directs *Au boutte du quai* (1978). Through the intermediary of his main character, a woman who becomes keenly aware of her socio-cultural status, Haché gives us a film which expresses several concerns essential to being Acadian: cultural pride; linguistic issues; tensions between the Acadians, the English and the Quebecois; the golden age before the Deportation, etc. Unfortunately, the subject matter tends to overwhelm the form in this film, indicating a limited mastery on the part of the filmmaker; Haché simply tries to address too many topics without any sort of unifying style.

It is worth noting that the first batch of films resulting from the French Regional Production Centre, "Régionalisation/Acadie," are predominantly fictional, as this means of storytelling seems to be best suited to describe the life of Acadian people and to express their imaginative and creative capabilities. This is the first time, in fact, that Acadians see their own image on screen in stories which place them at the centre of the plot. It is through the cinema that they become aware of life in other Acadian communities, but the act of filmmaking also sensitizes directors to their social, economic, and cultural reality. On the documentary end of the spectrum, three filmmakers – Laurent Comeau, Suzanne Dussault and Marc Paulin – decide to capture on film the events that take place during a popular festival in Cap Pelé. However, *Le frolic cé pour ayder* (1979) amounts to nothing more than a sort of television coverage in which the musicians participating in the festival end up being the most interesting aspect.

Central vs. Regional Tensions:
Problems and Threats

In the meantime, Acadia continues to pursue its struggle to have the Centre Acadien recognized as an essential component of the NFB. Montreal remains unsympathetic to its cause as several believe that the amateur nature of regional production devalues the quality of the NFB name. In the midst of all this controversy, a few filmmakers try as well as can be expected to extricate themselves from the situation and move ahead with their projects. The one that stands out is *Armand Plourde, une idée qui fait son chemin* (Denis Godin, 1980), a film about a priest who gets involved in politics by joining the Acadian Party. Also in the category of what can be called local cinema, *Arbres de Noel à vendre* (Denis Morisset, 1981), a documentary about a sivicultural co-operative, is well worth a mention. As the climate deteriorates between Acadie and Montreal, the head of French Production announces the temporary closure of the Moncton office and suspends all production. Thus, *J'avions 375 ans*, a film about the Acadian festival of 1980 begun by P. Comeau, will not be finished until 1982. Several months would be necessary to find a compromise to satisfy the Acadians' aspirations: to accomplish an authentically Acadian cinema, and to see the NFB respect both this desire and the idiosyncrasies of the region.

Production resumes in January 1982 under the guidance of a new producer, Éric Michel, who, intending to start with a clean slate, hires a number of new filmmakers. The Acadian new wave thus begins to take shape. Filmmakers begin to learn better script-writing skills, how to better direct their actors and guide their documentaries, while at the same time relying upon Quebecois professionals. The circumstances surrounding *Massabielle* (Jacques Savoie, 1983) or *Une sagesse ordinaire* (Claudette Lajoie-Chiasson, 1983) are good examples of this renewal. Realizing that music, literature, and theatre are alive and well in Acadia, Michel thinks that fiction best suits the Acadian tradition in that it offers artists a greater range of opportunities to explore their imagination. The success of *Massabielle* confirms his assertion. This short film is astonishing for a first work. The film succeeds due to Savoie's adept construction of the various levels of interaction between his characters and also his faithful rendering of the unusual atmosphere of the locale. The film speaks of expropriation, alienation, and survival, yet in a metaphorical context. Impressed with Savoie's first project, Michel encourages him to start preparing the feature film, *Le*

Journal de Céleste.[3] Michel also opens the door to a philosophy professor, Serge Morin, who directs *De l'autre côté de la glace* (1983). The result is less engaging due to the fact that the author attempts to bring concepts to life through images without any concern for their cinematic specificity. He continually insists upon the allegorical side of the images and situations yet cannot seem to get past their literal representation. We see a hockey team, representing the Francophones, facing off against the rest of Canada, the battle taking place in an abstract and overly aestheticized ice rink. The film garners a rather favourable reception in Francophone parts of the Maritimes, likely because the all the metaphors could be easily decoded in this eccentric yet straightforward project – one which nonetheless provides a cathartic occasion for the collective, a release from the tension between the English and the French.

In spite of the success of this activity after 1982, French Production does not give filmmakers in the region the means to actually shoot proper fiction films. As a result, there is a shift toward documentary productions, which are, minute for minute, less expensive. The case of *Une sagesse ordinaire* is a good example. In a style that is simple and warm, Lajoie-Chiasson introduces us to a nurse who, during her career, aided over three thousand women in delivering their babies at home. Among the other projects that will be completed in 1985, we discover a few themes with universal appeal born of Acadians' desire to broach topics which are not specific only to them. Lajoie-Chiasson expresses such a desire in *Une faim qui vient de loin* (1985), a film dealing with female obesity and a woman's acceptance or rejection of her body. The film is seen almost exclusively from a female point of view, a detail which constitutes the major point of interest of the project. Bettie Arseneault's cinepoem *Bateau bleu, maison verte* deals with another universal subject. Inspired by a photography exhibition which took place some time ago, she plays upon subtlety and simplicity by orienting her camera's gaze toward the chromatic variety of the boats and houses of Petite-Lamèque, while residents of the town explain in voice-over the importance of colour in their lives. The cohesion of this project makes this film an unequivocal success.

A New Structure:
A New Way of Working

During the time when the NFB is restructuring itself and French Production becomes The French Program, the Acadian Studio relentlessly pursues a renewal of its team of filmmakers and its program. A new era is heralded with *Toutes les photos finissent par se ressembler* (1985) by Herménégilde Chiasson, who arrives like a lightning bolt in a still-young production team. Chiasson is a multidisciplinary artist well known in his milieu and deeply rooted in the Acadian collective of artists. From the mid-1980s onward he has been the most prolific Acadian filmmaker. In *Toutes les photos*, a semi-autobiographical fiction, Chiasson speaks of the birth of modern Acadian literature and juxtaposes it with the political struggle of its people. He establishes, from the beginning, a style which will remain constant in his body of work: the use of archival footage, politico-cultural observations, self-referential discourse, and voice-over commentary, among other techniques.

The Studio has less luck with S. Morin's second film, *Sorry Pete ...* (1986). Due to its dreadfully amateur nature, this story of a village king, an ephemeral star in Acadian life, never really gets off the ground. Integrating the cinematic with the unusual and the fantastical is not as easy as it seems. In accordance with its plans, the Studio nonetheless makes progress on all fronts, even in animation. In fact, it produces the first professional film by Anne-Marie Sirois, a filmmaker from the Cinémarévie Film Co-op in Edmundston.[4] *Maille Maille* (*Stitches in Time*, 1978), a very colourful film with a somewhat naïve animation style, links the metamorphosis that happens during the knitting process with the lives of the women who practise the craft. This work portends an interesting career for Sirois, and the doors of the NFB's Animation Studio are opened to her. Among the films released during the course of the year, two projects by Claudette Lajoie are worth mentioning. The first, *Crab-o-tango* (1987), is an evocative film which uses a rhythmic, pulsating soundtrack and no voice-over to tell the story of a group of women who shell crabs in a plant in Grande-Anse. Her second and, arguably, more important film, *Femmes aux filets* (1987), portrays with great accuracy the working conditions of women employed in fish-processing plants in the Acadian Peninsula and their dealings with their labour union. This is social cinema, one engaged in women's issues and giving spectators a close and seemingly unmediated view of the life of these workers.

Les Années noires, Directed by Herménégilde Chiasson, courtesy of National Film Board of Canada.

Michel wants to increase opportunities for Acadian filmmakers to direct their own films and therefore suggests some co-production projects to his counterparts in Halifax. *Robichaud*, by H. Chiasson, is the best example of this collaborative effort. Michel also contemplates having Acadians participate in film projects which have no affiliation to the Centre Acadien. It is once again Chiasson who achieves a brilliant success and steals the show with a film dedicated to Jack Kerouac, *Le Grand Jack* (*Jack Kerouac's Road – A Franco-American Odyssey*, 1987). By allowing him to make a film within the series "Americanness" – in other words, entrusting an Acadian with a non-Acadian subject – the NFB explicitly indicates its desire to integrate the Acadian region in a "national" approach. In Chiasson's film, he makes connections between himself as a poet and Kerouac as a writer but, most interestingly, he makes an analogy between the Deportation that put an entire people "on the road" and Kerouac's wanderings across the United States.

In 1987, Éric Michel steps down from his position. His successor, Michel Lemieux, inherits a core group of filmmakers able to form a professional production team. He also chooses to explore co-production possibilities in order to make up for the modest amount of funds he has at his disposal, a fact which will be reflected in his following projects. First, a trilogy about "Acadianness" as compared with other identities, a project coordinated by Chiasson. Next is a series of six documentary films, "L'Acadie de la mer" ("Acadia of the Sea"), shot at a rate of two per year, the goal of which is to bring out all the influences of the sea in all aspects of Acadian life. In addition to these three series, four individual projects are in production: a medium-length documentary feature *Robichaud* (H. Chiasson), a fictional short *Pièces détachées* (France Daigle), a medium-length documentary *De Caraquet à Cheticamp* (Phil Comeau), and a documentary short *Photos de famille* (Joanne Gallant). We can also add *Madame Latour*, an historical fiction co-produced by the NFB and directed by Chiasson.

In *Robichaud*, the first of the above films to be released in theatres, the director's admiration for the man is palpable. Right from the title credits, it is obvious to the spectator that Chiasson intends this to be a film-memoir, as is customary for him. The film takes us back to the exemplary path taken by of this reformist Premier who brings his own Quiet Revolution to life in New Brunswick. Chiasson is full of so much admiration for the politician that he does not even dare condemn Robichaud for his weak support of Acadian issues, as claimed by some members of the community. One thing is certain: when the film is released its pertinence increases tenfold. Canada is in the midst of the Meech Lake psychodrama and, in New Brunswick, Premier Frank McKenna hesitates to adopt Bill 38 dealing with Francophone rights in his province.

One of the first concrete gestures made by Lemieux is to launch a co-production with Productions Phare-Est and Radio-Canada: four films from the series "Chroniques de l'Atlantique" ("Chronicles from the Atlantic"), which has just replaced "L'Acadie de la mer." Its goal is to showcase a more current and quotidian Acadian region, but one which moves beyond cliché. He believes that broadcasting the films on television will increase their visibility and impact. This decision will henceforth influence the structure and the aesthetic of a good number of Acadian documentaries. The first film, *Moncton/Acadie* (1989), sees Marc Paulin return to the NFB. The central issues of the film are French language, bilingualism, and culture in Acadia. Despite its traditional format built around "talking heads" and rather excessive symbolism (the railroad tracks that divide the city of Moncton), the film responds well to the objectives of the series as it points to the complexities inherent in Acadian identity. Each of the three other films explores individuals representative of contemporary Acadia. *Le Taxi Cormier* (H. Chiasson, 1989) tells the story of a taxi driver who makes the trip between New Brunswick and Montreal. The film serves as a pretext to enter into a discussion about Acadian wandering in which it is suggested that wandering is an intrinsic part of being North American.

At the other end of the province, in Madawaska, a place which rarely appears in Acadian cinema of the NFB, Rodolphe Caron shoots *À cheval sur une frontière* (1990), a film dedicated to a country singer who performs both in Canada and the United States. Caron uses this situation to question the concept of borders and belonging. He also touches on the topic of Acadian identity but from the perspective of a "Brayon" of Madawaska County, where Acadians do not seem to develop a victim mentality, as can be the case for those living in an Anglophone environment. On a completely different note, Ginette Pellerin proposes *L'Âme soeur* (1990), a profane look at a religious universe, and a woman's take on a woman's universe. The concept of the series demonstrates that filmmakers know how to move past formats that simply use reporting and interviews to ones that situate their discourse within the realm of metaphor and metonymy. The objectives initiated by the NFB have clearly been reached.

Instead of pushing the open program, which is dramatically stagnating, Lemieux orients his programming toward television, something which will have a great aesthetic impact on the films to be made. The success of "Chronicles of the Atlantic" prompts the NFB and Phare-Est to give it another try in an attempt to salvage their trouble-plagued production. Preparation is begun on "Acadie de la mer," a series about the Atlantic Ocean, at once an imaginary and yet a very real border in Acadia. In the first film, *Au mitan des îles* (1991), P. Comeau is interested in showing a Nova Scotian fisherman in his own environment. With *Marchand de la mer* (1991) H. Chiasson sketches the portrait of a processing plant owner, demonstrating that Acadians can indeed be successful in business. While there is nothing innovative in the above films with respect to production style, in *Les Pinces d'or* (1991), Renée Blanchar gives the impression that she is going to go even further than *Crab-o-tango* by opening her film with music by Bartok rather than the inevitable folk melody, and leads us to believe that a personal, even experimental film will follow. But after the success of this first sequence the film becomes didactic. As far as G. Pelerin is concerned, she gives us, in *Un jardin sous la mer* (1992), a portrait of the first Acadian woman to devote her life to cultivating mussels.

These four films represent an enormous backward step when compared with the preceding series. They move away from auteurist documentary, from inquiries on the field, from thoughtful contemplation of the subject, and from formal inventiveness. Here, four talented directors resort to filming without any kind of interior necessity, as if their projects were merely about earning a living, as if they believed that television is a medium which accepts anything and everything, including its adversary. Even worse is the fact that what we find in these films is a superficial Acadia, one which plays upon the regional accent and other obvious maritime details, things which could have easily been filmed by a non-Acadian. These are films in which the directors are not personally invested.

In early 1991, J. Savoie initiates a fiction feature film project bringing about his return to the Acadian region with a co-production between the NFB and his own company, Les Productions du Fado. Taking advantage of the NFB co-production programs with the private sector, he announces the shooting of a film entitled *Le Violon d'Arthur*, a fictitious episode in the life of Acadian violinist Arthur LeBlanc. This tele-film represents the most important film project shot in the region, one in which both Acadian and Quebecois artists and technicians participate. The director is Quebecois

(Jean-Pierre Gariépy), as is the principal actor who plays LeBlanc (Claude Gauthier). Upon the film's release in the fall, audiences give it an enthusiastic reception. Those in the film industry, however, denounce Savoie because he has resorted to Quebecois stars, and also accuse him of not encouraging Acadians to become involved with the film, believing that every Acadian film has to be 100 per cent Acadian. Savoie has just experienced the vulnerability of a very sensitive artistic community that also appears rather envious of the exorbitant amount of money devoted to a single film – especially considering that this community, at a loss for new film projects, is suffering the repercussions of an utterly weak NFB administration.

Another film to cause controversy is *L'Acadie à venir* (1992), about the by-election where Prime Minister Jean Chrétien, defeated in Shawinigan, tries to get elected in Beauséjour county. The film discusses Acadians' lack of political involvement and also the ways in which politicians use the Acadian people to their own political ends. The film is not a hit with everyone, however, and Chiasson is criticized for his lack of objectivity. A.-M. Sirois starts production on *Animastress*, an animated film showing the stress that farm animals endure. The NFB even adds a new film by S. Morin to its program, *Unis pour la vie*, on the construction of the Confederation Bridge linking New Brunswick and Prince Edward Island. Then in 1994 a new batch of films arrives on the big screen. *De retour pour de bon*, by Bettie Arseneault, is a documentary about Acadians returning home to the region and how they reappropriate their country. Although the cinematographic quality is lacking, the film relies mostly on what people are saying; its most interesting aspect (which may be too diluted for an hour-long television broadcast) is its topic.

Similar criticism – being too banal and too illustrative – could also be levelled at Monique LeBlanc's first film, *Le Lien acadien* (*The Acadian Connection*, 1995), a feature-length film about the LeBlanc family name, the most common of all Acadian surnames throughout North America. Fortunately she chooses her subjects with care, privileging their uniqueness and their humour, leading the spectator from California to the Maritimes, all the while highlighting the fact that the Acadians of the Deportation are not necessarily marked by pessimism but that they are, more than anything, a people in touch with the world. LeBlanc's biggest success with this film is that she manages to move beyond the local to cross borders and reach a wider range of spectators while still remaining firmly rooted in her Acadian heritage.

Such is not the case, despite appearances, for *L'Acadie retrouvée*, a film about the Acadian World Congress made by three different directors. We travel to France (to Nantes, directed by R. Blanchar), to Louisiana (G. Pellerin), and to Quebec (to Abitibi, H. Chiasson) to meet people preparing to attend the Congress and whom we will meet again later in the film while in the Maritimes. The film alternates between the three sections, giving us a glimpse into the preparations as well as the reasons why each participant is making the trip. The film tackles several subjects: Cajun life, Acadian organizations, genealogy, folklore, pride, etc. This is a commemorative film, an amalgam of almost everything that revolves around the concept of "Acadie" – but one that covers the same ground as television by merely prioritizing the recording of events as opposed to seeking original ways of shooting or putting ahead a point of view.

The NFB decides to launch a series of tele-films co-produced with Phare-Est (which is getting back on the saddle after a period of difficulty) that would deal with Acadian history from the Deportation and up to contemporary times. Two co-productions are the most interesting as well as the most personal projects. In *Les Années noires*, Chiasson takes us back to the one hundred months that followed the Deportation of 1755. He alternates sequences of testimonials by historians with documentary footage. His goal is to situate the facts in their historical context and on the larger scale of relations between New France and England; to deal with the Amerindian question; to show the Acadians before they became victims; to pay homage to their resistance and to their struggle (the English are obviously highly criticized). The film clearly states that the Acadians' refusal to swear oath to the English ultimately determined their fate. This act is part of their identity, of their rejection, as a people, of assimilation, and of choosing to assert their own distinctiveness.

G. Pellerin takes on an ambitious task in *Évangéline en quête* (*Evangeline's Quest*, 1995): showing the depth of Evangeline's presence, attacking the myth created by Longfellow in 1847 and, thanks to the contribution of her co-researcher, Maurice Basque, carrying out the work of an historian. In choosing to incorporate Evangeline as a character through voice-over narration, Pellerin cleverly gives the film a more vibrant feel. She explores Evangeline's every facet, from the implausible portrait of Acadie painted by Longfellow to the invention of her "rival" in Louisiana, Emmeline Labiche. She ridicules the ways in which the Evangeline myth has been used in painting, advertising, and religion. Above all, Pellerin depicts the evolution of the myth: an imaginary romantic heroine, Evangeline stole the Acadians' history from them, which in turn incited their irreverent attitude toward her, before being reclaimed in a more modern discourse in which this film participates. *Evangeline's Quest* is an undeniable success and signals a major evolution in Acadian cinema.

A More Institutionalized and Open Context

In the fall of 1994, a group of filmmakers from New Brunswick asks the provincial government to establish a film development office similar to the one that already exists in Nova Scotia and in other Canadian provinces. The NFB endorses the creation of New Brunswick Film, and even encourages co-productions between NB Film, the NFB and the private sector, as they did, for example, with R. Blanchar's *Ô Canada*. The NFB also believes that the more work there is in the region, the more technicians and filmmakers will be able to live from their trade, and consequently, all stages of the filmmaking process will be able to take place locally. This desire to develop a local production framework happens at the very time that the NFB as an institution is dealing with a major crisis – severe budget cutbacks throughout the 1990s. Its very existence is in danger and eventually survives at the cost of heavy cutbacks. As a result, fictional films are abandoned in favour of animation and documentary, and a restructuring plan called "NFB 2000" is unveiled.

What, then, motivates Acadian directors to make personal documentary films? Chiasson's *Épopée* is one example. This panorama of the history of song in Acadia – from footage of the St. Joseph choir from 1952 to Marie-Jo Thério, or to the Méchants masquereaux – is but a series of alternating filmed shows or interviews. As is his habit, Chiasson chimes in with a voice-over narration telling us of the saga of the Acadian people, of their long-standing struggle which infiltrates their music and which allows them to come out from the darkness, from these melodies that "carry in them all our promises of happiness." Chiasson's narration attempts to mitigate the shortcomings of his filmic content, but it does not quite do the trick. We have seen better "auteur" documentary filmmaking.

R. Blanchar takes an entirely different direction in *Vocation Ménagère* (1996). The subject could have easily lapsed into the anecdotal and the nostalgic, but Blanchar manages to pull it off with finesse. The housekeepers presented in the film are endearing, kind, and lively and they eloquently explain the nature of a job which some may find insignificant. Compared to the priests for whom they work, the housekeepers come out on top and the priests end up playing the foil. Blanchar also makes the intelligent decision to film the domestic interiors in a very stylized manner. The beauty of locations as banal as dining rooms, kitchens, and living rooms seems to somehow elevate the status of the cleaning women in question. Finally, Blanchar develops in counterpoint the theme of aging and even, very subtly, that of the place of religion in contemporary Acadian life. An elegantly powerful and emotional film.

After raising her personal bar high with *Evangeline's Quest*, G. Pellerin had quite a challenge on her hands with *Mathilda la passionara acadienne*. The portrait she creates of Mathilda Blanchard falls short of the possibilities of her subject in the sense that, by resorting several times to archival footage, we are given an interesting look into the militantism of this unionist, but we remain at the threshold of Mathilda the woman. Her relationship with her husband and children is barely mentioned, and certain choices are poorly explained, such as the moment where Mathilda defends British royalty; here Pellerin finds no solution other than to intervene in voice-over in order to tell us that "no one is safe from their contradictions." Yet the film does address important social questions in Acadian cinema which call to mind the reality of the factory workers and unionists in *Femmes aux filets* and *Marchand de la mer*.

NFB producers Pierre Bernier and Diane Poitras seek to move beyond the problems specific to Acadians by offering filmmakers in the region the most freedom possible. *Cigarette* (M. LeBlanc, 1997) is a case in point. This hour-long highly personal film takes the spectator from Cap-Caissie in Brussels, to Paris and New York. Also appearing are a poem by Gérald LeBlanc, a song by Jacques Higelin, an allusion to Serge Gainsbourg and a reference to Godard's *Breathless*. The Belgian New Brunswicker character can be irritating, but he nonetheless manages to stimulate debate for the spectator. His style creates distance within the subject, or rather generates a dual focus – one being the cigarette and the other the character himself – leading the spectator to take a side, whereas LeBlanc makes no attempt to identify with either of them. As for B. Arseneault's next film, *Fripes de choix, guenilles de roi* (1998), the first positive note is that she does not visit the usual Acadian region of New Brunswick, but instead goes to Nova Scotia, a place where, up to this point, only P. Comeau had ventured. The film techniques used are more or less conventional, but her topic – how second-hand clothing stores are creating new dressing habits and democratizing fashion – ends up surprising us. Lastly, Arseneault grabs the audience's attention not through the progression of her story, but by the manner in which she builds successive layers and overlapping cycles. We are won over by the scope and complexity of the experience she describes.

Twenty-five years after the creation of the Centre Acadie the situation has evolved a great deal. The NFB studio reaches a fragile state of maturity. Independent production companies are now consolidated and the creation of NB Film has allowed large amounts of funding to be injected into film and television production.[5] It is in this more comprehensive context that the NFB wishes to now operate. It claims to want to prioritize the production of creative and personal documentaries as well as to give filmmakers more room for creative expression than that allowed in the realm of television. The administration seeks to remain stable while at the same time encouraging change. In 1998, D. Poitras initiates, with the help of CBC Radio, the contest "Jeune documentariste." His successor, Jacques Turgeon, on the job since 2000,[6] tries to pursue a similar policy of finding balance between renewal, on the one hand, and encouraging experienced filmmakers on the other. Further initiatives toward openness and renewal include the "Tremplin" competition, created in 2005 to encourage the creation of short films, or the "AnimAcadie" competition started in 2004 which would help animated films to be produced professionally. A balance must also be struck between subjects of local interest and more universal ones. Such is the dilemma of Acadian cinema: to be a cinema that reflects the reality of its people while still being able to open itself up to the rest of the world, and also one able to give an Acadian perspective on topics of more general interest. For the past ten years or so, the Studio has attempted to maintain this delicate balance.

Let us now take a look at the new wave of Acadian filmmakers of the twenty-first century. For her first attempt, À demain, chères prunelles (1999), Aube Giroux, refusing to play the Acadian card, investigates the place and the impact of virtual images in contemporary life. Five years later, this Prince Edward Island native returns with Dis-moi ce que tu manges ..., which illustrates the reconciliation that has taken place between the food industry and the environment brought about by organic farming. As a co-production between the NFB and CinImage, this project takes advantage of the interdepartmental program for official language communities which helps young people make documentaries – a fact acknowledging that there must be an increase in resources to encourage production in the region. As for Paul Émile d'Entremont, his first film, *Seuls, ensemble* (2000), wonders what has happened to contemporary Acadian identity through two characters searching for their own identity while still asserting their difference: one a gay man and the other a girl looking for her biological mother. For his next film, *Le confessionnal réinventé* (2004), D'Entremont examines a variety of situations, from television to the internet, where people want to confide in others, to confess secrets in a public manner.

In *L'Éternité? ou la disparition d'une culture*, Marie-Claire Dugas, another representative of the new wave, courageously deals with Acadian assimilation in a context where globalization and the decline of the French language are at stake. Her answer, however, is disappointing. Chedly Belkhodja, along with Quebecois co-director Jean Chabot, interrogates, in *Tableaux d'un voyage imaginaire* (2002), the phenomenon of mass tourism as it is experienced in the Maritimes, where images of the region are consumed more so than their reality. In *Kacho Komplo* (2002), Paul Bossé speaks of a modern and dynamic Acadian region, completely turning his back on its folkloric past, by resurrecting, in a fragmentary manner, the glory years of the Moncton bar *Le Kacho*, incubator of Acadian counterculture. Through this evocation of the 1990s, Bossé argues that the vitality of Acadian culture must be maintained. He turns toward a subject of general interest by questioning, in *USAssez!* (2004), the military intervention of the United States in Iraq, and the arrogance of this superpower and its president. This subject is in stark contrast to the one chosen by Louiselle Noël in her film *Bonnes vacances* (2005), a documentary on the life of a child who goes to summer camp in northern New Brunswick.

We must not, however, let this new wave get our hopes up too high. The question still remains: is it possible to survive in the film industry in the Acadian region? It all depends on the kind of work one wants to pursue there. The NFB and television remain two pillars of production. The arrival of NB Film did nevertheless shake things up. The most revealing example is that of Rodrigue Jean. In order to direct the types of films he wants, this newcomer was obligated to shoot his feature films as co-productions in Quebec with Quebecois stars. His first film, *Full Blast* (2000), similar to the novel by Martin Pître of which it is an adaptation, constitutes a surprise in the landscape of Acadian cinema. Here is a film that no longer speaks of the fishery, the deportation, or survival, but of hopelessness, sex, and

Full Blast, Dir: Rodrigue Jean (2000), courtesy of Domino Film and Television.

drugs in an urban setting. Moving away from both pure entertainment and documentary, the Acadie portrayed here is far from cliché – an Acadie from which Jean must in large part distance himself for his second film, *Yellow-knife* (2002), a co-production between three provinces with action taking place throughout Canada. An extremely personal road movie, in which the characters' constant movement contrasts with their interior stagnation and despair, this film is a raw existential drift, punctuated by sex and alcohol, a cinema which reveals more a state of being than a social or political point of view about Canada. It is not surprising that Jean's third film deals with an Acadian poet, modern in both his themes and his writing style. *L'extrême frontière – l'oeuvre de Gérald Leblanc* (2006) fits into the group of films portraying famous Acadians (Durelle, Robichaud, Mathilda Blanchard, Anna Malenfant, Raoul Léger,[7] Emma Edmonds[8]) but it is less common that a cultural personality take centre stage in such a film.

On a tué l'Enfant-Jesus, directed by Renée Blanchar, courtesy of National Film Board of Canada.

Not everyone chooses to take their chances, like Jean, outside the Acadian region. Many try instead to devote themselves to developing the tools necessary to survive closer to home. The creation of production companies is an essential element of this strategy as it allows established filmmakers to pursue their careers while still encouraging newcomers. The leading company, and also one of the oldest (1988), is Productions Phare-est. Headed by Cécile Chevrier and Gilles Losier, with talented collaborators such as M. Paulin, H. Chiasson or G. Pellerin, Phare-Est works for television but in particular pursues a policy of co-production with the NFB where it is guaranteed a considerable level of participation in terms of creative content. The vitality of Acadian cinema depends upon the existence of this company. One has only to mention a few of its recent titles to get a good idea: *1604*, by R. Blanchar (2003), a docudrama on the first French establishment in the New World; *Durelle*, by G. Pellerin (2003), the story of Yvon Durelle, an Acadian boxer who was famous in the 1950s before dealing with several hardships; *Ceux qui attendent* (H. Chiasson, 2002), on the conflict between Acadian and Mi'kmaq fishermen, a situation in which both sides speak of survival but where the Acadians are seen as the oppressors; or *Le temps X*, by R. Blanchar (1999), about Generation X and its turbulent times.[9]

Other production companies have come into being over the last few years, contributing to the diversity of Acadian cinema. We must mention Jacques Levesque's Cojak Productions, to whom we owe Chris LeBlanc's *Libérateur libéré* (2002), a televised documentary about an ex-soldier returning to Holland fifty years after the war; and, from the same director, *Désoriental* (2004), which follows a theatre troupe putting on a show in Vietnam; as well as *La Légende Bricklin* on the American promoter who, in 1973, succeeded in convincing New Brunswick's Premier, Richard Hatfield, to get involved in the manufacturing of a new car. For her part, M. LeBlanc founds CinImage Productions in 1999, which will allow her to produce and direct just as much for television (the documentary series, "Artiste dans l'âme") as for the NFB. Her feature film, *Les chemins de Marie* (2005), takes a look at American society, one in which religion and violence, poverty and charity, racism and social sensitivity intermingle. Finally there is R. Blanchar's feature film, *On a tué l'Enfant-Jésus* (2007), co-produced by her company, Ça tourne Productions, and the NFB, which again illustrates an Acadian people united in solidarity, ready to defend its interests.

Conclusion

Several observers have already noted that artists within Acadian culture seem to have difficulty producing longer works, that poetry and song are more established forms than the novel, for example. Not wanting to speak for other art forms, I nonetheless note that, with the exception of Rodrigue Jean, the best films are not always the longest, and that the one-hour television format has occasionally led filmmakers to extend a piece that would have otherwise been more satisfying had it been condensed. This possibly explains why one often has the impression of being faced with a cinema which shows less concern for the formal aspects of the medium while instead emphasizing the communicative side. This also explains the importance of verbal discourse (narrator, voice-over) which allows filmmakers to enunciate instead of show, which is, after all, what cinema is all about. We must nevertheless recognize that the principal means of dissemination for

Acadian films, as well as Canadian documentary, for that matter, is through television (and recently DVD), that this fact is intimately implicated in the projects themselves, and is also that which creates limitations, as much with regard to the format and the style of the work as with the level of expectation of TV spectators. In the realm of Acadian cinema one often finds, beyond the themes dealt with, an underlying questioning of concepts such as "Acadianness," "Americanness," the weight or absence of borders, wandering, etc. It is necessary to remember that the Deportation constitutes the founding event in the historiography of the Acadians and determines their struggle for identity as well as their definition as a distinct people. Several films make direct reference to this history and to the linguistic specificity of Acadians. Numerous films also question Acadian history and society. During the early years of Acadian cinema, one has the sense that filmmakers have a conflict to resolve regarding the presence of the Catholic Church in their lives. But, with time, the revolt subsides and Acadian society begins to live in a less inward-looking manner. We thus find more films dealing with the Acadians' attitude toward the use of English and their possible assimilation in a more open society.

At the same time, many filmmakers feel the need to maintain their originality; therefore music, song, and literature are very prevalent subjects. It is recognized that Acadians struggled and continue to struggle to preserve their language and their culture. Traditional music is much utilized in their films, and if there is one professional whom the NFB never had to send to the Acadian region, it is surely a musician. In thirty years, the themes broached in Acadian films have significantly evolved. From an overt attachment to the sea and that which it provides, Acadian cinema has, since the end of the 1990s, started to turn its back on themes which made it appear rather folkloric, and urban subjects have been taking on additional importance. Even better, filmmakers are exploring an increasing number of non-Acadian topics, even those considered to be of universal interest. Better still, they no longer feel obligated to limit themselves to shooting in the Acadian region.

It is important to note that this is also a women's cinema. Female filmmakers make up a significant number of total filmmakers in the region, probably the highest in Canada in relative terms. Worth mentioning here are Anna Girouard, Claudette Lajoie, Bettie Arsenault, Anne-Marie Sirois, Ginette Pellerin, Renée Blanchar, Monique LeBlanc, and Cécile Chevrier. However, these women do not appear within the programs reserved for women, as is the case with female directors whose work draws from the NFB national budget. It must be noted that not a single Acadian film can be found in women's initiatives such as "Regards de femmes." Is it because they do not feel welcome there? On the male side of the spectrum, if they did not have the all-round champion Herménégilde Chiasson, promoted to Lieutenant-Governor of his province, the unique Rodrigue Jean, the tenacious Madawaskan Rodolphe Caron, or recently Paul-Émile d'Entremont, the output of male filmmakers would be much less, despite the contributions of those such as Phil Comeau or Jacques Savoie (both now active in Montreal), Claude Renaud, Marc Paulin, or Serge Morin. Even more numerous are films which revolve around women and which have women as main characters. It is especially when the political and the social are at the heart of their films that men are centre stage.

It has been said that, for the Acadians, wandering was at the root of the pain that pushed them toward self-expression and creation. It is clear that art plays a pivotal role in the collective consciousness raising being articulated in Acadia. Cinema does fall in line behind literature, music and song, but in thirty years it has made enormous progress. Acadian cinema has learned to move beyond folklore and the picturesque despite the fact that diverse forces have attempted to resurrect such themes. It has come to be in tune with its community and has overcome major crises tributary to the overall situation at the NFB. It has still not reconciled the fragmentation of the region, Nova Scotia and Madawaska still finding themselves confronted with Moncton. Acadian cinema now finds itself on the threshold of maturity and modernity, a threshold which the work of Rodrigue Jean has already crossed. It has learned to adjust to production imperatives which it did not always determine. I am therefore close to believing that fiction, but not necessarily the feature film, constitutes the mode of expression now best suited to articulate the Acadian imagination. It is not surprising that when the Acadian studio was created, its first films opted initially for fictional material while the majority of personnel sent to Moncton by the NFB head office to help filmmakers (except during the time of Savoie and Morin) were more experienced in documentary. The filmmaker's desire for fiction reflects the spectator's desire for fiction. Nor is it surprising that when fiction is no longer an encouraged mode of expression, filmmakers come to think that fiction is able give documentary discourse a better a grasp on the real; consequently, they have a tendency to fictionalize their material to better their relationship with the spectator. Acadian cinema invites us to clarify our understanding of both the regional and national imaginary, and to clearly see that, on the thematic level, the collective identity may indeed prevail over that of the individual.

NOTES

1 One needs only to think of *Tintamarre – la piste Acadie en Amérique* (André Gladu, 2004, 80 min.).

2 The NFB recently released a DVD box set dedicated to Forest's films and Rodolphe Caron has also made a 52-minute film about the director, *Léonard Forest, cinéaste et poète* (2006).

3 This 60-minute film project, cancelled in 1984, eventually becomes *Les Portes tournantes* (Francis Mankiewicz, 1988).

4 We must highlight the importance of independent production firms, whether they are co-operatives or not, in the training, development, and consolidation of Acadian cinema, and in the contributions that they provide the NFB. They especially allow for more continuity and regularity in providing work, as the few local films by the NFB would never allow for the development of a professional workforce. Another member of Cinémarévie, R. Caron, will become involved in several NFB projects as a cameraman.

5 Unfortunately for Francophone cinema, the director of NB Film, Sam Grana, allocated three-quarters of the organization's funds to Anglophone productions, to the great displeasure of the Acadians who demanded his resignation.

6 Until very recently, Turgeon's office had relocated back to Montreal, a decision which troubled many Acadians. The hiring of a Moncton-based producer, Murielle Rioux-Poirier, rectified this situation.

7 *Raoul Léger, la vérité morcelée*, by R. Blanchar (2002), is a film-inquiry about this secular missionary from New Brunswick who was mysteriously murdered in Guatemala in 1981 during the civil war.

8 *La vie secrète d'Emma Edmonds*, by Pepita Ferrari (2006), is about the adventurous life of a New Brunswick woman who disguised herself as a man to better act as a spy during the American Civil War.

9 The importance of this company has been recognized by the awarding to producer Cécile Chevrier the French government's prestigious Knight of the Order of Arts and Literature in 2006.

3

MOVING PICTURES AT THE OPERA HOUSE: THE INTRODUCTION OF MOTION PICTURES TO THE TOWN OF TRURO, NOVA SCOTIA, 1897-1914

GREGORY CANNING

There is a commonly held belief that rural areas have been less receptive or even resistant to new technology and to modern culture in general. The study of film history has also suffered from this belief since, in the 1970s, scholars began to look at the exhibition practices of early motion pictures.[1] This bias is not necessarily due to any particular lack of awareness on the part of historians, but because the documentation for early film history has centred mostly in the large cities; New York, Chicago, and Montreal all hold extensive archives for newspapers, fire maps, and company documents which made the research not only easier but also more fruitful. These early studies dispelled many of the myths about early motion picture history, such as the myth of the immigrant composition of early audiences and the theory that films acted as a "chaser" in vaudeville shows, to usher the audience out, rather than serve as one of the primary attractions. The myth of the rural areas remained, however, if only through the omission of any investigation into rural film reception.[2] More recently, authors such as Charles Musser, Gregory A. Waller, and Katherine H. Fuller have begun to address this omission.[3] Musser's study of itinerant film exhibition and Fuller's look at small-town American exhibition have opened the way for further studies into the reception of film in the areas outside the major metropolis. My own study follows in the framework set out by Fuller and Musser: that the rural areas of North America can provide a unique approach to the early history of film exhibition and can offer an interesting view of the interaction between audiences at the dawn of new mass culture and the beginning of the twentieth century. This emphasis is important not only in filling a gap in the history of film exhibition, but also because, until the middle of the century, it was the rural areas where much of the population in North America lived. In the case of Nova Scotia at the beginning of the twentieth century, only 28 per cent of the population lived in an urban setting.[4]

Truro, in 1901, was a town situated on the edge of this rural-urban split, with a population of 5,993.[5] Settled by Irish Presbyterians from the American colonies, the lands around Truro were and still are among the most fertile in the province, making Colchester County a desirable destination for both the American settlers and the Scottish Presbyterians who were fleeing Scotland in the 1770s. The importance of Truro started to become more evident around the beginning of the nineteenth century with the provincial road-building program. The town sits at the crossroads between Pictou, Amherst, and Halifax, making it an ideal resting spot and inviting the building of many of the structures that are associated with highway towns in the nineteenth century: hotels, shops, and blacksmiths. This new role for the town caused it to become less reliant on agriculture and more reliant on small-scale manufacturing and trade. The next major step in this history was the building of the provincial rail line in 1858. By 1875, Truro was a progressively led incorporated town in the newly minted nation of Canada. The railway, along with the town's central location, made it an ideal place for many small industries and services. Because of its position, Truro was selected as the location for the regional high school for Colchester County, the Normal School (Teacher's College), and, in 1905, the Nova Scotia Agricultural College. Along with location, Truro was able to boast a water system, electrical generation plant, new schools, and churches to meet the growing population, making it a truly modern town in rural Nova Scotia at the turn of the twentieth century and an ideal case study for the emergence of cinema going.

Between 1875 and 1900 there was a period of unprecedented growth in Truro. A combination of out-migration from the surrounding rural areas, students coming to the new schools in town, and an influx of entrepreneurs taking advantage of the location took the population from just over 2,000 in 1871 to nearly 6,000 in the 1901 census.[6] All of this rapid change – the combination of a new working-class population and the transient group associated with the schools – gave rise to a desire for moral guidance, a role filled by the Presbyterian Church. Presbyterians shared Truro with Anglicans, Catholics, and Baptists, though it was the Presbyterians who held the central position among the spiritual groups from the days of the town's founding, and maintained it by having the largest congregation in the town.[7] Through the temperance societies and the YMCA, the churches in Truro were very active in providing distraction for the population's increased free time.

It is through the *Truro Daily News*, the only surviving newspaper from the turn of the century, that it is possible to investigate the entertainment habits of Truro.[8] Founded in 1891, the *Daily News* was much like any small-town paper in Nova Scotia, consisting of four pages in the early years, with a focus on local and county news and gossip. The entertainment section of the paper was often in the advertisements, typically placed on the third page along with notices and reviews that inhabited the same page, usually in the opinion section. The *Daily News* did not, however, offer opinions on the theatres, unlike the urban papers that Paul Moore investigates.[9] The Truro paper covered entertainment in the town in ways that appear like advertisements, without any critical comment on the shows or the composition of the audiences. The town's only theatre was Gunn's Opera House, built in 1894 as a combination vaudeville and opera house, an 850-seat theatre that occupied the top story of the Gunn block, owned by Daniel Gunn, a local entrepreneur. "The Gunn," as it was locally known, had upholstered seats in the balcony, steam heat and electric lighting, and also boasted five complete sets of scenery painted by Boston's L.L. Covele & Company.[10] In spite of this luxurious description, the theatre lists itself as a middle-class theatre in the newspapers, and the historical works about Truro do nothing to challenge this assertion. The conspicuous displays of wealth that are flaunted in the ads and records do not conform to the Presbyterian teachings of thrift and productive labour, though the design is consistent with public architecture of the era. Even the name Gunn's Opera House appears to place the theatre on a slightly higher plane. However, since the theatre was built in 1894, it is less likely that Daniel Gunn was interested in placing his theatre in highbrow culture, and more likely that he was trying to make audiences equate his theatre with quality.

In a 2005 article published in *Cinema Journal*, Gregory Waller argues that the film exhibitors in America played a special role in the small towns of the 1930s.[11] Using trade papers and a serial story from *The Saturday*

Evening Post as his sources, he illustrates how small-town theatres, whether owned locally or part of a chain of theatres, were given a greater chance at success if the managers let themselves be better known in the community. Prominence in the community on the part of theatre managers would raise the profile of the venue and decrease the likelihood of local censorship and protest and increase the loyalty of clients. Waller's argument is that this is what may have protected many theatres from both the Great Depression and the censorship battles of the era. This assertion is well founded, though I would argue that this is a lesson that was learned long before by theatre owners. The goals of theatre managers in Truro appear to be consistent with this history.

The Gunn was the first theatre in Truro, and it appears that Daniel Gunn was quick to learn the importance of becoming a community leader. He was known in the community before opening his theatre, being a landowner and businessman in the town. He owned the building along with his brother Jesse, and both hailed from Earltown, a Scottish-settled enclave 30 kilometres north of Truro. The Gunn was a centre of the community, which is not surprising as it was the only theatre in the town.[12] This theatre was able to position itself as a pillar in the town through charity shows, local talent shows, and tailoring the incoming entertainment to the local audience. Shows would often not start until after 8 pm at the Gunn, to allow for the church meetings that often went until 7:30. It is also obvious from the types of shows that there was some influence either from the churches or from the town leaders. Prior to the arrival of the first film projector the shows were the regular vaudeville fare that one would expect, from "The Great Harry Houdini,"[13] who performed two shows at the Gunn in 1896, to the travelling dramatic companies that regularly toured the region.[14] The common theme in the advertisements for these shows was both the moral quality of the program and the success that the show had in other towns. This theme is illustrated in an ad from January 6, 1897: "The John E. Brennan Co. will play Gunn's Opera House commencing on Tues. the 12th ... continuing all week. This company has met with unusual success in St. John, and other cities, and the stagework is attractive, witty, clean and clever."[15] Many ads for the travelling shows commented on how "clean" the acts were, assuring the audience that what they would be shown would not offend them. If the people of Amherst (200 km north of Truro) or Saint John, New Brunswick, thought that the show was acceptable, then those in Truro could be assured that it would not offend them.

MOVING PICTURES AT THE OPERA HOUSE

One of the assumptions that is often held about Nova Scotia is that most things originate in Halifax and spread into the rural areas from this urban centre. This assumption is not necessarily true, especially of the travelling shows that were moving around the region in the late nineteenth and early twentieth centuries. When, in September 1896, the Edison Vitascope was exhibited in Halifax, one would expect that the operator would have toured the province from this point. However, since the Halifax show was a failure due to electrical problems, it was nearly a full year before the moving pictures came to Truro and other regions, including Sydney, Amherst, and Yarmouth.[16] On July 19, 1897, the first exhibition of the Edison Vitagraph arrived in Truro with Rice's Comedians, a travelling vaudeville troupe.[17] The interesting thing about this show, aside from the fact that it was the first moving picture show in Truro, is that there was no mention of the films in the published review. The notice from July 20, 1897, was of course positive but with no mention of the first local screening of what was to become the dominant entertainment form of the modern age: "It was the universally expressed opinion of those who were at the Opera House last night that it was the best thing that had ever been there, and that Rice's Comedians should have a full house tonight."[18] The absence of film might appear surprising, but it should be remembered that, although in hindsight the Vitagraph was an amazing machine, the audience at Gunn's were more interested in the comedy. The advertisement also notes that the Edison Vitograph was slated to play all week, showing that it was indeed a draw for audiences, though it was not the most important aspect of the performance.

The first show was enough of a success to invite the return of motion pictures four times over the next year, all playing multiple days (suggesting audience appeal and popularity), and all changing their programs nightly. Among these shows appearing in 1897 was Wormwood's Monkey Theatre, showing scenes from Queen Victoria's Jubilee, one of the most popular shows of the first two years of film exhibition in Truro. According to a review in the *Truro Daily News*:

> In addition the latest projecting machine showing animated pictures of the Queen's Jubilee Procession taken by the Lumiere Cinematograph Co., of Paris.
>
> See the Queen in the grand parade, also the Colonial and Indian troops, a sight of a lifetime. Not just a panorama, but

life size pictures in motion, true to life, just as though you were present during the Jubilee.[19]

Of course, this show was offered great reviews, though the commentary was not on the images shown, but on the quality of those images, stating that they were "fine and lifelike," emphasizing the representation of the Queen rather than the fact of cinematic representation itself.[20]

An indication of the type of shows that were being appreciated at the Gunn comes from a short note in the December 7 paper from 1897: "The Queen's Diamond Jubilee Procession views have no connection what ever with the Corbett-Fitzsimmons Kinetoscope Show. These views have the approval of Her Majesty and are beyond anything ever shown in Truro in this line."[21] This note can indicate at least two things. First, that the Gunn Opera House was not interested in showing the boxing match, which was one of the early and much-discussed draws of the Kinetoscope and the Vitagraph. This absence is rather remarkable, since in the studies done on film exhibition in the United States, the Corbett-Fitzsimmons fight and subsequent boxing films were huge draws.[22] Audiences flocked to see the boxing since they were unable to see the fights live. As well, the films were an ingenious way around the prohibitions that many towns had for boxing. Despite being one of the most popular sports in America, it was banned in most municipalities, and the films proved to be the only way that many could see the fights (though it did not take legislators long to catch on to this and place bans on boxing films). However, in Truro, the films were taboo, and the fact that they might have been confused with the Queen's Diamond Jubilee pictures caused enough concern at the Gunn that the managers put a note in the paper. The second thing that this note suggests is that the people in Truro were aware of the Corbett-Fitzsimmons fight and that there was an element in the town that was interested in seeing this, yet were unable to, at least in Truro.

The pre-Nickelodeon period in Truro is interesting mostly for what was highlighted in the ads. That the Corbett-Fitzsimmons fight was not shown becomes understandable in the context of what other films were popular. The most often-noted films come not from America, but from France and Britain. The Pathé films rank rather high in the ads, a fact that is not surprising since Pathé was the world leader in filmmaking prior to the ascendancy of Hollywood-style narrative.[23] Most of the other films were actualities, with subjects like the Queen's Jubilee, the Boer War, or the San Francisco earthquake.

In this early period of film exhibition, the managers of the Gunn and the editors of the newspaper seem to be taking great pains in illustrating the redemptive value of the motion pictures. Repeatedly in the ads and reviews the films and shows are referred to as being uplifting and intellectual. The films and the shows are also used to cement the role of the theatre in the community. Not only does the Gunn provide entertainment, but it also acts as a fundraising venue for local causes. The DJTA (Diamond Jubilee Temperance Association), one of the more successful local temperance associations, took advantage of the Gunn at least twice prior to their getting their own auditorium in 1899 to stage fundraising and awareness lectures. The Gunn was also the site where, in 1900, the Indian Relief Fund was held. In this instance, the theatre was working closely with the *Daily News*, attempting to raise funds for famine relief in India. "FOR FIFTY CENTS you can get fifty dollars worth of entertainment and five thousand dollars worth of instruction; and at the same time your fifty cents will help save some fellow man from the tortures of death by starvation."[24] The draw for audiences was both communal pride and a desire to see the popular Biograph War pictures. The show was advertised as a chance for Truro citizens to show their support for the starving Indians and to raise more money than was being raised in Halifax by the *Halifax Herald* with their own fundraiser. "Truro is one of the most generous towns in Nova Scotia. It has already given several hundreds of dollars to the Patriotic Funds for the Canadian 'soldiers of the Queen,' but has not yet made any specific contribution for the four millions of our fellow citizens who are suffering the horrors of starvation in India."[25] With this show the Gunn appeared to be using both communal pride and a tinge of guilt to sell the idea of seeing films for a charitable cause. That films were the main draw for this fundraiser shows that this was an established and popular form of entertainment in Truro.

The Gunn begins to lose its place in Truro's entertainment scene when, between 1902 and 1905, there appears to be a change in the entertainment desires of the town. Truro appears, during these three years, to be returning to the churches, or at least staying away from the theatres. The churches were never far from the population, but there is a lull in secular entertainment, while at the same time a rise in advertisements for church-sponsored activities – lectures, concerts, or meetings. There is also a rise in the importance of the YMCA and the Metropolitan Rink. When the Gunn burns down in late 1905 there is barely a mention of it in the paper. For such an important cultural institution, the Gunn fades rather quickly in the popular discourse in Truro.

When the Gunn burns down there are already replacements poised to take on the mantle of the entertainment centre for Truro. It already had competition from the DJTA Hall, operated by the local temperance association, which opened in early 1905, slightly before the fire, and from the Metropolitan Summer Theatre, opening in 1905. In the winter this was the local ice rink, though in the summer of 1905 it is converted to theatre featuring vaudeville, concerts, and moving pictures. As might be expected, these two new theatres competed to be the cultural centre for the town, and both promoted the middle-class lifestyle that Truro espoused. Both featured vaudeville and travelling performers, though it was the DJTA that offered shows in the winter, while the Metropolitan was converted back to a rink.[26]

The first site dedicated exclusively to motion pictures opened in Truro on June 13, 1908. On June 8 the DJTA first placed announcements in the paper that the theatre would be changing its name to the Nickel and would be providing "Animated Pictures and Illustrated Songs" with continuous performances every day, 2 to 6 and 7 to 10 o'clock. Also advertised was the changing of pictures every Monday and Thursday.[27] Prices at the Nickel were decidedly less than the former DJTA or the Metropolitan. Five cents for admission or reserved seats for 10 cents was a significant change, making the theatre more accessible for townspeople. The Metropolitan, Gunn's, and the DJTA all charged between 25 and 50 cents for seats for film performances. The other major change was the end line on the initial ads for the Nickel: "Come when you wish. Stay as long as you wish."[28] This feature was something very new to the people of Truro. Yet there was no backlash coming from the churches or the town leaders to the effect that films were a bad influence or that they were in any way undesirable.

In contrast, early American film exhibition history has many stories about censorship and controversy surrounding the nickelodeons, the most famous coming from both New York and Chicago beginning in 1907.[29] These protests were not evident in Truro, perhaps because of the size of the town, its homogeneous population, or the lack of a substantial immigrant presence. Although Truro was situated at a major crossroad in the province and was the regional hub for a large rural area, the town appears to have retained its traditional control in this early period of mass entertainment. As well, the lack of a legal drinking establishment seems to indicate that the leaders of Truro had a solid grip on the morals of the town.

By late 1908 there is still only one theatre in town, though for a period between 1907 and 1908 the Nickel and a new theatre, the Wonderland, operate at the same time. After the closure of the Nickel in mid-1908 the Wonderland becomes the home of movies in Truro, though it operates as if there is major competition.[30] The ads consistently remark on the cleanliness of the theatre, the films, and the live shows. In one advertisement it even states that the manager goes weekly to Halifax, at his own expense, to hand-pick the films to show in his theatre. The theatre appears to be going to extreme lengths to prevent people from seeing it as anything other than a clean middle-class site, suggesting the degree to which censorship is integrated into everyday life rather than externally imposed.

The Wonderland remains the only film site in Truro until 1909 when the Lyric opens along with the Metropolitan Summer Theatre to offer competition. The difference between the three theatres is interesting. The Wonderland and Lyric appear to be modelled on the nickelodeon model that other cities had, playing films and vaudeville, placing their focus on family entertainment. The Metropolitan Theatre is different, a much larger facility, since it also acted as a rink in the winter months, and thus it was able to stage larger productions as well as films. The grand opening for the theatre in 1910 advertises:

> "Along the Kennebec," the latest successful play of New England life will be seen in this town on Monday night, May 16, at the Metropolitan Summer Theatre. Like all New England plays, laughter must intermingle with tears and the humor is so carefully blended with sentiment that just as you are on the verge of tears something humorous happens, which turns the tide to [excruciating] laughter. No play of recent years has had more [sumptuous] production in point of scenic detail and the production in this city will be given with careful attention. As an advertising feature the company [carries] a fine band.[31]

The Metropolitan Summer Theatre was often advertising productions from New England or New York, giving it perhaps an advantage over the other theatres which often labelled their productions as coming either from Montreal or New Brunswick. The Summer Theatre was also able to offer a grand opening at the start of every show season, giving audiences the illusion that every year it was a new theatre, or at least a novelty.

When the *Daily News* ran the notice that the Queen's Jubilee was not to be confused with the Corbett-Fitzsimmons Kinetoscope Show, it was only the first boxing film to cause a problem for the people of Truro. In June 1910, the Metropolitan Summer Theatre started another round of discussion over the showing of fight films when they displayed the epic Nelson-Wolgast Fight.[32] The film only showed for one night, on June 6, 1910 (perhaps an indication of the controversy and popularity of these films in Truro), but shortly after its showing the letters started appearing in the newspaper. The first was published three days after the event, in the Local and General section of the paper, where the matters of the town were discussed. Using news from Halifax that the Local Council of Women petitioned the Mayor to ban fight films, the paper further editorializes that money spent on renting these films would be a "bad investment."[33] It is perhaps telling as well that this is the last film shown at the Metropolitan. The theatre continues to function for 1910, offering live shows, but there is no advertisement for films.

On July 22 the *Daily News* brings the issue of fight films to the public once more, using this time quotes from Regina's Chief of Police. Chief Zeats is quoted by the paper as saying that he doubts he has the power to stop the exhibition of any film in his jurisdiction, and further opines that there is no municipality in Canada which has this right. The fight film in contention was the famous interracial bout between Jack Johnson, the black heavyweight champion, and Jim Jeffries, the white former champion who was coaxed from retirement to defeat Johnson.[34] Chief Zeats argues that the cities in the United States that were taking action against fight films were vested with more power than the Canadian cities, and moreover, the fight between Johnson and Burns, another interracial bout, was shown in Regina without incident and there was no reason to prevent this film. The paper, though, had another opinion. The last paragraph of the article offers advice to the "Solon of Regina" to stay out of the "legal-prediction business" and cites Ontario's Premier Sir James Whitney, who found the legal grounding to ban these films.[35] The editorializing of this news item indicates that the citizens of the town were still not meant to see these films, and that certain elements of Truro were continuing to pressure the theatres in the area into not projecting these films and were hoping to persuade audiences to avoid them as well.

The theatre business in Truro in 1910 gets more crowded when two new theatres open to compete with the Lyric and the Metropolitan Summer Theatre. Both the Royal and the Orpheum open in August 1910, though the Royal is not a new theatre, only a renovated Wonderland, and curiously only appears once in the paper, announcing its opening, never to appear again. These new theatres appear to operate essentially as vaudeville houses, showing nightly films and live acts. This gives the Lyric and the Metropolitan competition, and each deal with it in a different way. The Metropolitan Theatre essentially ceases to function as a movie house after the July showing of the Nelson-Wolgast fight film and closes as a theatre in October, never to open again.[36]

The Lyric first attempts to solidify its position as the local theatre, offering in mid-August a picnic for children. Leaving from the theatre at 10:45 on Wednesday, the 18th, 205 children of all ages "formed into a marching order" and took to Victoria Park, the central park in Truro founded in 1887. The day was spent playing games and eating food catered by M.E. Bates, a local caterer, and the children were escorted home at 4 o'clock. J.W. Stanley, the manager of the Lyric, was certain to attach his name to the notice about the picnic, which in the paper reads more like a news item than an advertisement.[37] This was only the first of two major attempts by the Lyric to retain its position in Truro as the entertainment centre. By mid-September, the Lyric closes for renovations, announcing that the theatre will reopen on October 1.

The renovations that the Lyric undertake are not substantial, as they had just prior to the summer added ceiling fans to the theatre and made some aesthetic changes to the interior. These new renovations appear to be done both to improve the show and to improve safety. Stanley advertises in the *Daily News* that he will install a new Edison Kinetoscope, maintaining that this will make the picture "absolutely flickerless" and that the new machine will make "film fires impossible."[38] The advertisement also states that the theatre will now be contracted with the Kinetograph Company of America to maintain a continuing supply of the latest films and songs for the audience. The note closes with the assurance that the Saturday matinees will return when the theatre reopens, letting parents know that their children will still be an important part of the Lyric's clientele, and is signed by the manager, Stanley.[39]

ORPHEUM.

JAMES WATERS

In his very clever and exceedingly funny character,

"GENERAL COHEN."

Full dress uniform and all his medals.

Mr. Waters is an Impersonator of rare ability. His performance is all comedy and he is a never failing laugh creator.

OUR NEW PICTURES
THE PONY EXPRESS

Big Western Feature Cowboys, Indians, Bands. A wonderful story of the West, full of thrill and stirring situations.

Salutary Lessons	Hank and Hank
Another excellent feature by the very popular Biograph Co.	A comedy scream by the S and H. Co. "OLD LOVES and NEW." A beauiful drama by Ediaon

2 Vaudeville Acts Tomorrow

Wesson, Walters and Wesson	Leslie Feather
Featuring Master Wesson with Champion Juvenile Buck and Wing Dancer.	In a very clever acrobatic and hand balancing act

LIVE BABY GIVEN AWAY
Save Your Coupons

The person holding the LUCKY TICKET on Saturday night will be presented with a REAL LIVE BABY   See the reading column

AFTERNOONS 5c.	EVENINGS 10c

Truro Daily News 26 November 1910, p. 4. Nova Scotia Archives and Records Management, PANS MFM 2084. Digital image restoration by Kristine Richer.

These measures by the Lyric start what can only be described as a battle between the two remaining theatres in Truro, the Lyric and the Orpheum. The two have different formats, the Lyric operating solely as a film house and offering the occasional musical slide show. The Orpheum, though, maintains itself as both a vaudeville house and a nickelodeon, often showing films and vaudeville on the same night. All through October and November, the two appear to fight for audiences, each trying to outdo the other with the quality of the shows. As well, the Lyric starts to offer gifts with the shows, beginning in late October with the giveaway of school supplies to children at the matinees on Saturday.[40] This scheme is not new; giveaways had been a part of the theatre experience in Truro for at least the previous five years, often coinciding with a holiday or special event. The difference here is that it is being used not to coincide with a holiday, but specifically to compete with another theatre.

The Orpheum responded to the Lyric's giveaway of school supplies by offering watches. Each paying customer could retain their coupon for a draw for two watches, but there was little other difference between the two theatres in the advertisements. They were both geared to the same audiences (though the Lyric did cater more to the children of Truro), and were both showing similar film programs at identical prices, though the Orpheum did offer a live vaudeville component to coincide with the films. The difference was really in the items given away. While the Lyric offered school supplies, the Orpheum's giveaways were like a raffle. Perhaps the oddest and seemingly the most controversial item "raffled" at the Orpheum was first advertised in the paper on Wednesday, November 23, 1910. Highlighted in the second last paragraph of the article advertising the coming weekend's entertainment is a giveaway of "A REAL LIVE BABY." To compete with this grand adventure, the Lyric was hosting an amateur contest, looking for the most talented person in Truro, whether a dancer, bag piper, or singer.[41]

The baby giveaway was real. The following day, the ad for the Orpheum repeats the call, only this time, offering a little more detail:

> Do you want a real, live healthy, white baby? The Orpheum management are going to give one away on Saturday night. No home is complete without a baby, and if you have not one in your home, now is your chance. It's a pretty baby, too and of good parentage, and the winner will have just reason to be proud

of the prize. Save your coupons, and bring them with you on Saturday night, when the drawings will be held, and the prize will be awarded.

NOTE, – This is not the baby left at the Town Office a few days ago. This one is being given away. It's parents are no longer able to support it.[42]

Although this adoption by raffle may appear shocking, it did not even garner a mention in any other section of the paper. It does not appear to be a hoax, or merely a stunt to get people to the theatre. First, the show offered has nothing to do with babies or parents; it is a double bill of vaudeville along with three films, "The Pony Express," "Salutary Lessons," and "Hank and Hank." This was common for theatre giveaways, as they rarely in this period connected to the entertainment offered.[43] Second, on the following Monday the name of the winner is given, Charles Yuill of Commercial Street, and the census records indicate that he does have a one-year-old nephew in 1911 living with him and his brother and sister-in-law.[44] The 1911 census indicates that Charles was a young man (his age was not given) and that his brother, Harry (who is twenty-three) has the son, Frederick, who is one year old in 1911. The next giveaway at the Orpheum is less spectacular, but similarly odd, if practical. In December, the prize offered to audience members is fifteen live chickens. Yet it is not the chickens that are the real draw, according to the ads, but the manner in which they are given to people. It is never specified what the "new and original manner" is, but audience members are guaranteed that it will be a source of "unlimited fun and laughter."[45] This history we can only imagine.

The Lyric does not appear to be able to compete with such advertising, because after a change in management in November the theatre shuts its doors in December 1910. The new manager, Percy C. Gillingwater, places an ad in the *Daily News* on December 10 to tell the citizens of Truro that the town is too small for two theatres to operate profitably.[46] The Orpheum was the theatre of choice for the people of Truro in 1910. The closure of the Lyric may have been necessitated by lack of audience; however, this may not have been because of the size of the town, but the type of theatre. Both the Lyric and the Orpheum offered similar films, a mixture of travelogues, actualities, comedies, and, as the medium matured, melodrama and western films. In Fuller's *At the Picture Show*, she indicates that the transition between non-fiction film and narrative fiction that occurred around 1908 (in the United States) was met with some resistance from rural audiences, as indicated by letters to trade journals by theatre managers. This frustration over the lack of non-fiction films, she observes, continued until at least until 1920.[47] Fuller concludes that this is evidence that there was a difference between the rural and urban audience in America. Although there is no correspondence from the theatre owners or the audiences about the types of films they were watching, the advertisements in the newspaper indicate that there is no real change in the programs in Truro. The programs advertised do, increasingly over the period studied, carry more and more narrative fiction, but there is no call for the end of costume dramas and society pictures, as Fuller notes. These films simply do not appear. The managers of the Truro theatres are able to satisfy their audience's desire to see travelogues and actualities with no problems well into 1912. What concerns the citizens of Truro is not the quality of the films or the type of film, but the size and style of theatre. That the Orpheum survives may have been because its mixture of vaudeville and film gives residents the opportunity to retain at least a portion of live entertainment.

In November 1911, nearly a year after the Lyric closes its doors, the *Daily News* publishes a plea from an American company for more amusements in Truro. The letter is written by the staff of the paper as an opinion piece and indicates that one of the "enterprising Yankees" who are connected with the new shoe factory in Truro is willing to front a "liberal" sum of money for the establishment of an opera house. The letter indicates that what Truro needs to attract skilled workers who are required to operate both the new shoe factory and many of the small industries that were being developed in town is "clean vaudeville, moral drama and educational pictures." To compete with towns in Quebec, New Brunswick, Nova Scotia, and New England, the article argues, Truro needs more than a "small picture show" to attract and entertain workers.[48]

The response to this letter comes a mere five days later. Mr. T.G. Spencer of Saint John proposes a solution to the lack of amusements. Spencer is no stranger to the theatre business, as the owner of a chain of eleven theatres in New Brunswick and Nova Scotia, including the Orpheum in Truro. Six weeks prior to writing this letter, he states, he opened a 400-seat motion picture house in Amherst, and will, on December 1, open a 1,200-seat theatre again in Amherst. Spencer does not own the buildings, though; he operates them on long-term leases from citizens of the town, thus avoiding any fear of outside control. The theatres, Spencer states, were constructed by

"Amherst citizens who are interested in the entertainment conditions of the town, believing that such is necessary and desirable to interest new citizens who are daily coming to this enterprising manufacture centre." What is offered in this letter is a business proposition to the yet unnamed "Yankee." Spencer will accept the "liberal sum of money" and join in communication with any other residents of Truro about the construction of a new, modern theatre. Although he does state that he will be making extensive changes to the Orpheum, adding seating and modernizing the building, he argues that only a new theatre will meet the needs of the town.[49]

This theatre was never constructed to the specifications mentioned in the November 9 letter, but the correspondence does shed light on business practices and the role of the movies in small town Nova Scotia early in the twentieth century. There is one more theatre that opens in Truro prior to World War I, the Princess, another movie house operated by Spencer and the managers of the Orpheum. As Truro moves from a rural crossroads to a small manufacturing town and educational centre, the nature of the entertainment of the citizens remains surprisingly static. Although new theatres open and old ones close, there is no real alteration in the style of entertainment offered, unlike in the theatres in larger urban centres. The theatres still offer a mix of vaudeville, movies, and music, all with little controversy.

Theatres in Truro attempt to retain authorship of the shows in order to satisfy the local market and to prevent the censorship battles viewed in other areas. The theatres do not attempt to align with churches through the exhibition of moral plays and religious entertainment. Churches do, however, increasingly attempt to compete with the secular culture as they begin to host their own entertainment, though there is no call in Truro for the censoring of films – there is no fear of "foreign influence" in the town, the only expressed fear is of boxing films, as indicated in the *Daily News*. The theatre managers of Truro appear to have done an excellent job of meeting the entertainment needs of the townspeople and have done so with minimal challenge, their major expressed concern being the cleanliness of their theatres and their shows. That the clergy and the various community groups do not protest the theatres proves that at least on the surface, this small town was adjusting well to the influence of this form of modernity.

NOTES

1   Both the groundbreaking Peter Morris, *Embattled Shadows: A History of
Canadian Cinema* (Montreal: McGill-
Queen's University Press, 1978), and
Robert Sklar, *Movie-Made America: A
Cultural History of American Movies*,
revised ed. (New York: Random House,
1995), show this bias toward urban film
exhibition.

2   Ben Singer, "Manhattan Nickelodeons:
New data on audiences and exhibitors,"
in Lee Grieveson and Peter Krämer, *The
Silent Cinema Reader* (Routledge: New
York, 2004), challenges the assertions
that have been made about the composition of the Manhattan nickelodeon
audience, though he does not go so far
as to again place the main popularity
of the shows in the hands of immigrant
populations. The Chaser theory is described and debunked in many of the
works about early film practices, including Charles Musser, *The Emergence of
Cinema: The American Screen to 1907*
(New York: Charles Scribner's Sons,
1990), and Eileen Bowser, *The Transformation of Cinema: 1907–1915* (New
York: Charles Scribner's Sons, 1990).

3   Charles Musser and Carol Nelson,
*High-Class Moving Pictures: Lyman H.
Howe and the Forgotten Era of Travel-
ling Exhibition, 1880–1920* (Princeton,
NJ: Princeton University Press, 1991);
Kathryn H. Fuller, *At the Picture Show:
Small-Town Audiences and the Creation
of Movie Fan Culture* (Charlottesville,
VA: University Press of Virginia, 1996);
and Gregory A. Waller, "Imagining and
Promoting The Small-Town Theater,"
Cinema Journal 44(3) (2005): 3–19.

4   Canada, Statistics Canada, *Population
urban and rural, province and territory*.
5 January 2005, 16 August 2006, http://
www40.statcan.ca/l01/cst01/demo62d.
htm. According to this table, the population of Nova Scotia in 1901 was 459,574,
of which 129,383 lived in areas with over
1,000 people per square kilometre.

5   David E. Stephens, *Truro: A Railway
Town* (Hantsport, NS: Lancelot Press,
1981), 62.

6   Ibid., 55.

7   Ibid., 63.

8   Though the *Daily News* is the only
paper to survive, there is evidence that
other papers were published in the town;
however, none was of the importance or
circulation of the *Daily News*.

9   Paul S. Moore, "Everybody's Going: City
Newspapers and the Early Mass Market
for Movies," *City & Community* 4(4)
(2005): 347.

10   Colchester Historical Society, *Historic
Colchester: Towns and Countryside*
(Halifax, NS: Nimbus Publishing, 2000),
85.

11   Waller, "Imagining and Promoting The
Small-Town Theater." Kathryn Ober-
deck also illustrates similar conclusions
for Sylvester Poli's theatre in New Haven,
Connecticut. Kathryn J. Oberdeck, *The
Evangelist and the Impresario: Religion,
Entertainment, and Cultural Politics in
America, 1884–1914* (Baltimore, MD:
Johns Hopkins University Press, 1999).

12   The Gunn is also a major source of advertising for the only newspaper. *The
Truro Daily News* had ads for the Gunn
nearly every day in the late 1890s; even
when the theatre was inactive between
travelling shows, the ad for the Gunn remained in the paper, apparently reminding people that it was still active.

13   Colchester Historical Society, 85.

14   These shows were commonly coming
from New England and Quebec, though
it was not typical for them to list where
they originated, only where they had
played locally.

15   Publicity, "At the Opera," *Truro Daily
News*, 6 January 1897.

16   Musser, *The Emergence of Cinema*,
129.

17 Advertisement with notice for Edison's Vitascope appears in *The Truro Daily News*, 13 July 1897.

18 Review, *The Truro Daily News*, 29 July 1897.

19 Review, *The Truro Daily News*, 24 September 1897.

20 Ibid., 25 September 1897.

21 Ibid., 7 December 1897.

22 For a view on the importance of this fight to the American film industry, see Musser, *The Emergence of Cinema*, 194–200.

23 This is a fact that Richard Abel articulates in his work *The Red Rooster Scare: Making Cinema American, 1900–1910* (Berkeley, CA: University of California Press, 1999).

24 Advertisement, *The Truro Daily News*, 14 March 1900.

25 Ibid.

26 This was not to be considered a bad switch for the Metropolitan, since hockey was an important and popular sport in Truro in this time.

27 Advertisement, *The Truro Daily News*, 8 June 1908.

28 Ibid.

29 For Chicago, see J.A. Lindstrum, "'Almost Worse Than the Restrictive Measures': Chicago Reformers and the Nickleodeon," *Cinema Journal* 39(1) (1999) 90–112. The New York experience is perhaps one of the most documented in early cinema. See also Bowser, *The Transformation of Cinema, 1907–1915*.

30 The Nickel's last advertisement in the *Daily News*, on June 22, 1908, gives no evidence of its closing, yet the theatre ceases advertising in the paper while the Wonderland continues steady advertisements throughout 1908 and 1909. Advertisement, *The Truro Daily News*, 22 June 1908.

31 Advertisement, *The Truro Daily News*, 11 May 1910.

32 Local and General, *The Truro Daily News*, 6 June 1910.

33 Ibid., 9 July 1910.

34 Lee Grieveson, "Fighting Films: Race, Morality and the Governing of Cinema, 1912–1915," *Cinema Journal* 38(1) (1998): 44.

35 Local and General, *The Truro Daily News*, 22 July 1910.

36 It is not obvious why the Metropolitan stops advertising in the paper at this time, nor does the paper mention the theatre closing. Additional information about this theatre is not available, so there are several conclusions that can be drawn from its disappearance. One could be that the paper barred its advertisements after the fight film exhibition, though more likely the theatre closed after the film to focus on its winter activities.

37 Advertisement, *The Truro Daily News*, 18 August 1910.

38 Ibid., 12 September 1910.

39 Ibid.

40 Ibid., 21 October 1910.

41 Advertisement, *The Truro Daily News*, 23 November 1910.

42 Ibid., 24 November 1910.

43 Alexandra Keller notes that film viewers were part of the commodity fetish that was becoming increasingly part of modern life, yet they were unable to leave the theatre with any item aside from their theatre tickets. Theatre giveaways like the child were a way for at least one member of the audience to leave with an item. Although this is an extreme example, giveaways were common in the Truro theatres throughout this period. Alexandra Keller, "Dissemination of Modernity: Representation and Consumer Desire in Early Mail-Order Catalogs," in Leo Charney and Vanessa R. Schwartz, eds., *Cinema and the Invention of Modern Life* (Los Angeles: University of California Press: 1995), 163.

44 1911 Census Data, http://www.automatedgenealogy.com/census11/Test16.jsp?id=70921.

45 Advertisement, *The Truro Daily News*, 3 December 1910.

46 Ibid., 10 December 1910.

47 Fuller, *At the Picture Show*, 75–76. For more information on the change to narrative cinema, see Tom Gunning, "The Cinema of Attraction: Early Film, its Spectator, and the Avant-Garde," in Robert Stam and Toby Miller, eds., *Film and Theory: An Anthology* (Malden, MA: Blackwell Publishing, 2000), 229–35.

48 Local and General, *The Truro Daily News*, 9 November 1911.

49 Ibid., 14 November 1911.

4

DOCUMENTING THE SEAL FISHERY: A SHORT HISTORY OF NEWFOUNDLAND FILM

NOREEN GOLFMAN

In an op-ed piece for the *St. John's Telegram*, journalist Bob Wakeham wrote that "Sam Peckinpah, the cantankerous hard-drinking but brilliant film director, would have loved to have walked the Newfoundland ice floes during the sealing season with one of his million-dollar cameras, recording and savouring every stomach-turning image of carnage."[1] Wakeham's essay abandons the usual defensiveness Newfoundlanders have long practised in the face of the annual vigorous anti-sealing campaign, arguing that such an approach has been "invariably a battle of retreat." Instead, he proposes an aggressive Peckinpah-inspired counterattack, one that pushes the bloody image of the twitching seal pup "in the face of every hypocrite who has ever chastised sealing."

Wakeham's immodest proposal has not yet been taken up by government or the image producers, but with arguments about the necessity and history of sealing having fallen on deaf ears for decades, several Newfoundland filmmakers have recognized a responsibility to fight back, image to image. That said, no history or record of the seal fishery off the waters of Newfoundland and Labrador will ever be complete, at least for the foreseeable future. The annual early spring seal hunt has been a highly contested event for at least thirty years, but the intensity of the so-called debate around the event has been radically increasing since the dawn of the millennium. What has been a localized ritual serving a modest economy is now a highly magnetic international spectacle, attracting scores of reporters, animal rights enthusiasts, and an assortment of fringe-group voyeurs of various ideological bents.[2] In 2006, a Beatle himself turned up, albeit with his then fervidly anti-sealing wife, to add to the chorus of the indignant and the offended. To be sure, when a Paul McCartney pays a visit to an Atlantic ice floe and tries to make meaningful eye contact with a seal pup then the world sits up and pays attention, no matter how self-conscious or even geographically challenged he might appear.[3]

It is fair to say that until very recently, the struggle to own the moral high ground has favoured the anti-sealing protesters, led, most famously, in the 1970s by a gorgeous French film star and her legions of adoring fans. That edge of victory, so to speak, has been wholly dependent on an obviously successful and ongoing visual campaign, as stirring and seductive as it is often deliberately misleading. Without a by-now hackneyed visual inventory of white seal pups looking plaintively at the filmmaker or photographer's lens it is doubtful that the rest of the world would ever have paid attention to the hunt in the first place. Certainly, Brigitte Bardot – whose sometimes hysterically declared love of animals might have resulted from the frequency with which she had been described as a "sex kitten" in the sixties – managed to parlay a second career as an animal rights activist by single-handedly targeting the seal hunt. Psychologists could argue that Bardot has long been repenting for her notorious breakthrough performance as a rabbit-loving vixen in *Et Dieu … créa la femme* (1956), but such speculation should be the subject of another study.

Today, just over thirty years after the International Fund for Animal Welfare (IFAW) launched an international campaign against the fishery, virtually shutting it down and occasioning an annual clamour of arguments both for and against a cull or harvest, seals have become, as Umberto Eco has said about all signs anchored in media, unavoidably "charged with cultural signification."[4] But while the seal emerged at the end of the last century as the cuddly icon of environmental protectionism, today the animal is often demonized by Newfoundlanders, many of whom, including political leaders, have openly blamed the under-harvested seal population for the decline of the ground fishery, and notably, for the almost complete disappearance of the biomass of cod stocks.[5] As a culturally loaded sign, in some sense the victim of a more complex global war over shifting definitions of the natural, the seal has come to embody an unambiguous meaning – depending on one's point of view, of course.

Because the struggle for ownership of the winning side of the debate is so fiercely dependent on images, it is not surprising that filmmakers – amateurs and professionals – have long claimed their own right to capture the truth of the event, especially as evidence of exotic spectacle, at once ennobling and primitive, necessary and fearsome. The modern film industry in Newfoundland and Labrador is still in development, but people have been making films in the province for as long as the camera itself has been around. There are several ways of understanding the way film has attempted to catch or has inadvertently caught something of the history and experience of the region. It is especially fruitful to consider that because of Newfoundland's unique place in the Confederation of Canada, filmmakers are especially conscious of a responsibility to correct long-held prejudices about the island's history and culture in particular, and to dispel or even correct the stereotypes that fuel bad or offensive jokes.[6] Arguably no subject is more fraught with controversy or loaded with visual signification than the annual seal hunt, and so tracing the developing story of the industry through its approach to this confused subject, a Newfoundlander's notion of lingering "troubles," helps us understand how Newfoundlanders themselves are using film to work through and reappropriate the visual field.

Any study of the signifying properties of the seal owes a great deal to Roland Barthes' classic examination of the way signs accrue meaning – or mythologies – as they circulate through our everyday lives.[7] Indeed, the sign of the seal operates so neatly along Barthes' analysis of signification that it offers up a template of how myths evolve, assume ideological weight, and eventually take hold of the popular imagination. On the primary level, as Barthes defined it, the seal is what it is – a sea-loving mammal. But bearing the weight of a socially constructed history, the seal has acquired the status of a myth, the characteristics of which have been largely shaped by the shrewd propagandists of the animal rights movement. A scan of the Web pages of the IFAW, to take the most prominent example, proves how much more emphasis the seal commands as a victim of human folly than almost any other animal for which the organization serves. Furry, relatively small, and endowed with large, brown, watery eyes, the seal, especially the white-furred baby version, quickly became both an icon of vulnerability and a symbol of what humanity is capable of destroying in acts of greed and depravity.

But whereas the fifty-four subjects of Barthes' analysis – from French toys to soap – were seen to be participating in the production and validation of the bourgeois nature of cultural myths, the seal has conveniently come to signify the natural, and the threat of the natural, in opposition to a monstrous humanity. This inversion of the values and properties normally associated with Barthes' interrogative project has conveniently helped mask the way the seal has been renaturalized, as it were, as a figure of innocence at the mercy of bourgeois culture. It is therefore not hard to see why an outspoken celebrity like rock singer Chrissie Hynde would write that "the commercial seal hunt that takes place every spring is an off-season cash bonus for a handful of big-business fishing companies."[8]

It has not always been this way. The seal has acquired its iconic status as sign and symbol of a natural innocence only recently, albeit powerfully, and perhaps irretrievably so. Tracing the triumph of the sentimentalization of the seal is most fruitfully achieved by reaching back to the origins of the fishery on film. In particular, it is critical to re-examine a cinematic milestone, the release of *The Viking* in 1931, a marker of feature-length achievement, the first Canadian "talkie," famously shot just off the icy, punishing coast of Newfoundland. *The Viking* can be and has long been identified as a Canadian feature film for the convenience of cinematic taxonomy, but, in fact, when director Varick Frissell, an upper-east-side New Yorker and a Yale-educated adventurer, brought his camera crew north, he set up production in territory that was still a colony of Britain. In 1929, Newfoundland was a good twenty years away from entering Canada and as remote from Ottawa as the New York City skyline. These historic ironies pale besides the driving force of Frissell's film itself. *The Viking* was vivid expression of an urge to capture through this relatively new medium called cinema the astonishingly dangerous labours of the annual seal hunt off the north shore of Newfoundland. As most Newfoundlanders soon come to know, real life has a way of intervening with epic force, and *The Viking* was to be Frissell's most ambitious, and ultimately his last, cinematic undertaking.

Like many privileged New England men after World War I, Frissell had earlier answered a call of the wild, travelling far away from the bourgeoning urban traffic of New York City to the forbidding landscapes of the north.[9] In particular, the rugged uncharted interiors or Labrador held an uncommon allure for Frissell, who ended up spending summers in and shooting dramatic features of the region, even discovering and naming the surging Yale Falls.[10] Film historian Peter Morris, who has arguably done more for the reputation of *The Viking* than all the production marketers in Canada, aptly describes Frissell's "neo-Rousseauesque concern for those

Varick Frissell from the film *White Thunder*, courtesy Victoria King.

parts of the world as yet untouched by the hand of industrialization,"[11] a concern Frissell shared with Robert Flaherty, whose work he admired and with whom he hoped to collaborate on a film about the "'Indians,' of the farthest far northwest."[12]

The Viking, then, was to be the fulfillment of Frissell's long developed and socially popular ambition to document the exotic landscapes of the north and the people who sought their livelihood from and by it. Frissell had already produced an astonishingly graphic documentary that came to be called the *Great Arctic Seal Hunt*. Forty minutes in its final release version, this film is nothing less than a black on white tone poem of the seal hunt of 1927. Frissell himself had to participate in the hunt directly if he wanted to film it, and so the documentary assumed the narrative shape of the frightful journey aboard the S.S. Beothic, on which Frissell sailed. About the *Great Arctic Seal Hunt* the *New York Times* observed that it contained "infinitely more drama than many a Hollywood piece of fiction," while the *New York Post* claimed it was "even more realistic" than *Nanook of the North*.[13] Perhaps, not surprisingly, the experience of a vicious hurricane, frozen ice, and eventually the brutal slaughter of the seals themselves inspired Frissell to carry the original proto-filmic event over into the dramatic structure of *The Viking*.

In the late 1990s, Newfoundland filmmaker Victoria King took up the challenge of situating Frissell's rightful place in the history of cinema, and so in collaboration with the National Film Board and inspired by the creative hothouse atmosphere of the St. John's–based Newfoundland Independent Filmmaker's Cooperative (NIFCO), she set about to create a documentary about Frissell's own documentary urges. It would have been tempting to tell Frissell's story as being typical of the privileged outsider's exoticizing – othering – of a people so different from his own class, race, and culture, but King was less interested in ready-made postcolonial spin than she was in the filmic strategies Frissell deployed to feed his creative ethnography. It is worth noting that at the moment King threw herself into the project at the end of the 1990s the IFAW had submitted gory videotapes of the hunt as evidence against specific Newfoundland sealers accused of inhumane acts. These tapes, lurid, sensational, and conspicuously edited with no fewer than seventy-seven cuts as they were, became part of the IFAW's most ambitious campaign since the 1970s, aimed at both exposing the alleged atrocities by seventeen specifically identified sealers and shutting down the remnants of the fishery once and for all. Tellingly, in 1999, a Newfoundland Supreme Court judge declared the submitted twenty-three minute tape to be inadmissible, calling the cameraman "a sophisticated con man." The court's judgment openly called into question the authenticity of the material, the tactics of the IFAW and of other animal rights groups – by extension Greenpeace and other internationally established organizations to which many if not most Newfoundlanders could not contribute in good conscience.

And so it is no coincidence that in that very heated and public war over the rightful representation of images, a war that continually engages Newfoundlanders as much as the language debates of the 1970s and 1980s consumed Quebecers, Victoria King turned to Frissell's masterwork for her inspiration. The poetic title she gave to her film, *White Thunder*, comes directly from Frissell's own original title for *The Viking*. In effect, King's film not only serves to locate Frissell prominently in the historical line of national documentary cinema but also to animate his own initial commitment to honour the staggeringly difficult labours of the sealers of Newfoundland. When Frissell's film was finally released in 1931 by Paramount, the director himself was already the crystallized vapour of tragic history. In March of that year he had returned to the ice fields of the northern shores to capture additional footage for his film, then still identified as *White Thunder*. A Hollywood test screening of the film had confirmed his own view that the documentary footage of the sealers in dangerous action on the undulating sea of the North Atlantic worked; the studio-added melodramatic storyline, mapped flimsily and awkwardly onto his original raw footage, did not. The romantic trappings of a love story had been pressed onto the film, against Frissell's better judgment or experience, by his Paramount producers who believed that audiences were less interested in ice than they were in a kind of *Broken Blossoms* scenario of sentiment and longing. To be fair, Paramount was certainly attracted to the raw, compelling footage of sealers dancing dangerously across the icy North Atlantic, but the repeated success of contemporary romance genres, in which every narrative demanded the romantic coupling of a put-upon man and woman, was too forceful to ignore.

Frissell, although obviously directly indebted to D.W. Griffith for the wisdom of his framing and editing, was energized and inspired by the spectacle of nature, not of the stage.[14] When the test audience clearly rejected the shabby artifice of Hollywood for the gripping documentary footage of men on a frozen sea, Frissell was not only vindicated but called back into service to rejig the script and return to his original conceit for the film. This meant returning to the ice floes and acquiring more footage. Tragically, it also meant the end of the line. The ship the crew had sailed in 1931 out of St. John's harbour, *The Viking*, blew up, presumably ignited by the dynamite aboard the vessel that was to be used to clear the ice for the ship's passage through the crusty North Atlantic waters. Frissell and twenty-six of his crew were wiped out. Partly because of Frissell's own privileged background, and partly because Paramount had its own interests to protect, news of the disaster made international headlines. The producers quickly renamed the film *The Viking*, releasing it complete with sappy melodramatic trappings and an already fraught legacy of attractions. As one erstwhile Web reviewer recently commented, "the film is important but still bad." The typically casual Web chatter goes on:

Why does the film feel so Canadian? Well it's badly acted, thinly plotted, yet beautifully photographed. What could be more Canadian than that? Ok, ok, not all Canadian films are that bad, but "The Viking" is. That's not Frissell's fault, he fought to keep out the love/jealousy story that ruins the film. But all joking aside, I think the reason "The Viking" feels so Canadian (even to us Canadians) is unfortunately because it has all the stereotypes of our country that American audiences expect: cold barren landscapes, lots of snow, and rugged, but jovial people.... Like I mentioned before it is stunningly photographed, and without the current story, and with more emphasis on the seal hunting (the way Frissell intended), it could have been a very good film. One that I would have been glad to call Canadian no matter where it came from.[15]

One reads a lot of this sort of conversational comment on the Web, of course, and it might be worth examining the emergence of an entire discourse of online reviewing to uncover how and why assumptions of cinematic value circulate and maintain their currency, but as this equivocating sample shows, power still resides in the sealing footage after all these years, and in spite of the IFAW's campaign to degrade the activity.

Victoria King's documentary, produced some seventy years after the explosion that took Frissell's life, forcefully reanimates that power. *White Thunder* both directly harnesses and implicitly confronts not only Frissell's tragic story and the achievement of *The Viking* as a feature film but also a lurid history of anti-sealing mythology. In effect, *White Thunder* offers up a correcting mirror to that mythology, and to the most sensational vehicle of its transmission – that is, a graphic Web-based pictorial history against the entire fishery. Even a cursory glance at the photographic images, but especially the short films featured on the well-travelled IFAW Web sites, reveals what one might be so audacious to call seal snuff footage. These alarmingly manipulated images of white seal pups languorously sunning themselves on ice floes or apparently winking or smiling or pouting for the cameraman's – and Web browser's – gaze, are figured prominently in spite of an international ban against the harvesting of these very young pups. It is worth nothing here that one of the films to which *White Thunder* is also indirectly addressed is an earlier documentary that finds sympathy with King's, and Frissell's, perspective, a sober view that demands respect for the labourers who had to endure the hardships of the hunt. The NFB had already produced that rather well-meaning but morbid documentary in 1991, part of its "Atlantic People's History" series called *I Just Didn't Want to Die: Newfoundland Sealers*. The film, essentially a short compilation, is most interesting for its reliance on the original still photography of the famous and disastrous hunt of 1914, in which seventy-eight sealers died and almost a dozen were severely disabled for life. Its extended narrative drama is punctuated with a series of mezzotints by well-known Newfoundland artist David Blackwood, whose own contribution to the visual repertoire of Newfoundland tragedy is worth bearing in mind.

White Thunder is therefore a relatively recent attempt to foreground the unforgiving aspects of the hunt by reminding viewers of its tragic history, countering the anthropomorphizing campaign of the IFAW and its allies with a resolutely determined focus on the men and their work, not on the animals that are a distraction from the socio-economic nexus in which the hunt operates. King's documentary functions at some level to ennoble the hunt by directing sympathy back to Frissell's fascination and admiration for it, part of what is now an actively evolving myth-making process of representation, one reproduced in a variety of ways and in variation through a whole series of documentaries made not only by the National Film Board but also by the private industry that wishes to recruit labour to mine the ore from Labrador, the oil from the sea, and so on.

White Thunder is arguably the first accomplished feature documentary in this region to draw on the time-honoured practice forged by John Grierson to tell the truth with, if not a club, then a hammer. For here we have a familiar and fairly conventionally choreographed hour-long National Film Board product, replete with voice-over narration of a decidedly stoic kind, of the even tone and delivery that Bill Nichols best characterizes as "stoic understatement ... [deliberately] laconic to underscore a possibly overly rigid or doctrinaire text."[16] Indeed, the intermittently heard, informing voice of the documentary belongs to none other than Newfoundland filmmaker Mike Jones, director of *Secret Nation*, the 1992 feature-length drama starring his sister Cathy Jones about the search for the conspiracy behind the province's vexed entry into Confederation. Recessed within Jones's own voice-over account of Frissell's ill-fated experience with *The Viking* is the imagined presence of Frissell himself, as another actor (this time Sebastian Spence) reads directly from Frissell's letters home to his mother. This double voice, so to say, lends a "real-life autonomy" to the animation of a now long-dead filmmaker and helps reinforce the film's sober realism, a realism quite opposed to the phony evidence of the IFAW film footage and its crude strategies of propaganda. The "fusion of direct and indirect address sequences" in *White Thunder* also lends material weight to the accumulated evidence of archival footage, interviews with experts, and such respected talking heads as film historian Kevin Barnouw, and the always clever juxtaposition of Frissell's gorgeous black and white documentary footage of the late 1920s and contemporary colour footage – matched to underline the still untrammelled beauty that characterizes much of the provincial coastline.

In these examples, the filmmaker's harnessing of the power of Frissell's original images of all that undulating ice, of the tiny black shapes of the men who dared to bob up and down on its dangerous edges, the epic sweep of the long shots which contained an entire world within the frames of its possibility, the awesome grandeur of icebergs and blistering cold, one can appreciate an attempt to let the seal fishery regain the nobility Frissell and others once recognized in its activities. Resolutely faithful to the sanctioned conventions of so many NFB-stamped films of the past century, *White Thunder* preserves what Nichols calls "the place of the subject at the level of the desire to know." The film invokes the subject him/herself at the very heart of the structure of the film, casting the spectator in that place stretched, as Nichols also says of what he calls "expository cinema," between a "hope and a memory," a hope of a restored and prosperous fishery of the future, a memory of something lost, erased by the forces of a suspect environmentalism.[17] The film is, to be sure, a gesture of nostalgia, invoking both a lost filmmaker and a vanishing traditional local practice. But in repeatedly punctuating her documentary with Frissell's own grandiloquent footage of the fishery that he lost his life attempting to capture, King deliberately delivers a subversive counter-discourse to the dominant repertoire of the anti-sealing campaign, fighting ice with ice, one might say, and thereby adding yet another document to the growing inventory of images attending to the seal ritual.

An even more recent contribution to that inventory is a locally grown documentary film, Anne Troake's *My Ancestors Were Rogues and Murderers* (NFB, 2006). Produced in part by the same team at the National Film Board as did *White Thunder*, *My Ancestors Were Rogues and Murderers* is really the first extended and direct artistic argument against decades of IFAW propaganda.[18] The film operates brilliantly on several levels, all working in a graceful balance to undermine decades of effective IFAW

My Ancestors Were Rogues and Murderers, courtesy of director Anne
Troake.

myth-making. The title, openly borrowed from the filmmaker's loquacious,
witty grandmother, Jessie Troake Drover, underscores the film's dead serious playfulness. It is at once highly entertaining, beautifully shot, and
informative without being didactic or boring. What we have here is an implicit defence of the sealing industry, but at its core the film is really about
the outport people who have long lived with its harsh realities, specifically
the director's family based in the seaport of Twillingate. Whereas *White
Thunder* personalizes a long-dead filmmaker and his almost forgotten intentions, *My Ancestors* works exclusively with and through the personal to
fight back.

The impetus for Troake's film was direct and clear. In 2000, in a tragically recurring drama, the raging sea took the lives of Twillingate residents
Roger Butler and Gary Troake, the latter the director's cousin and a well-
known spokesperson for the industry. Gary had spent most of his adult life
working up an impassioned discursive position, determined to contest the
doctrines of the IFAW machine on the world's stage, a self-styled David
among the well-funded Philistines. Inspired by Gary's life, a life snatched

cruelly and too soon, Anne Troake decided to honour him and what he stood for. Fortunately, by the time he died Gary's profile was high enough to have generated a sufficient amount of surviving media material, and so he is revived as fully as possible by this film, speaking from beyond his watery grave with characteristic wit and passion. Indeed, Troake is astute to have made Gary one of the central "voices" of her film, articulating an incisive analysis of why Newfoundland suddenly became the victim of a misguided environmentalism. What is especially appealing is Gary's tough ability to nail the hypocrisy of the IFAW anti-sealing campaign, pointing out, for example, that their celebrity advocates care no more about seals than he does about the spiders in his woodpile. Demystifying the romance of the seal is a daunting challenge, but Gary's blunt rationalism is a powerfully persuasive hammer.

Offsetting Gary's forceful outrage is the self-effacing charm, as mentioned, of the director's grandmother, fully alive to the camera and her curious granddaughter. This bright, wry older woman's story captures almost a century of life in Twillingate and the long-standing dependence of the community on the annual seal harvest. Her account of her own youthful first encounter with a seal is at once moving and amusing, while director Troake matches her voice with fascinating archival images to prove it. Central to the older woman's narration of her childhood is this startling encounter with a seal, and indeed her own first kill. That this woman, whom audiences are easily inclined to admire, can speak with such graceful candour about such a politically incorrect experience goes a long way toward disarming a spectator's prejudices about the necessities of the hunt and about an entire way of life most audiences would know little about.

We are also reminded of how insecure and unsophisticated a young Newfoundland girl must have felt in the bustling world of Montreal, where she somewhat reluctantly trained to be a nurse. Homesick and out of water, so to speak, she carried her cultural difference around like an unshakeable anchor. Listening to her story, the audience comes to appreciate the vulnerability of the outsider, a sympathy that carries over into a deeper understanding of just how vulnerable the sealers and their families would be to an aggressive international campaign against their livelihood. Even more to the point, that campaign not only targeted the business of the harvest but it also demonized, and continues to demonize, an entire people.

To its great credit, Anne Troake's film serves to humanize the bloody, messy business of sealing. It is neither sentimental nor romantic, preferring to let Garry and his family speak plainly and for themselves, underscoring the laws of nature and necessity that have informed their lives for so long. At some point even the most skeptical viewer must recognize the absurdity of Brigitte Bardot and her ilk campaigning against people they have never met, whose lives essentially mean nothing to them. Unlike Bardot's self-important camera-hogging posturing, the unpretentious candour of the Twillingate subjects is obvious and endearing. The blunt force of the film has itself generated a torrent of hostility, and Troake herself was for a time the vulnerable victim of hate mail and even bricks thrown through her St. John's windows, evidence of just how serious the battle for control of the images of the hunt have been and continue to be.

The film is structured around Gary's presence, and tragic absence, gradually building a portrait of the tough, self-reliant life in outport Newfoundland. Sealing has always been one way such communities could sustain themselves, relying wholly on a natural world that offered sea animals, berries, and a modest degree of farmed food. An implicit irony teased out by the film is that this time-honoured practice of living so dependently on nature should be threatened by a remotely generated movement claiming nature as its first principle. Gary's father, Jack Troake, is also granted considerable voice in the film, as he colourfully describes the bare mechanics of the hunt, without apology or regret. These and other interviews, informed by handsome images of land and sea, are shrewdly juxtaposed against the noisy declarations of the anti-sealing protesters, who emerge in this framework as obviously out of touch, self-interested, and dangerously deluded.

In the words of Newfoundland writer Ray Guy, for all the rhetoric of embattled sealers and their champions in Ottawa or London, sealing is about as critical to Atlantic Canada "as cuckoo clocks are to the main economic activity of Germany."[19] But as anyone east of Quebec well knows, all of this is not about the economy, after all. It is about who has a right to speak for and produce images of a place where people live and work, about who is representing what, when, and for whom. To be sure, as Bob Wakeham notes in his column, the "video age and the proliferation of the professional protester, have made the seal hunt a television gift, and inspired a yearly and understandable gravitation of the international media to the ice, hard to resist scenery, passion and blood."[20] Urging his readers to "forget the sheepish, sanitized defence," Wakeham calls for the kind of response both King and Troake have taken up, albeit without the wild machismo fury of a Peckinpah.

In many ways the emerging history of Newfoundland film of whatever genre or duration is best understood in light of *White Thunder* and *My Ancestors Were Rogues and Murderers*. Perhaps not surprisingly, each of these films marshals the infrastructural strengths of a venerable institution like the NFB to contribute to the nation-building project that is Newfoundland itself. That project, like the seal hunt, is far from over.

NOTES

This chapter is an extended version of a paper first delivered at the annual meetings of the Film Studies Association of Canada in Halifax, Nova Scotia, May 2003.

1   Bob Wakeham, "Sealing ain't pretty, so let's show it like it is," *The Telegram*, 11 March 2007, A6.

2   A useful historical overview of the seal hunt can be found at: http://www.heritage.nf.ca/environment/sealing1_e.html.

3   In a widely broadcast debate with Premier Danny Williams on Larry King Live, McCartney and his then wife Heather Mills apparently did not help their cause when they failed to realize they were speaking from the province of Prince Edward Island, not Newfoundland. McCartney's discomfort at his wife's manner was also obvious and widely commented on afterwards.

4   Umberto Eco, *A Theory of Semiotics* (Bloomington: Indiana University Press, 1976), 267.

5   Notably on record is former provincial Natural Resources Minister John Efford, who liked to attend national meetings wearing a sealskin coat, and often spoke about "harp seals ... munching on 300 million baby northern cod per year – more than 12 times the size of the Canadian population." News release, http://www.releases.gov.nl.ca/releases/1998/fishaq/sealing.htm.

6   See my critical survey of the provincial industry in *North of Everything: English Canadian Cinema Since 1980*, ed. Bill Beard and Jerry White (Edmonton: University of Alberta Press, 2002), 46–59.

7   Roland Barthes, *Mythologies*, trans. Annette Lavers (New York: Harper Collins, 1972).

8   Chrissie Hynde, "Don't hide behind Inuit in pursuing seal hunt," *Globe and Mail*, 4 March 2007, web-exclusive commentary. http://www.theglobeandmail.com/servlet/story/RTGAM.20070404.wcomment0404/BNStory/National/

9   See Ronald Rompkey's work on Sir Wilfred Grenfell, which best captures the time-honoured impulse to have an adventure in Labrador. *Grenfell of Labrador: A Biography* (Toronto: University of Toronto Press, 1991).

10 Peter Morris, *Embattled Shadows: A History of Canadian Cinema 1885-1939* (Montreal: McGill-Queen's University Press, 1992), 206.

11 Ibid., 204.

12 Ibid., 205.

13 Ibid., 207.

14 See "The Cinema of Attractions: Early Film, Its Spectator and the Avant-Garde," in *Early Film*, ed. Thomas Elsaesser and Adam Barker (British Film Institute, 1989), 56–62.

15 Daniel Yates, "Important, but still bad," Review of The Viking, 15 April 2002, http://www.imdb.com/title/tt0022537/.

16 Bill Nichols, *Ideology and The Image: Social Representation in the Cinema and Other Media* (Bloomington: Indiana University Press, 1981), 197.

17 Ibid., 205.

18 For an overview of the provincial government's rationale for the seal hunt, see News Releases, Government of Newfoundland and Labrador. Speaking points for John Efford, Minister of Fisheries and Aquaculture to The Rotary Club of Ottawa, 9 February 1998, http://www.releases.gov.nl.ca/releases/1998/fishaq/sealing.htm.

19 *The Boston Globe*, "An early melting hurts seals, hunters in Canada," 1 April 2002, A1.

20 Wakeham, "Sealing ain't pretty."

5

A PAROCHIAL NEWFOUNDLAND: GORDON PINSENT'S FILM TALE ABOUT TRADITION, PROGRESS, AND RESISTANCE[1]

MALEK KHOURI

Gordon Pinsent's 1987 film *John and the Missus* presents a fictional account of the historical events that changed the lives of thousands of people in Newfoundland in the early 1960s. At the time, the province's infamous premier Joey Smallwood decided that small outport towns, like the one shown in the film, were economically unviable and therefore should be permanently shut down. Some people in these areas would actually sail the ocean with their houses floating on barges to move them to other areas, leaving behind their family legacies and their traditional way of life and work. The film itself is set in the working class community of Cup Cove, where the town faces the prospect of resettlement as a direct result of the provincial government's decision to fold up the local copper mine – the town's only source of income. The mine employs the majority of the town's working inhabitants, and John, a local miner and the film's main protagonist, incurs the fury of the townspeople when he initially rejects the settlement money offered by the government. Eventually, John, his wife Nan, and his newly wed son Matthew and his bride Faith accept the inevitable and adapt to the harsh reality of forced displacement. The film adapts Pinsent's own 1974 novel and his 1976 play of the same title. While the novel differs slightly from the subsequent play and film variations, it nevertheless maintains a similar sense of a nostalgic personal homage by Pinsent to his own roots in the outports of Newfoundland.[2]

Director, Writer and Actor Gordon Pinsent, courtesy of Pinsent's agent
Penny Noble of Noble, Caplan, Abrams.

A Theoretical Framework

When the earlier version of this chapter on this film was first published in 2000, several colleagues of mine criticized what they saw as heavy-handed theoretical overtones that marred my analysis. Some of them frowned upon what they conceived as nostalgia on my part for the bad old days of psycho-Marxism in film criticism. Of course, by the late 1990s, while the rise of Cultural Studies within cinema criticism reaffirmed continued interest in the social and political effects of cinema, notions such as ideological interpellation were largely marginalized. Gramsci's conceptualization of hegemony, common sense, and agency, all of which represented critical theoretical thrusts within new Cultural Studies, was frequently pronounced antithetically to earlier attempts, particularly by Louis Althusser, to define ideology and ideological workings of culture. Commonalities between the dialectical thrusts in both Marxist thinkers' theoretical outlooks (that is, despite their undeniable variations) were greatly exaggerated, mostly by eliminating the political (and specifically the anti-capitalist and socialist gist) from Gramsci's cultural analysis.

Althusser consistently emphasized the notion of 'overdetermination' to press the point about how ideology reinforces or modifies the relation between people and their conditions of existence within class society. The structural dialectic between the 'unconscious' and 'conscious' (the 'imaginary' and the 'lived') as seen by Althusser represented his way of theorizing Marx's explanation of ideology as a locus of political struggle which allows people "to become conscious of [and active within] their place in the world and in history,"[3] a concept which is by no means antithetical to Gramsci's notion of 'agency.'

Critical assessment of film is neither a mere semiotic resistance, nor an isolated ideological struggle against cultural policy as Lyotard suggests.[4] It is rather a process within which specific cultural practices within historically specific hegemonic relationships are re-contextualized. Such a process cannot but appraise what a film manifests by way of ideological intelligibilities; and as a historically based practice, such criticism brings to the fore the contradictions of an 'Other's' hegemonic reading, and illuminates the tensions that mar the dominant reading of the film as a cultural product, introducing in the process an interested reading which is open to contestation. While many cultural studies critics concentrated on how certain cinematic plots allowed for 'resistant' common sense audience reception, it is my view that such conceptual preoccupation on the part of some critics also risks falling into critical and political reductionism. One aspect of this reductionism relates to its deprivation of the notion of hegemony, common sense, and agency of their political edge and eventually reducing them into ideologically 'neutral,' and ultimately politically and culturally meaningless processes.

Pinsent's largely overlooked film offers an excellent example of how a notion such as 'free will' (as common sense) is used to specifically function as an ideological reaffirmation of capitalist hegemony within a Canadian (and specifically Atlantic Canadian) historical and economic political context. The film's plot offers rich and complex variations of the contradictory social and political dynamics under late capitalist conditions; it depicts a declining working class community in a marginalized region of an advanced capitalist society where contradictory aspects of economic, political, and technological changes lead to major social and cultural upheaval. The ideological positions associated with the film's main characters and with its plot structure reflect their actual inseparability from the structure of the socio-economic body in which they exist (i.e., the capitalist formation), their inseparability from this body's formal conditions of existence, and even from the instances it governs. As such, the film inadvertently illustrates how ideological allusions are affected by capitalist body formation, determining, but also determined within the same movement, and by the various aspects of the social formation they animate:[5] what Althusser usually refers to as 'overdetermination.'

This chapter situates Pinsent's film within the common-sensical/ideological intelligibilities of the period that the film's plot depicts (1962), the period of its release (1987), and the historical framework of late capitalism in general. More specifically it attests to the film's ideological framework as manifest in its sympathetic depiction of personal 'resistance' (associated with 'free will'), and by extension, non-collective resistance as common sense; it also explores the plot's delineation of social and class resistance as 'non-sensical,' and as old-fashioned obstruction of progress.

Between History and Fiction

Interweaving a hegemonic 'common-sense' reading of notions such as technological evolution, social change, and preordained progress, the plot and the visual codes of this mid-1980s film inform and are informed by key facets of Canadian and world events and politics from the period in which it was produced. By inscribing the town residents' submission to shutting down the town and the resettlement of its inhabitants as free will – and this 'free will' as resistance – the film etches a tale about the inevitability of social and political submission. As such, the film's fictional inscription of a specific period in Newfoundland's 1960s history also projects the ideology of the time of the film's production; that is, a 1980s version of this history. The film affirms ideological intelligibilities that, at the time of production, were just beginning to dominate hegemonic Canadian political discourse.[6] With the beginning of the collapse of the so-called socialist bloc in the late 1980s and early 1990s and the subsequent rise of neo-liberalism and right-wing rhetoric on 'the end of socialism,' such intelligibilities were progressively shaping and enhancing dominant Canadian political discourse. To assess the discrepancies between the film's and the 'historical' version of its plot I will survey some key elements that led to the events that took place in Newfoundland in the early the 1960s.

In 1949, the year Newfoundland joined Confederation, it had close to 1,500 rural communities – most of which had fewer than 300 residents. Between 1953 and 1965 the Smallwood provincial government initiated an extensive program to amalgamate these communities into and within larger communities and semi-urban locations on the island, citing the cost and difficulty of providing roads and other services to the remote outports. Financial assistance was provided to residents when 100 per cent of the community ratified their willingness to resettle. By 1965, however, the plan had only succeeded in resettling 115 communities comprising fewer than 7,500 people. Only after making some revisions to its strategy was the government successful in closing 119 further communities and relocating an additional 16,114 residents.[7] Describing the unfolding of these events, David Macfarlane presents an image of a virtual uprooting of the lives of entire communities in Newfoundland:

> [The resettlement program] reached its dizzy heights in the 1950s and '60s when poor outport communities that were too thinly populated to justify the construction of a road or a causeway were simply uprooted and moved to more convenient locations. Entire houses – their china shaking, their drapes billowing, their pots rattling, their dogs barking at the upstairs windows

– were put up on floats and pulled across bays to be transplanted to more central communities.[8]

The real effect on the lives of people in these communities was substantial and devastating. But while it resulted in negative economic and emotional consequences for most of the resettled, for others (particularly those with better access to money), the government program presented an opportunity for economic profit. Describing his own family's status, Macfarlane writes:

> At times it seemed as if the entire island was for tender. The Goodyears were in the right place at the right time with the right occupation. The family's move to the interior had been prophetic. They built roads, and when people travelled on those roads they ended up at one of the Goodyear's stores. It looked like the beginning of a dynasty.[9]

Assessing the crisis in Newfoundland's economy from the late 1950s to the early 1970s, Fredrick Johnstone suggests that issues of economic dependence on the island at the time should be considered in the context of issues of underdevelopment in so-called Third World societies. Johnstone rejects the conventional account on "traditional backwardness," and instead draws attention to the capitalist nature of economic development in Canada. He writes: "people were poor because wealth flowed out of their regions, due to resources being controlled by profit-seeking business in other regions."[10] The process of economic deprivation in Newfoundland was therefore the legacy of a neo-colonialist type of penetration of the area. Johnstone reminds us that after World War II: "[There was] uneven development of regions and unequal exchange between them. The rich areas got richer at the expense of the poor areas, because they controlled resources, credit, and the terms of trade. The capitalist core actively 'underdeveloped' the Third World periphery over a long period of time. The Third World did not arise naturally; it was created."[11] Much of the discourse on Newfoundland's economic development, however, presents itself as an inquiry into the island's problematic embrace of progress and modernization. While acknowledging the significant obstacles to regional growth – noting, for example, the foreign exploitation of provincial resources, the alteration of aqua-environments, and the challenges of geographical isolation – this discourse "tend[s] to reserve the most vigorous finger-pointing for Newfoundlanders them-selves."[12] Newfoundland workers, for example, have been consistently be-rated for harbouring the underdevelopment of their region "through their lack of support of government-sponsored growth initiatives."[13]

For its part, as it tackles directly a situation where a working class community faces virtual displacement, *John and the Missus* presents an ideologically specific interpretation of history, progress, and resistance as common-sense philosophy. The drive to resettle Cup Cove's residents, for example, is constructed within the confines of a specific predicament: on the one hand, while it is "logical" for the town's inhabitants to move into larger and more advanced dwellings, it is not desirable (or logical) that they leave behind the traditional social, familial, and traditional ties they have devel-oped in the community over several generations. To resolve this dilemma the film seeks out an alternate paradigm. While John the hardrock miner is presented as a character who embraces and is proud of his class identity,[14] his form of subaltern resistance is ultimately reconfigured to herald at once the notion of 'change' as embrace of inevitable modernization and progress *and* the notion of individual struggle (free will) by way of absorbing the negative consequences of this progress.

Change as the Vehicle Linking the Past, the Present, and the Future

The plot of the film sets the stage for a common-sense resolution of the resettlement dilemma within the parameters of espousing (or 'resisting') modernization by Newfoundlanders. Cup Cove's residents enter a period of instability after the decision by the town's mine owners to layoff workers, and they are challenged to come up with their own response to the new situation. However, a major explosion occurs in the mine causing several casualties, including the death of Alf, John's closest friend. To keep the mine open under these circumstances is clearly impossible, and ultimately, sustaining life in Cup Cove as it was before the explosion becomes an unre-alistic and even dangerous choice.

A common-sense interpretation of history tends to transform it into a homogenized past. History is conceived as an abstruse moment with a muddled relation to the economic, political, legal, and philosophical prac-tices within a specific setting. It is transformed into an elucidation of the past necessitated by the ideological intelligibilities of the present. As the notion of 'change' and evolution is customarily conceived to be inevitable, nostalgia becomes the commodified version of what Althusser labelled as 'historicism,' which on the one hand promises continuity and stability, and on the other 'interpellates' the 'ideal' social subjects that are essential for maintaining the economic and social order of the day.

This way of interpreting history, and for that matter the history of class relations, is not unique to this Atlantic Canadian film. Examples extend from the Canadian classic *Goin' Down the Road* (Donald Shebib, 1970) to *The Bay Boy* (Daniel Petrie, 1984), *Margaret's Museum* (Mort Ransen, 1995), and *The Hanging Garden* (Thom Fitzgerald, 1997). As John Mc-Cullough points out in an analysis of another Canadian film, *Rude* (Clement Virgo, 1995), the tendency when it comes to presenting characters with a working-class background is to subsume their struggles within narratives about moral redemption, which usually translates into an "idealist fantasy that equates human progress with moral evolutionism."[15]

The opening segment of the film brings together John, his wife Nan, and the 'historicist' (from an Althusserian viewpoint) face of Mr. Fudge. The Past (history) is introduced as a memory, and is merged into the present through the image of Nan's touching hand introducing us to John in the present. Lost in his memory, John relates the continuity of the present (his wife) to the comfort of the reassuring hand of an early settler (Mr. Fudge). The scene sets out the couple's facility to freely move across the inevitable process of change from the past to the present by inextricably intertwining the 'transformation' of Mr. Fudge's hand into the hand of the Missus. In conjunction with constructing Nan's point of view as that of the audience as André Loiselle suggests, the film also consistently re-identifies us with her role as the mediator between the past and the present.[16] Nan is the one who heralds the ensuing evolution that eventually leads John (albeit based on 'his own terms' as we will see later) to agree to leave Cup Cove.

Nan's unspoken sympathy with the idea of moving out of Cup Cove is matched by Mr. Fudge's passive observance of the unfolding of events over which he has no power. Toward the end of the film, and as John throws Mr. Fudge's black hat into the water in a gesture of his break with one symbol of the past (Cup Cove), Nan utters a painful sigh. John puts his arms around her in a reassuring display of continuity between a preserved past (the house, and his marriage), the present-change (moving away from Cup Cove), and the future (the open possibilities). The presence of Nan becomes the natural 'substitute' for the absence of Mr. Fudge's hat (the past-present-tradition).

Thus, change in the film is rendered open: to move toward the past as much as away from it. This supposedly free flow in the relationship between present/future and present/past reconfigures the preoccupations of the present not merely as those of the present historical moment but rather as eternal and timeless preoccupations. They become significant for the past, the present, and the future, all part of one all encompassing homogenized moment. As such, the film's notion of tradition becomes part of a process of de-historicizing history, and conceiving change and modernization as synonymous only with predetermined continuity rather than with historical dialectics. In this context, the film depicts the need to recall tradition to impact the present (i.e., recalling the tradition of early settlements, family, hard work, community etc.,) by way of preparing for an evolutionary, non-threatening, and common-sensical form of change.

Technology and Continuity

A crucial element in the film's depiction of continuity in change is its incorporation of the role of technology. Technology (as signifier of the future and of change) assumes a particularly privileged position in Canadian cultural discourse. While it varies in how it perceives this signifier, this discourse generally maintains invariable assumptions in relation to technology as a formative vehicle for progress and change. In most cases we tend to look at technological progress as the way through which we accept the inevitability of change, and we do that without giving weight to understanding and considering how social forces and dynamics that control, enhance, or interact with technology also impact the process of change itself. Within this context, change as technological progress is 'imagined' as one with universal utility and infinite prospects and is therefore conceived as desirable. While it is occasionally rendered as a thinly disguised chaos which undermines the principles of an orderly society (rhetoric about the negative effects of information technology provides examples of such caution), change as symbolized through technological progress remains a condition of individual innovation and breakthrough upon which the Canadian entrepreneurial imagination is constructed. In the words of Arthur Kroker: "What makes the discourse on technology such a central aspect of the Canadian imagination is that this discourse is situated midway between the future of the New

World and the past of European culture, between the rapid unfolding of the 'technological imperative' in the American empire and the classical origins of the technological dynamo in the European history."[17] Yet, society under late capitalism remains largely guarded about the notion of change, because it also implies possible disorder, interruption, and lack of direction. To resolve this apparent contradiction, *John and the Missus* depicts the past as it moulds itself into the future through evolutionary technical innovation.

The film delineates this linkage as part of a non-threatening transformation. Change as technology signifies 'natural' progression between young and old, primitiveness and innovation, past and present. In one scene John etches a tree branch into a whistle pipe and hands it over to his friend Alf's young boy Robert. The boy is suddenly distracted by a loud sound, and as he looks up to discern the source we see a supersonic plane buzzing across the sky above. The shot of young Robert looking upward is immediately followed by the image of John looking in front of him at one of the town's newly abandoned houses. "Wouldn't be bad for young Matt," John tells the boy's father Alf. The scene's reference to technology exemplified in the plane does not perceive it as a threatening omen, but as continuity and as part of an evolutionary change which incorporates tradition through familial ties. The boy's interest in the newer form of technology (i.e., the plane) is juxtaposed with John's mastery of a different form of traditional technology (the pipe). The two seemingly contradictory interests of the two generations are depicted in a rather complementary manner suggesting a natural displacement of progression between one generation and the other.

The film nevertheless makes consistent connections between youth and progressive technology. For example, John's son Matthew is introduced as the young man with the blue car, while his wife Faith is presented as the young woman with the photographic camera. The couple are fascinated with the beauty of Cup Cove (the past). The way they express this fascination, however, is by driving their car through the town or by capturing its sceneries on film (i.e., utilizing the technical instruments of the present-future). The film's interest in technology and its symbolic embrace by youth places both of them as elements of the inevitable or fate, of a natural progression identical to the generational displacement between the young and old. To quote Kroker again: "It is the gamble of the Canadian discourse on technology that, in disclosing the full horizon of the technological simulacrum within which we are trapped, and in revealing possibilities for transforming technique in the direction of human emancipation, Canadian thought partakes of the 20th century by posing the question of the human fate."[18] Such characterized inevitability generally associated with the Canadian discourse on technology complements the common-sense conception of social and political resistance.

Into the Future:
Submission as Resistance

In the 1960s many Newfoundlanders looked at the proposed resettlement program as a scheme to help big business exploit the cheap labour of the impoverished and newly displaced settlers.[19] Local folk culture in the island maintained and acquired a significant repertoire of anti-resettlement poetry and songs which articulated this experience as a tragic break in a historical way of life.[20] While major difficulties characterized labour and independent political resistance in Newfoundland in the 1950s and '60s, various forms of collective resistance on the island were not totally absent as the film implies. Describing the nature, size, and impact of labour activities around that period in Badger (a town less than fifty kilometres away from the fictional setting of Gordon Pinsent's Cup Cove), David Macfarlane writes:

> In January 1959, twelve thousand loggers struck against the paper mills in Newfoundland. It was a vicious, bitter dispute, and when premier Smallwood called in the RCMP and a young officer in the royal Newfoundland constabulary had his skull cracked open at a violent demonstration on the main street of Badger, my grandfather concluded that, if Newfoundland was any indication, the world had finally gone mad.[21]

In an island with less than half a million people labour action of such magnitude could not but have some impact on the collective political, social, and cultural memory of the community. For its part, *John and the Missus* inscribes a common-sense perception of Cup Cove's residents' opposition to the government's resettlement plan; it draws a trajectory linking the impossibility and/or worthlessness of collective action with the willingness to submit to the new order under the guise of individual and free will resistance.

The film's delineation of resistance on the island projects a nostalgic appreciation of family, hard work, love of the place of birth, and fidelity to social and cultural values and heritage as moral high grounds for resisting the recklessness of progress. At the same time, the film presents progress as an inevitable fate: an inconvenience, but nevertheless a desirable destiny. Under late capitalism, 'change' is equated with 'natural' and inevitable technological and economic evolution. Within such a paradigm, social and political passivity is conceived as a sensible way of dealing with change. However, self-determination (both individual and collective) remains an important aspect of bourgeois values which needs to be adapted if 'change' is to occur without causing major social upheavals. In other words, being part of the late capitalist concept of change one needs to be prepared to articulate his/her own way of surviving the ordeals that come with major economic change (read, adjusting to capitalist corporate strategies): one needs to negotiate ways of coping with the benefits as well as with the repercussions of change and progress.

When John and the rest of workers are told about the possibility of closing the mine and about the resettlement plan, John's own conception of his future as historical nostalgia (staying in Cup Cove with his wife and his son's family by way of continuing earlier settlers' tradition) is contrasted with the more dynamic notion of change as present (resettlement). His initial rejection of such interruption in the chain of evolutionary continuity in his own version of past, present, and future becomes the high point in the subsequent dramatic development of the film.

The explosion in the town's copper mine results in the death and serious injury of several miners. The incident creates the pretext which prompts the owner (Tom) and the government representative (Danny) to begin implementing their plan to resettle the community in another part of the island. Independence, love, the possibility of procreation, and ultimately change, are posed against the rigidity and the sterility of hanging on to the past (in this case, the option of staying in Cup Cove). John's attempt to resist the government's decision is clearly doomed to failure. Lying down on his death bed after he is fatally injured in the explosion, John's friend Alf appeals to John to accept keeping the mine closed down.

As John carries Alf's coffin for burial, his voice is heard in the background speaking to his departed friend while simultaneously contemplating his own fate: "Your feet could only go wherever you wanted to go, just like mine ... till now. Now, you have to go where [they] say you go, and you have no say about it. What would you think of that ... imagine that ... no say in the matter...." The bitterness expressed here by John reflects his own genuine inability to change the course of the events around him. 'Progress,' just like death, is sealed as inevitability, a fate and natural evolution, and John – just like his dead friend – has "no say in the matter."

The inevitability of submission is also marked forcefully in the role played by John's son Matthew. The son's problematic relationship with tradition is suggested early in the film when he hesitates to make love to his wife Faith because they happen to be sleeping in Matthew's grandfather's bed. Later, in an intimation of his father's isolation, Matthew, along with other town workers, picks up his resettlement application form and walks out, leaving the old man standing behind alone in the town hall where he was professing staying in Cup Cove. Youth (the present-future) has opted for the hegemonic and common-sense alternative of inevitable change.

At this point the film becomes a measure of the possibilities available for an entire community; a 'collectivity' of the subaltern faced with the determined will of the guardian of progress: the capitalist power structure. The film sets in motion a chain of events leading to the town's consent to resettlement and finally to the symbolically significant consent by John. While various sites are posed as expression of resistance, the film depicts those sites as parochial and anti-progress.

John rejects angrily the government's offer for resettlement. But while this position gives him a moral high–ground, his 'resistance' is, nevertheless, destined for failure. John's motivation for rejecting the offer appears intertwined with clinging to the graves of the elders: his vision of the future (clinging to the past) is synonymous with death. As he challenges the government's official at the town hall meeting, John points his finger toward the town's graveyard while holding his father's clock in the same hand and says: "will anybody recognize my grave? ... you sir are telling me where to die!" The film, therefore, presents defiance and resistance against the new imposed order as identical with hanging on to a dead past (ancestors' grave). Submitting to the 'reality' of progress and accepting the impossibility (or worthlessness) of collective resistance, however, leads the town residents to accept the resettlement offer, despite John's appeals both inside and outside the town hall meeting.

But without resolving the impasse of the main protagonist in a common-sensical way, the film's plot would be 'problematic'; John's submission to the new fate would amount to surrendering to oppression. By way of rationalizing this submission, failure in instigating collective resistance is supplanted by another form of 'resistance': individual free will. The film sets out to reflect the idea of moving to the future without disregarding the past (i.e., maintaining the dignity of the past/tradition as an element of stability and continuity). So when John is convinced that something has to be done in regard to the future, he tells his family, "we're staying." This time, however, John incorporates 'rudiments' from the future to sustain continuity: he suggests building a new extension for his son's new family at the back of his own house. This 'defiance' feeds our sympathy for his position because it upholds respect for an important component (i.e., the past-tradition) in the chain of progress (past-present-future). But John fails in convincing his family of his plan, and this failure is directly linked to his conception of the future, which does not go beyond recreating the past (i.e., clinging to Cup Cove). Furthermore, the future, embodied in John's own son, interferes to reject the father's proposal: "I'm not staying!" Matthew avows. In their search for new living grounds, Matt and his wife Faith want to get as far away from the current temporal (the past) and geographical (the island) as possible. However, the limits to their desired journey are already determined by the fate of the entire town.

The notion of change here once again assumes the shape of destiny or fate, one that no one can possibly defy. As admitting to submission is not viable, the film articulates a common-sensical accommodation which still allows John to move away from the past-tradition and toward the future while maintaining his own individual 'free will.' This becomes John's own way of rejecting servility. When forced to recognize the worthlessness of his attempt to mobilize collective defiance (by trying to convince the town's people and his son's family to stay in Cup Cove), John offers a new version of resistance. He does that through pronouncing his own 'free willed' intention to move toward the future while upholding his own past and tradition. The ensuing stretch of the film re-establishes stability in the chain linking past and present with the future by having John and his wife Nan physically move their house and belongings, setting them on a journey across the Notre Dame Bay – a journey which complements the present-change as envisaged through John's rejection of resettlement.

John's history is consequently rewritten through a journey which leads him back to another collective imaginary symbolic of the island's traditional form of resistance: the 'dream' of abandoning the island for the big city or the mainland. John and Nan's reinstatement of the past (the house and each other) restores stability and continuity to the previously disrupted chain of progress. However, this is a stability associated with one's own 'authentic' (read, consensual) inscription of the past, the present, and the future within the framework of existing power relations. The couple's fate embodies the prescribed role of the working class under capitalism as disposable labour power. It is a fate that the working class (within the ideological framework of capitalism) has no alternative but to accept and re-adjust to.

While the unspecified dimension of the journey (the film does not make clear John and Nan's resettlement plans) reflects the couple's own version of their free will, their goal subscribes to the same notion of progress to which everyone else in Cup Cove has already succumbed. As John and Nan sail offshore and arrive at their first destination (Shoe Cove), Nan goads John to move on. "It looks like home, doesn't it!" John tells his wife. "Yes," she replies, and urges him to continue on. As their actual destination becomes an open-ended question, the journey itself is rendered a culmination of the infinite possibilities that they (as a working class couple) hold: a voyage which exemplifies their ultimate personal triumph in choosing their own destiny. The journey reinstates John and Nan's relationship; it also marks the intense emotions we expect them to bring to the renewed substitute for the happiness they left behind in Cup Cove. Furthermore, the journey also rationalizes the couple's submission to a 'new lifestyle' which was forced upon them by the government's resettlement program.

The haunting presence of the 'old folks' and Mr. Fudge throughout the film indicates John's longing for the past as present-future. It symbolizes John's loathing of the logic of the authorities. John rejects the present-change as he is disinclined to enter the future as proposed by the government. Yet while he initially drops out of the collective common sense of his town peers, he remains bound by the larger ideological framework of the town's consent. John's logic of 'independence' does not go beyond the idea of personal freedom as conceived within the paradigm of bourgeois common sense.

The climactic stand which allows John to show personal defiance in contrast to other working class members of his community who already succumbed to resettlement is denoted in his insistence on physically dragging his own house (his personal space) across the bay to a vocation that only he can identify. The journey essentially privatizes the notion of struggle: it helps John and Nan maintain their peace with themselves and with the world by incorporating the possibility of a prosaic future of a likely wanderer.

The mainland and the world outside the island add yet another symbolic dimension to the ideological options provided by the film for the people of Cup Cove. References to these symbolic spaces (the photographs in the travel brochures, the travel fables told by Fred, and the stories of success uttered by the baker who left the island to open a successful business in Hamilton) are all used as the standard against which other characters and their experiences are probed. In this context, these spaces are found either morally lacking and thus rejected as anti-tradition (as in the case of John), or considered agreeable and hence undertaken as the only destination option available. As the ultimate imaginary traveller and the never-settled (or resettled) islander, Fred is the one character who does not belong to the past (as nostalgia), the present (as consent), or the future (as false hope). His dreams become ideological signifiers of the impossibility of articulating imagination (and consequently, agency) into reality. Fred's last stand culminates in his death. After throwing away his travel brochures and 'souvenirs' he embarks on the only 'voyage' he could realistically take: his departure from life.

Conclusion

Politics and economics are always concerned with history. But history in the context of capitalist hegemony is given a specific epistemological dimension. Examples are studies of the colonized world and cultures which mould them into narratives about 'ancientness' and 'primitiveness' in comparison to the modern (or postmodern) and progressive colonial culture. Societies and cultures are irrevocably placed on a temporal pitch, a movement within history – some upstream, others downstream. Civilization, evolution, development, modernization (and their cousins, industrialization, urbanization, and technological progress) are all terms whose conceptual content derives from an evolutionary perception of history.

Within the same framework, history under late capitalism re-inscribes the past that is recovered in the name of change, making it as harmless and non-threatening as possible. However, for the past to be consumed for the sake of the present, it has to be first transformed into 'tradition.' As such, tradition becomes an element in an uninterrupted chain which is linked to the idea of evolutionary modernization, one which provides familiarity and stability. The construction of tradition as an ideological entity is nevertheless subdued so that the view of reality seems inevitable, natural and, more importantly, common-sensical. This moulding of history into tradition erases the dynamics of the past, while projecting it as a moment of clarity and sameness in which the interests of the present (i.e., current production relations) are rendered natural and eternal.

When *John and the Missus* was produced over two decades ago, then Canadian Prime Minister Brian Mulroney was selling the Free Trade Agreement with the United States as the sensible way of competing and functioning in a new global economy. As it provided an outlook at the history associated with the events that took place in the early 1960s in Newfoundland, the film also offered a cohesive epistemology on Canadian society and economy seen from a late capitalist hegemonic perspective. It alluded to changes that have become characteristic of the late capitalist condition since the late 1980s and into the new millennium: economic downsizing, global corporate expansion, free trade agreements, the explosion of information technology, and what accompanies these features in terms of increased polarization between those who benefit from these changes and those who suffer and struggle with them. By exploring change as fate and as a vehicle within an uninterrupted process linking the past, the present, and the future in the chain of evolutionary history, *John and the Missus* inscribed a common-sense story of dissent in a marginalized working class community. By traditionalizing this community's struggle for survival, it re-inscribed submission as 'free will,' and 'free will' as resistance. Perhaps not a very outdated lesson for future generations of disposable workers?!

NOTES

1. This chapter is based on my publication "*John and the Missus*: Progress, Resistance, and 'Common Sense'" in *CineAction* 49 (1999): 2–11. It has been revised to include a refocusing of the main argument and to contextualize the analysis of the film in light of recent research on similar films dealing with the history and lives of Canadians from the Atlantic region as well as Canadians of working-class origin.

2. For further comparative analysis of the three versions of the story, see André Loiselle's study "Novel, Play, Film: The Three Endings of Gordon Pinsent's *John and the Missus*," *Canadian Journal of Film Studies* 1 (1994): 67–82.

3. See Louis Althusser's *For Marx* (New York: Verso, 1990), 233–34.

4. Jean-Francois Lyotard, *The Postmodern Condition*, trans. G. Bennington (Minneapolis: University of Minnesota Press, 1984), 76.

5. See Louis Althusser's elaboration on the notion of 'overdetermination' under capitalist conditions in his book *For Marx* (New York: Verso, 1990), 101.

6. For a discussion of the marginalization of working-class experience in another contemporary Atlantic Canadian film, see my article "Other-ing the Worker in Canadian 'Gay Cinema': Thom Fitzgerald's *The Hanging Garden*," in *Working on Screen: Representations of the Working Class in Canadian Cinema*, ed. Darrell Varga and Malek Khouri (Toronto: University of Toronto Press, 2006), 134–47.

7. Ralph Mathews, *There's No Better Place Than Here* (Toronto: Peter Martin Associates, 1976), 2–3.

8. David Macfarlane, *The Danger Tree* (Toronto: Macfarlane Walter & Ross, 1991), 125.

9. Ibid.

10. Fredrick Johnstone, "Bones and Bare Cupboards: Dependency, Class and Crisis in the 'New Newfoundland,' An Overview," in *Contrary Winds*, ed. Rex Clark (St. John's: Breakwater, 1986), 176.

11. Ibid., 176–77.

12. Lisa Sullivan, "No Part of Our Life; Local and Official Construction of Meaningful Work in Contemporary Newfoundland," *Labour/Le Travaille* 34 (1994): 189–90.

13. Ibid., 190.

14. See David Frank, "In Search of the Canadian Labour Film," in *Working on Screen*, 36.

15. John McCullough, "*Rude* and the Representation of Class Relations in Canadian Film," in *Working on Screen*, 263.

16. Loiselle, 77.

17. Arthur Kroker, *Technology and the Canadian Mind* (Montreal: New World Perspective, 1984), 7.

18. Ibid., 18.

19. Ottar Brox, *Maintenance of Economic Dualism in Newfoundland* (St. John's: Institute of Social and Economic Research, 1969), 67.

20. Sullivan, 204.

21. Macfarlane, 156.

6

GUYS WITH BRYLCREEM DISCUSSING FISH PROCESSING: FORM, COMMUNITY, AND POLITICS IN THE NFB'S NEWFOUNDLAND PROJECT

JERRY WHITE

> They were teachers, social workers, film-makers, and they were not only prepared to teach with film, they were also prepared to help ordinary people to make their own films. That bothered Grierson. That was carrying things too far. – *Colin Low*[1]

I owe the title of my essay to my wife, Sara Daniels. As I was working my way through the films of the NFB's Newfoundland Project (1967–69), she came into my office and watched a bit of the film *Two Cabinet Ministers* with me. This is a particularly dry piece, comprised entirely of footage of a conversation between Eric Jones, then MPP for Fogo Island, and John Crosbie, then Minister for Municipal Affairs and Housing (appointed Lieutenant Governor of Newfoundland and Labrador on February 1, 2008, after a long career in both Newfoundland and federal politics), as they range over the economic complexities of the Newfoundland fisheries and how the people of Fogo Island in particular might make the best of their situation. When the film was over (and it's long as the films of the Newfoundland Project go, checking in at about 20 minutes), she tried to tactfully ask if all the films were like this. *Like what?* I asked. *Um, well*, she said, *are they all about guys with Brylcreem discussing fish processing?*

From the film *Children of Fogo Island* (Dir: Colin Low, 1967), courtesy of the National Film Board of Canada.

GUYS WITH BRYLCREEM DISCUSSING FISH PROCESSING

The NFB has itself certainly encouraged people to think of the films of Colin Low's Newfoundland Project, sometimes called the Fogo Island films, in this way. They have been remembered (by historians, by the NFB, and by those involved with the production of the films) as dry exercises in community building; the discussion of the work is remarkable for its disdain of aesthetic considerations. I want to offer a modest corrective to this consensus, and recover these films not only as examples of community-based media making (although that is an unquestionably important part of their identity), but as an aesthetically sophisticated form of non-narrative, poetic cinema. This kind of cinema, and these Fogo films, were very much in line with the work done by the NFB's elite Unit B of the 1960s, and with that of Canada's liberal avant-garde (an avant-garde resident in government-funded institutions like the NFB or the CBC) generally. It is a truism that form follows politics and vice-versa; the Fogo Island films are actually quite wonderful examples of artworks that are equally complex formally as they are politically. Continually emphasizing the latter and ignoring the former really does a disservice both to the filmmakers and to their audience.

Fogo Island

Fogo is an island community off the northeastern coast of Newfoundland. It has ten villages, many of which, at the time of the production of the Newfoundland films, had their own school boards (the amalgamation of school boards is a constantly recurring theme in these films). The island did, however, have an improvement committee, and was working very hard to both found a fishing co-operative and attract fish processing onto the island itself. These efforts were due largely to the desperate economic straits in which Fogo found itself in the 1960s. The infrastructure on the island had deteriorated to such an extent that the government in St. John's was considering evacuating the island, and many residents felt that the provincial government had begun to withhold services in an attempt to get people to move off on their own. The NFB recognized this situation as an opportunity to use film as a social catalyst, as a means of improving communication between island residents and between these residents and the St. John's-based government. Colin Low wrote, in an untitled 1968 report to the NFB, that "I selected Fogo because: (1) It had many problems, social, economic, educational; (2) The policy of the government towards this area was being formulated. In effect its future was uncertain."[2] This opportunity to enable people to intervene in an evolving political situation did indeed speak to the highest ideals of the *Challenge for Change*, a programme with which Fogo Island would be forever connected.

Challenge for Change

The Newfoundland Project was the flagship initiative of the *Challenge for Change* programme, which the NFB began in 1967. The original mandate of the programme was twofold: regionalization and increased collaboration between filmmakers and their subjects. Gary Evans, in his history of the NFB *In the National Interest*, writes that the Board "envisioned the project as a forerunner to initiating a regional production-distribution-advisory scheme, where films would be the catalyst to precipitate social action."[3] Although a few other films were produced during that first year of 1967 (such as *Encounter at Kwacha House – Halifax* and *Pow Wow at Duck Lake*), Evans dismisses them as "not impressive cinematically."[4] It is clear that they were nowhere near as ambitious as the 28-film Newfoundland Project, which has come to be seen as the flagship of the programme.

Challenge for Change emerged in the fallout surrounding Tanya Ballantyne's 1966 film *The Things I Cannot Change*, and indeed of the whole documentary film moment which produced it. Ballantyne's film documented the domestic and economic troubles of an underclass Montreal family named the Baileys with an attention to detail that was quite uncommon in 1966. When the film was televised the family was horribly embarrassed. Evans also recalls how "[w]hen John Grierson saw [the film] he hated it for revealing a person's private life without that person deciding that he or she be fully known. Colin Low agreed; the family was at a fundamental disadvantage because they were vulnerable and easy to exploit."[5] *The Things I Cannot Change* was a film whose fly-on-the-wall intimacy was made possible by the increased availability of lightweight camera gear and (perhaps more importantly) portable synchronous sound recording, and was thus very much implicated in the emerging aesthetic changes and ethical conundrums of cinéma-vérité. *Challenge for Change* really must be seen in the context of this technical-aesthetic revolution. Lightweight sound gear enabled filmmakers to get close to their participants, but an ethical framework for this new technology was still emergent. "In the aftermath of *The Things I Cannot Change*," Janine Marchessault writes, "an ethical dimension was incorporated into the documentary process."[6] Allan King's portrait of a home for mentally ill youth, *Warrendale*, also released in 1967, is part of the same attempt at an incorporation that would lead to filmmaking practice based in knowing, active collaboration between filmmakers and their subjects. Slowly, the aspiration of many Anglophone filmmakers became making films with people, not simply about people.

This built on, of course, a long-standing interest in these sorts of ethical concerns on the part of Francophone filmmakers. The signature case here is Jean Rouch's *Chronique d'un été* (1961), which was revolutionary (among other reasons) for the way in which it integrated the commentary of those being filmed about the ways they were represented in the footage; it is a clear precursor of the "Fogo Process." The cameraman on that film, Michel Brault, went on to co-direct, with Pierre Perrault, *Pour la suite du monde* (1963), another clear precursor to the Fogo process. The connection between all of Pierre Perrault's films about Île-aux-coudres, and especially *Pour la suite du monde* (1963), and the Fogo Island films, is to my mind a very rich one indeed; it breaks my heart that I do not have the space to take it up here.[7] Strangely, the only example of a Perrault-Low connection in the scholarly literature that I know of is the work of Pierre Pageau. In a 1986 essay he compared *Pour la suite du monde* and Low's *City of Gold* in terms of their treatment of historical narration, speech, nationalism, memory, and images of childhood.[8] The absence of the Fogo films from his formulations is baffling. But Pageau made up for lost time in 2006, writing in an essay called "Colin Low, un anglophone au Québec" that "[l]es liens entre la trilogie de l'Île-aux-coudres de Pierre Perrault sont ici plus perceptibles; en effet, avec cette série de films sur les habitants de l'Île Fogo, nous retrouvons des thèmes, des personnages, une utilisation de la parole que nous rappellent les films de Perrault " [the connections between Perrault's Île-aux-coudres trilogy are here more noticeable; in effect, with this series of films on the inhabitants of Fogo Island, we rediscover the themes, the characters, and a usage of speech that reminds of Perrault's films].[9] But even more important than Perrault's recurring interest in island communities, or his much-discussed interest in a *cinéma de la parole* [cinema of speech] was his notion of *le cinéma vécu*, lived cinema. In a 1963 interview about his Île-aux-coudres films Perrault told Fr. Léo Bonneville that "j'aurais pu faire du cinéma-fiction et construire un scénario. Nous avons opté pour un cinéma-document. Moi j'appelle ça du cinéma vécu. On ne peut pas mettre sur papier à l'avance une année à vivre." [I could have made a fiction-film and built a script. We opted for a document-film. I call that lived cinema.

You can't write up in advance a year of living.][10] This emphasis on spending time in a community over the exigencies of commercial filmmaking is key to the ethic of *Challenge for Change*, key to the programme's desire to move away from a cinema that saw people and communities as fodder for exploitable images. Perrault's cinema, and especially his Île-aux-coudres films (including the 13-part 1958 TV series *Au pays de Neufve-France*) depend centrally on his investment in the community itself, his closeness to the participants and his ability to live with them rather than simply appear and disappear when the filming is done.

Duly chastened by *The Things I Cannot Change* and following this Francophone example, it was clear that NFB filmmakers could not simply "parachute" in to as isolated and tightly knit a set of communities as Fogo Island. The involvement of Memorial University of Newfoundland's Extension Service, then, was instrumental. An anonymous 1967 report for the NFB (*Fogo Island Film and Community Development Project*) states that:

> In effect it can be stated that this project reflects a logical culmination in the thinking and action of the Extension Service of Memorial University at St. John's, Newfoundland, and the Challenge for Change program....
>
> By the spring of 1967 the National Film Board and Memorial University were in the preliminary stages of negotiating a three-year agreement for collaboration in pioneering a new approach to film in community development. The first stage was launched in May, 1967, on Fogo Island.[11]

Donald Snowdon, as director of the Extension Service, was the lead on this connection; Low noted in his 1972 report *The Fogo Island Communication Experiment* that "Don Snowden of Memorial who had taken me to Fogo Island helped me understand some of the basic philosophy of community development."[12] But for Low and the Fogo project, Fred Earle, identified in the film *Introduction to Fogo Island* as one of the Extension Service's community development officers, was their real insider. The opening voice-over of *Introduction to Fogo Island* states that Earle "was born and raised on Fogo Island. He knows, and is known, by all its people." The voice-over goes on to say that "we, as outsiders, felt that we could never go into such a community without the help of such a person." But Low's report is more blunt (and this is characteristic of his writing both inside and outside the NFB, both in English and French): "I went to Fogo Island mainly because I was impressed by Fred Earle. I had an idea that if nothing more happened I could make a film about a fine community development worker who would help justify our involvement."[13] Earle is ever-present in these films, acting as a sort of Virgil to Low's Dante.

The Fogo Process

These films were made with a very small crew, and emphasized flexibility and the unobtrusive integration of the filmmakers into the community. An anonymous 1968 NFB report recalls that "[a]fter initial research in May [1967, Low] went to Fogo Island in late June to acquaint himself with the Island and at the same time to find subjects to be filmed. Only on August 1st, were a cameraman, soundman, and assistant cameraman assigned to Fogo Island. They filmed continuously for five weeks, accumulating over twenty hours of material."[14] D.B. Jones, in his history of the NFB *Movies and Memoranda*, points out that "the shooting ratio of 4:1 was quite low for documentary."[15]

The most well-remembered element of the Newfoundland Project is its use of "feedback," the insistence on the part of the filmmakers that the islanders be shown raw footage and be given input into the final shape of the films. The opening voice-over of *Introduction to Fogo Island* states that "*Challenge for Change* is an experiment in the role of communications in social change. As part of this experiment, we filmed local people talking about the problems of a changing community, and played back these films in that community." Likewise, Low identified the use of "playback" and "communication loops between the community and government via film" as the two unique aspects of the project.[16] Low, in his untitled 1968 report, states that "[i]ndividuals must know that they could if they chose impose censorship on their material prior to its exhibition. Film would always be screened in advance for those people that are uncertain about their statements or their appearance during the filming."[17] Snowden's 1968 report to the U.S. Office for Economic Development makes the circular nature of the "feedback" more explicit. He has 15 points that describe "The Newfoundland Experiment," and numbers 4–9 are particularly illustrative of the core elements of the "Fogo Process":

4. People filmed are promised they will have first rights to edit for content, and this promise is kept.
5. After processing and editing for technical reasons, film is returned to the area as quickly as possible.
6. Local screenings are arranged – well advertised – in places convenient to the area's deprived people.
7. Screenings are arranged for the area's "power" people – whose planning, policies, or neglect affects the lives of the people already on film. The community workers and film makers involved in the project must be available at screenings to explain, substantiate, reassure, suggest. "Power" people are not only those whose role is recognized as such, but those whose interest, time and help can be marshalled to alleviate the conditions of poverty, but who are not themselves poor.
8. Filmed responses may be made from the "power" people and attached to pertinent reels. Or the "power" people may choose to answer directly in public meetings.
9. Such filmed material is widely distributed among the area's people and may serve as an effective linkage point for mutual discussion and action, where this does not already exist. If possible, there should be participation at all screenings by community development workers, social and behavioural scientists, and the filmmaker.[18]

Low similarly sums up the process:

> In all, we filmed about twenty hours of material. Back in Montreal, we edited to six hours of cutting copy blocks on various themes, subjects, or personalities.... Three months after filming, we returned to the Island for playback of material. This was done in a different village every night for about a month and a half. Screenings usually included a general discussion. Fred Earle and Bill Nemtin of our NFB distribution staff were usually involved.... I have never been to more exciting film screenings. The appreciation was extensive, the discussions animated. We invited people to help edit the material, remove sections or add to it. In six hours of material, three minutes were removed because they were considered "unfair."[19]

Appendix B of the anonymous *Fogo Island and Community Development Project* report lists each of these screenings and gives attendance figures and provides an indication of the scale and ambition of this project. They were held from 22 November 1967 to 29 January 1968. There were 39 screenings altogether, some with as many 300 people, and none fewer than 30.

Evans recounts how "Low's method became the model for most of the future Challenge for Change films," and indeed this use of "feedback," was central to the philosophy of the programme.[20] Low was at pains to distinguish this from mere liability considerations, writing that "[t]here have been situations where film has been played back to subjects before the completion of a film in order to obtain permission to use the material. But never before had such a systematic effort been made to involve a complete community."[21] In his untitled 1968 report he wrote that these advance screenings "would contribute to the establishment of the confidence that is necessary for this kind of work."[22] This kind of confidence between subjects and filmmakers, and the freedom and agency that it can lead to, was something that was very much lost when technology shifted again and the *Challenge for Change* programme began using portapack video recording equipment. Indeed, Marchessault's critique of this later, video-based period of *Challenge for Change* is that "the interactivity and participation that video delivered instituted access without agency. It instituted a particular form of self-surveillance rather than transforming the actual institutional relations of production and knowledge."[23] I take Marchessault's point here, and agree that the idealism around the ability of *Challenge for Change* to create democratic agency was largely unfulfilled. But it also seems clear that a lot of the historical discussion around *Challenge for Change* has focused neither on access nor on agency, but on *process*. This really is the nub of the problem of the way in which these films are remembered.

Access or Aesthetics?

The aspect of that historical memory that seems to me the most problematic is that the Fogo films, like the work associated with *Challenge for Change* in general, has been discussed by historians and filmmakers alike purely as a process, not as a group of films at all. Marchessault writes of the video revolution of the 1970s that this electronic medium "redefined the film director's role. No longer an authorial agent, the director became a social animator whose chief function was to provide technical training to select communities."[24] But even in the celluloid era of the late 1960s, this writing was on the wall. We see this in the way in which the NFB and those involved in the Fogo films represented their work, and then in the way in which historians analyze the period, sometimes quite harshly.

Those attached to the Fogo films almost always insist that these films are about social change, not about filmmaking. The anonymously written 1972 booklet *Fogo Process in Communication* states simply that "[i]t is crucially important to appreciate that the films are subsidiary to the purpose they serve and that the process deals with community action rather than film making."[25] In case there's even the slightest doubt about the utilitarian approach here, we also read "in this process, film is quite simply a tool, a means to an end and part of a total approach."[26] A booklet by Sandra Gwyn, ostensibly meant to document a workshop on the Fogo films (*Cinema as Catalyst*) states that "[f]ar more important than the films themselves, was the process of making them. More important still was the process of screening them, a month or so later, for the people of Fogo."[27] Even though Gwyn, in a rare cinephile lapse, writes that Low "became the D.W. Griffith of the Fogo Process," cinematic considerations are basically absent from the internally generated discussion.[28] Even Low himself seems to disown his non-narrative, poetic documentary roots, so celebrated in films like *Corral* (1954), *Universe* (1960), *Circle of the Sun* (1960), or the *Labyrinth* project (1967/79); Gwyn quotes him as saying "I'd always been more interested in using [film] for poetic document. But in Newfoundland I discovered something very different."[29] Echoing this in a 1996 French-language anthology on documentary, he writes in the section of his essay devoted to the Fogo project that "[l]e cinéaste « artiste » et le cinéaste « animateur social » sont deux personnes differentes" [the "artist" filmmaker and the "social animator" filmmaker are two different people].[30]

Historians of the period have followed suit. Thomas Waugh has summed up the frustrating nature of this discourse by writing that "[t]here is a received wisdom that has accumulated over the years both in [Film Studies] and in the corridors of the NFB itself, that yes Challenge for Change/Société Nouvelle was indeed an interesting experiment, vindicated by its offshoots Studio D and Vidéographe, but practically flawed as well as ideologically and theoretically naive, and moreover no great shakes cinematically speaking."[31] D.B. Jones' assessment bears this out: "the Fogo *process* became more widely known than the films themselves."[32] Jones deemed even this aspect of the Fogo project specifically something of a failure, writing that "the project was not a cost-effective model. Traditionally, films have seemed to make economic sense when used as mass communication…. And though the twenty-three films were produced at a cost comparable to what the Film Board spends on a typical one-hour television documentary, the amount of money represented no trifle and the audience differential was quite large."[33]

This consensus is further emphasized in the arguments about how the Fogo work should be distributed; nobody seemed to think that these films had any hope for wide distribution, any hope of being interesting to anyone not invested in these specific political situations. Evans writes that "[t]he films were supposed to be a series of modules with relevance to Fogo Island and Newfoundland, but not much to the rest of the country."[34] Jones writes that "[t]wenty-three films useful mainly to a small community of five thousand people constituted very expensive social change."[35] Fair play to these historians; they are only following the way in which the distribution was constructed by the filmmakers and administrators themselves. An NFB "Request for Funds" document dated 31 March 1968 (which indicates in the affirmative for the question "The Production work covered by these finds has already been initiated," and which refers to "26 films varying from 1 to 3" reels and thus seems to be for the core Fogo films) states: "[t]he completed films will hopefully fill regional needs and will be released almost entirely for local distribution." An NFB internal memo from Bill Nemtin to "Distribution Representatives in field and H.Q." dated 3 October 1968 reads that "[w]hen the Fogo material was being made we did not envisage that it would be distributed beyond that community," and says that rather than the film having relevance for areas other than Fogo, "[m]ore likely is the use of the films as examples of the Fogo Island process." Snowden concurs that "some film which is very effective in the region has very little value for a broader distribution simply because it might be boring to a wider audience. Cinematic values and showmanship enter into a broader use of materials."[36] Barry de Ville's 1972 report called *Distributive Targets for the Fogo Island Films* holds out some hope for the wide distribution of Roger Hart's 1972 retrospective look at the project *Memo from Fogo* (the report suggests it be shown on TV), but states that "[s]uch films as *Songs of Billy Cobb* [sic; he means *The Songs of Chris Cobb*], *Children of Fogo*, and *When I Go* … are obviously less comprehensive and, with the exception of *When I Go* … would suffer from relative antiquity and monochromatic listlessness in any general appeal to a potential viewing public."[37] Recounting a terrifying encounter at a seminar being given by John Grierson, Low recalls His Grey Eminence's response to watching *Billy Crane Moves Away*:

> "What," Dr. Grierson wanted to know, "was the value of the film off Fogo Island? Was it good for television? Mass media? What did it say to Canada?" I was deflated. "What did it say to the world?"
>
> I had to admit that the film wasn't worth much outside the context of the situation – outside the mainland of Newfoundland. Billy Crane's accent was hard to understand. It had some specialized value in Ottawa, but it did not say much to farmers in Alberta, except that centralization and central decisions of government are not always right.[38]

The only respites from this consensus regarding the films' utter parochialism, irrelevance, and, *in the NFB's own words*, "monochromatic listlessness," come from surprising places, including a dissenting view from Snowden himself. Comparing the core Fogo films with the videos made on Fogo Island by Memorial's NFB-trained film unit, Stephen Crocker recalls that "Snowden has described these projects as more 'information oriented' than the Fogo films which he characterized as 'impressionistic' and aesthetic in orientation, probably as a result of Colin Low's professional filmic interest."[39] Crocker also acknowledges the aesthetic quality of some of this material, writing that "[i]n addition to films that dealt with difficult social problems, there were also more lyrical films such as: *The Songs of Chris Cobb, Jim Decker's Party*, and *The Children of Fogo*."[40] Just to see the word "lyrical" in the discussion of the Fogo films feels like a revelation. Dissent regarding the irrelevance of the films to outsiders comes from the islanders themselves. In his 1968 report, Low recalls how "[d]uring the filming, Fogo people everywhere asked me if their statements were going to be run off the Island. Many people were concerned that the statements receive a broad distribution."[41] In his subsequent 1972 report, he recalls how during the discussions in the villages that were so central to the "Fogo Process," "[p]eople continuously asked us to run the film off the Island – particularly to government."[42]

The sense that these films are purely instrumental, with nothing to say to non-Newfoundlanders, is a historical error of significant proportions. As Marchessault documents so vividly in her analysis of the portapack-era of

Challenge for Change, access by no means equates to democratic action, *particularly* when we are talking about access to mass media. And anyway, access as such was not even the goal here. Grierson famously dismissed *Challenge for Change* as "eight millimetre films for eight millimetre minds," presumably because he assumed that it would involve training people to use consumer-grade film equipment without much sophistication.[43] Training people to make their own films, training them to replace the artists of the NFB, was, for Grierson, as Low recalls in the epigraph of this chapter, carrying things too far. Jones (a diehard Griersonian in many ways) sees it as a betrayal of the NFB overall, writing that "[t]he shift in authority from filmmakers to 'the people' had aesthetic implications as well, not just for the programme but for the whole Film Board."[44] But it is essential to understand that, at least when we are talking about the NFB's Newfoundland Project, this is not at all what happened. The programme was not originally a media training programme, along the lines either of the portapack projects of the 1970s or the Super-8 projects launched in the high Arctic.[45] While the NFB did train some staff of MUN's Extension Service who did go on to shoot footage on the island, for these first Fogo films, an actual NFB project, *filmmakers* shot the footage, mixed the sound, and so on. They were not simply there to show islanders how to turn on a camera. In this way, the introduction to Gwyn's *Cinema as Catalyst* is quite misleading as far as the Newfoundland Project goes, even if it does seem to confirm Grierson's worst fears about the *Challenge for Change*. Claiming that film equipment was far too complex for most people to operate, Gwyn writes that "the arrival of cheaper and simpler equipment ... means that anyone can learn to be an operator in an hour.... Instead of writing a report explaining how Mrs. Snook got the road fixed, Tom O'Keefe can flick a switch and let Mrs. Snook tell about it herself."[46] Low, in the same essay where he distinguishes between "le cinéaste « artiste » et le cinéaste « animateur social »," implicitly acknowledges this. He writes of the islanders that "[l]es gens se montraient très amicaux, mais modeste quant à leurs capacités à contribuer au film" [the people proved themselves very friendly, but modest as to their capacity to contribute to the film].[47] Islanders were collaborating closely with filmmakers, but they were surely not *replacing* them. Low and his team brought a skill-set quite a bit more complex than the ability to turn a camera to the "on" position.

Fogo and 1960s Canadian Nationalism

This purely instrumentalist understanding of the Fogo films is not only a matter of getting the aesthetics wrong; it also gets the politics of the films wrong. No film in the series illustrates this more vividly than the series' final, "resumé" film, *Winds of Fogo* (1969). This film is the only one of the series that is in colour, and it is one of the most poetic, and indeed the most visually oriented, pieces in the series. The original "Request for Funds" document proposing the film (then to be called *Journey to the Funks*) even has "General" written on the "Intended Audience" line, which as I have shown, is noteworthy in the context of the internal NFB understanding of the Fogo films. The film is on one level an evocation of the life of William Wells (who is at the centre *William Wells Talks About the Island*, where we mostly see him talking as he putters around his shed). *Winds of Fogo* spends a lot of time with Wells out on the sea with his sons. One of the most startling of these sea-bound sequences is an extreme long shot (which seems to be shot from another boat) of his boys undertaking a very dangerous disembarkment from a small boat onto the Grand Funk. There is also some mesmerizing footage of the boys working on the deck of the fishing boat as it rocks back and forth in the slightly choppy seas. The next sequence is a series of highly composed images of his boys building a boat in their garage (sequences that also feature a very sophisticated combination of synch, non-synch, and semi-synch sound). The film is also peppered with images of the waves crashing against shore near his home, whose interiors Low also shows us (often in the form of images of quotidian objects such as sewing machines and fishbowls bathed in soft light).

But the crowning sequence of the film comes at the end, featuring images of kids flying kites as adults look on. One kite is made from a Canadian flag, at that time not quite three years old (having been approved by Parliament in 1964, it was officially ratified by the Queen in February 1965). Images where the kite shoots up through the air and then slowly rambles downward are graceful and kinetic, like so much in the film. Low has the younger Billy Wells say in the voice-over narration to this scene that "I like to make believe ... teach my father ... you know ... wonderful flag.[48] Oh-h-h ... ! *don't like the look of it, do you?* Not that he don't like the look of it, but he just don't like the flag. Oh, he still likes the Union Jack. All the old people are like that." Over a slow zoom out on the airborne Canadian flag, we hear the elder Wells say on voice-over, "I'd rather see the Union

Jack. More colour. There's no blue." The younger Wells protests, "the sky is blue!"; his father responds: "Red White and Blue; I'll ever be true."

The politics here, obviously, are complex. The maple-leaf flag which is here seen literally flying over Fogo replaced a flag that integrated the much older Union Jack on a red background, and that replacement spoke to an emerging post-British consciousness throughout English Canada. But the emergence of such an identity has special complexity in Newfoundland, whose historical ties to Britain are so different from the rest of Canada's. The province, after all, had joined Canada only in 1949, as the result of a referendum as divisive in its day as the more recent referenda on Quebec separatism. And yet, its ties to Britain had been the source of considerable strife, given the degree to which the pre-Confederation Newfoundland government had been alternately neglected and micro-managed by a distant London.[49] Thus, it is not entirely surprising that one of the last images of the film is the elder William Wells raising the Canadian flag on his fishing boat as he and his sons set out for the day. The message there seems clear: the new and modernity-oriented Canadian nationalism is the reality of present-day Newfoundland, even if it remains important to acknowledge that there is a different historical memory still alive on the island.

This desire to balance difference and national cohesion that is so clearly the subtext of this sequence of *Winds of Fogo* is absolutely of a piece with the ideology of Trudeau-era multiculturalism, a multiculturalism that emerged in no small part as a response to Quebec separatism, a much scarier phenomenon for Canadian elites than lingering fondness for the Union Jack on Newfoundland. And *Challenge for Change*, with its desire to regionalize, to build stronger communities, and with its ability to work together with a French-language partner (the Francophone counterpart of the programme, set up in 1969, was called Société Nouvelle), is classic Trudeau-era. Marchessault writes that:

> It is well known that Trudeau's bicultural and multicultural policies were implemented to dissipate the burgeoning forces of the separatist movement in Quebec as well as the increasing demands of Canada's diverse ethnic and native communities. It is easy to see how *Challenge for Change* is entangled in that web of coercion and consent, technologies of domination and technologies of the self, which define the functioning of power in a liberal democratic state.[50]

No wonder, then, that the flagship programme of Challenge for Change went to a place where a sense of nationalism was present but the Quebec separatist movement was strongly disliked. G.A. Rawlyk writes that most Newfoundland newspapers argued in 1967 that "Quebec nationalism threatened the very basis of Newfoundland's attachment to the federal state – the ability of Ottawa to redistribute the nation's wealth in the interest of its less fortunate parts. This, after all, the argument went on, was what Confederation was all about."[51] It was not, for Newfoundlanders, about accepting assimilation or absorption into a unified Canadian identity. This pragmatic approach to being part of Canada, so devoid of the sentimental patriotism that Quebec nationalists were reacting against, must have seemed, at the time, a perfect foil for separatism, a perfect way to dissipate that burgeoning force without having to oppose that movement's most emotionally affecting arguments about community or collective belonging.

This sequence in *Winds of Fogo* is to my mind the most explicit example of such entanglement to be found anywhere in the series. It acknowledges Newfoundland's status as a "distinct society" (I can feel the shudder of anxiety washing over the reader with the mere invocation of that term) by lingering not only on traditions of fishing and boat building, not only by extensive use of images of people speaking Newfoundland English, but by focusing on *national* differences, on lingering connections to a different nation-state. And yet, these conflicts are resolved. The recently adopted symbol of Canadian modernity *does* fly over William Wells' fishing boat. More importantly, there is no *anger* about the results of the 1949 referendum expressed in any of the Fogo films; given that this highly divisive moment was a living memory for a lot of the people in this series, that certainly is a noteworthy absence. What we see in *Winds of Fogo* is that differences, while not erased, are smoothed over as part of the work of a multicultural nation-state that recognizes how it has failed people materially but which clearly wants to do better.

This is quite consistent with the way that historians have explained Newfoundland's adjustment to Confederation. Rawlyk writes that in 1967, "[e]ighteen years as a Canadian province had not undermined the strong Newfoundland sense of community and close identification with the local perspective. Nor had it forged any strong emotional link with the rest of Canada."[52] But he also writes that because standards of living had changed so much during this brief period, "[i]n 1967, most Newfoundlanders wanted Ottawa to become even more powerful, and decried anything which threatened the federal power."[53] Raymond Blake also writes how in the immediate post-1949 period, as Confederation came to be seen as inevitable, "those who had demanded a return to self-government and fought against union quickly dropped their struggle and threw their support behind the union.... In their first electoral campaign, they promised to negotiate better terms with Ottawa rather than undo the union."[54] This combination of local nationalism and federalism is, really, the defining characteristic of the Newfoundland of Low's films. Fogo is shown here to be a distinct society, and yet one that is now fully of a piece with Canada as a whole. The paradox of the cultural mosaic, the community of communities, seems resolved. *Winds of Fogo*'s optimistic Canadianism is a good example of what Blake argues Canada as a whole saw in its inclusion of Newfoundland. He writes that Confederation was "an expression of a new mood felt throughout Canada.... Canadians expected a good life and welcomed the coming of the welfare state. Union with Newfoundland must be seen as an expression of this new-found confidence and ambition,"[55] a confidence and ambition that would, in the 1960s, find expression in such things as revitalized set of national symbols such as the maple leaf or, a bit later, a national anthem that made no reference to the monarchy.

Rather than the populism or individualist empowerment that critics of *Challenge for Change* seemed to have feared, the politics of the series, as borne out so clearly by *Winds of Fogo*, are quite state-ist. This is in no way in contradiction to its populist or empowerment-based mechanisms. "Low's notion of subject participation paralleled the liberal interpretation of cultural development," Marchessault writes, "and would play an essential role in the state promotion of community culture in Canada."[56] That *Winds of Fogo* walks this ideological tightrope so central to Canadian liberalism through the language of sound and image (the kite, the use of voice-over, the use of the Newfoundland-accented voice, the images of the other-worldly landscape of the Grand Funk) is entirely consistent with the way that all the Fogo films emphasize *both* the political and the visual, *both* the communication and aesthetics, and refuse to sacrifice one for the other.

Readings

This integration of communication and aesthetics is borne out simply by *looking* at the films, by trying to make sense of their visual language. This sounds obvious, banal. Alas, it is not. Arguing for the fundamental complexity of the *Challenge for Change* films, Waugh writes that he wants to "demonstrate the indispensable role of textual study in this process, of actually looking at the films and the videos."[57] He is almost alone is calling for such textual study. Indeed, he is very much opposed to scholars such as Jones, who writes that "[t]he craft of filmmaking, developed laboriously over three decades at the Board, began to lose currency.... *Challenge for Change*, which sprang in part as a recoil from the aesthetics of self-expression, got rid of aesthetics, but not the self-expression."[58] I want to answer Waugh's call, and show that the Fogo films in no way got rid of aesthetics. Rather, these films made a significant contribution to political documentary filmmaking in Canada, as is borne out particularly well by several key Fogo films. They are excellent examples of the craft of filmmaking that had indeed been developed so laboriously at the NFB over so many years.

One crucial element of these films is their "vertical" structure, a concept that Low used to distinguish them from conventional documentary. The anonymous 1968 *Fogo Island Film* report emphasizes the centrality of this, stating that "[t]he major decision in editing was to cut the material vertically rather than horizontally. In other words, the films were based on personalities discussing a variety of issues, rather than an issue incorporating a variety of personalities."[59] Jones, drawing on an interview with Low, describes the approach thusly:

> The traditional documentary structure was, in Low's word, "horizontal," moving from one scene to another, cross-cutting between different points of view. Invariably, no matter how conscientiously the filmmaker tried to present a balanced, objective picture, the editing would introduce an element of bias. Any scene would invariably seem to be a comment on the one that preceded it. The "vertical" approach of expressing each point of view in a film of its own alleviated this problem.[60]

My interest here is not in how the "vertical" approach alleviated the problem of bias. I do not accept that, and frankly neither does Low, who told Jean Pierre Lefebvre that "[i]l est en effet impossible de demeurer parfaitement objectif face à un sujet quelconque, on y ajoute toujours un point de vue personnel, et si ce n'est pas au stade des prises de vue, c'est à celui du montage" [it is in effect impossible to remain perfectly objective with whatever subject; you're always adding a personal point of view, and if it's not at the filming stage, then it's at the editing stage].[61] I understand how Low was trying to cut down on montage in the Fogo films, and avoid cross-cutting between views on specific issues, but as Low knows perfectly well and clearly states to Lefebvre, point of view, editing, and any of the literally countless inevitable decisions that *every* filmmaker makes always leads to some sort of distortion, some sort of point de vue personnel. It is disappointing to see him assuming a stance so much more naïve than the one that he seemed so comfortable and confident with a few years earlier. All that said, this vertical, or non-linear form really did represent an inno-vation in documentary structure. These Fogo films are unusual in the way that they simultaneously cohere and fragment, in the degree to which they are simultaneously linear and episodic.

The film *Introduction to Fogo Island* illustrates this structure vividly. The film begins didactically, with images of Fogo and a voice-over narra-tion that introduces Fred Earle and explains the basics of the Fogo process. Even though the traditional documentary voice-over is present throughout the film, the film's imagery does not simply illustrate the soundtrack. In-stead, there are a number of images that recur throughout the series. As the voice-over discusses how social and religious divisions persist, we see images from *A Wedding and a Party*, a ten-minute portrait that is part of series. The aerial images that follow this recur in the film *Children of Fogo Island*. The sequence that follows uses footage that reappears in *Dan Rob-erts on Fishing*. Sequences that shortly follow those again use images from *A Wedding and a Party*. The film, then, is less of an introduction to the island – although in a way it is that – than it is an introduction to the *series*. The voice-over talks about the topics that will recur again and again: the divided school boards, the need to get a co-op started, the dependency of people on welfare payments, etc. The imagery is very heavy on material that we will literally see again and again. I would suggest, then, that rather than a "vertical" structure, the series has a circular structure, with *Introduction to Fogo* Island serving as the hub. A rough sense of chronological order can be established, since in some films – *The Merchant and the Teacher, Citizen Discussions, Jim Decker Builds a Longliner, Two Cabinet Minis-ters, The Fogo Island Improvement Committee*) – there is discussion of the struggle to establish a co-operative, something we see actually happen in the film *The Founding of the Co-operatives*, which is basically a record of the meeting that sets up these co-ops (although even in this fairly dry film, there is a very lyrical opening sequence of men dry-docking boats, one that recalls the opening sequence of Pierre Perrault's *Pour la suite du monde*). In that way, then, *The Founding of the Co-operatives* could be said to come "after" these other films. But other than this, these films are as completely independent of one another (you don't need to see any of them to understand any of the others) as they are interconnected (together they form a detailed portrait of the island, its landscape, its language, its economy, and its politics).

This non-linear structure brings the films out of the realm even of non-narrative cinema and seems closer to a medium like television (although I will argue at the end of this chapter that it is actually radio that we are being brought closer to). Small wonder that the emphasis of the *Challenge for Change* project shifted to video and then community television in the 1970s; that form already seemed visible in the structure of this flagship project. Small wonder also, then, that the Newfoundland Project's greatest influence was felt in community TV circles. Crocker's discussion of the Fogo process takes its televisual quality for granted; it opens by saying that once the NFB and MUN had done their work, "[t]his locally produced *televisual* image would then become a medium for communication with distant decision makers, such as governments and financial institutions. The Fogo Process … created a very effective *televisual* public space for addressing social and political concerns" (emphases mine).[62] This was the influence that it had in Ireland; the community video experiments of the 1970s that led eventually to the establishment of a TV station in Irish Gaelic (via a series of pirate TV broadcasts in Irish Gaelic) were strongly influenced by *Challenge for Change*. And it was also its primary influence in the United States. When Low and Snowden went to Farmersville, California to act as consultants on the war on poverty, their efforts were written up in the *Washington Post*. Michael Kernan quotes Herbert Kramer, public affairs director for the Office of Economic Opportunity, by way of explaining the Fogo Process: "Kramer said it 'doesn't have the drawbacks of Whitey's TV station.' It cannot be compared to the 'lily-white' TV man who goes into a ghetto for a documentary that may be effective or less than effective because the TV man may not know what it is like to be poor or black or uneducated."[63] Internationally, as domestically, the series tends to be remembered for procedural rather than cinematic reasons. (The *Post* even uses the Billy Crane film to illustrate this, although at least mentions some photographic consideration via the use of light: "The camera acts like a neighbour, looking at Billy while he talks, watching him coil some line and putter around his boat, but mostly just focusing on his rugged face in the grey Newfoundland light.") And internationally, as domestically, these procedures seemed to lend themselves to analogies with the less linear, more open-ended format of television.

But this is a different kind of television, one with a more complex sound-image relationship, for instance, than what one would expect from TV news. Even though *Introduction to Fogo Island*, for example, serves as something of a didactic hub for the series, the connection between sound and image is far from straightforward. Many times in the film there is a conflict between the two that approaches the dialectical. One of the most highly composed of these is a zoom into a very tight close-up of a bride, who is wearing an elaborate veil; the narration over this image says "in its problems of isolation, Fogo is a microcosm of all of Newfoundland, and perhaps of other encapsulated communities that are symbolic islands." This is, of course, not an image of isolation at all, but of intimacy. As the camera gently moves to re-frame the image to include the groom, the voice-over says, "but Fogo is also an old community. It has been settled for almost 300 years, and its people have a deep sense of history and tradition." Again, the wedding may be part of communal tradition on Fogo, but these are not *old* people we are seeing; their connection and the life they have yet to build together – their youth, in short – is precisely the point of this image, even though the sound is discussing something very different indeed. And the next sequence, which is also repeated from *A Wedding and a Party*, has narration that talks about how there is no future for young people on this island set over images of the bride and groom emerging from the church; again, the sound and image are in conflict, since this is an instantly recognizable image of celebration that is set to narration that is non-celebratory to say the least.

I am not trying to recover this as an example of Soviet-style contrapuntal filmmaking; the sound-image relationship here is not exactly comparable to Dziga Vertov's *Enthusiasm* (1930). But nor is it simply a matter of voice conventionally or even lucidly illustrating image. The voice-over narration in *Introduction to Fogo Island*, like that of *Winds of Fogo*, exists as a kind of companion piece to the imagery; it is connected (talk of the flag when the kite is flying in *Winds of Fogo*, talk of ceremony when we see images of a wedding in *Introduction to Fogo Island*), but it is different (it is the unseen Union Jack that we are actually hearing about in *Winds*; it is about at a very different stage of life than the subjects of the imagery that we are hearing about in *Introduction*). Rather than assuming a passive viewer, a viewer who seeks only basic information – the viewer, in short, that seems to be assumed by all of those writers who so ignore any cinematic elements of these films – these films leave some space between their constituent elements, space for viewers to make some meaning, space for viewers to do some interpretive work. There is, then, something of Peter Wollen's "first avant-garde" (which he writes "can be loosely identified with the co-op movement," as opposed to the second avant-garde of Godard or Straub-Huillet) in the Fogo project.[64] Writing of this movement's connections to Cubist painting, Wollen points to "a semiotic shift, a changed concept and practice of sign and signification, which we can now see to have been the opening up of a space, a disjunction between signifier and signified."[65] Again, I am not trying to claim these Fogo films as works of radical, fragmented aesthetics; the co-ops that Wollen is talking about are pretty different from the co-ops that we hear about in these Newfoundland films. But these films do open up the space that he is talking about, abandoning both linear (or horizontal) form and facile sound-image relations in search of something different, in search of renewed connections between filmmakers, subjects and viewers. This ethic of a search for the new is equally visible – and I do mean *visible* – in a number of the films themselves.

This ethic is most evident in *Children of Fogo Island*, the most explicitly "poetic" of these films. The film opens with aerial images of Fogo (again, the same images as in *Introduction to Fogo Island*) and is followed by hand-held, zoom-y images of boys carrying a large frame of a boat up some rocks. The sound is clearly wild, but it is non-synchronous (none of the boys' chatter ever connects to any one boy's moving lips). This opening is a good indication of the way the film moves and is organized overall; there is a lot of documentary-style footage (characterized by hand-held imagery and sharp zooms), a lot of footage that is familiar from other Fogo films (the next sequence is a montage of children flying kites, strongly reminiscent of *Winds of Fogo*), and, most important, a pervading sense of montage over continuity. Although there are sequences that feature long takes or are edited along lines that resemble continuity cutting (we see a long shot of boys sailing toy boats, then Low cuts to a slightly different angle of a long shot of the boys at play, then a series of close-ups of the boats, then a water-level shot of boys swimming nearby), the sequences do not between themselves cohere into anything linear. Indeed, Low moves back and forth between a few sets of imagery – the boys carrying the frame, kids walking on stilts, kids in a rowboat towing the boat that this frame seems to have become – several times, in addition to using sequences that depict everyday life on the island or depict its landscape. Almost all of this is set to music; there are a few sequences that have the sort of semi-synch sound I described above, but not many. Overall the object of the film is to create associations between these discrete sets of images: kids at play, the landscape of the island, and the rhythms of life in a place where boating is a core component of the everyday. A lot of this imagery, as I said, adopts the visual style of *vérité* if not its emphasis on synch sound. On the other hand, a lot of it is highly composed; one shot has the camera slowly panning up the frame of an old boat to reveal the bay between a gap in its planks. Another shot features a boat slowly floating screen left to screen right in the foreground with a group of people working on another boat in the background; as an example of composition-in-depth and graceful horizontal motion it recalls both Lumière Brothers actualités and the famous sequence on board the boat at dusk in Jean Vigo's *L'Atalante*. The next sequence – a montage of houses – also features some very highly composed shots of houses in soft, magic-hour light. But even the less-composed vérité-style sequences have very real power. The next sequence, for instance, features the boys working on the frame sitting on some rocks, playing the harmonica and jigging. Camera work is shaky and makes frequent use of zooms, but there is also a sense of real intimacy, real connection, achieved largely though close up. This sense of connection is a big part of what makes vérité affecting, and it's no wonder that its filmmakers were so often attracted to musical performance, whose kinesis adds an extra layer of excitement to this sort of intimacy.

It is precisely this element of vérité aesthetics that *Jim Decker's Party* and *A Wedding and a Party* draw upon. These are two fairly straightforward films; they document communal events using the kind of semi-synch sound that I have already described. *Jim Decker's Party* opens with a shot of Fogo's landscape at night and then shifts to images of a man and a woman dancing to an accordion that we hear but whose player we do not immediately see (this first woman we see, though, is also a central participant in the discussions of *A Woman's Place* and *Discussion on Welfare*, films that are more or less "talking heads," or discussion films). The camera is always in motion during the dance sequences, weaving in and out of dancers in a crowded living room in a way that feels almost vertiginous. A lot of the work is choppy – again, many sharp zooms and shaky movements – but it is a small marvel of vérité aesthetics in terms of the motion that it captures and the intimacy to which it aspires. One shot about midway through the films is quite wonderful; the lens zooms just slightly in and the dancers are all framed in a blur of bodies in motion; as they move in and out the musicians become visible as gaps momentarily appear. There is a very similar sense of energy and intimacy in *A Wedding and a Party*. The post-wedding party scenes (which also feature dancing) are not quite as kinetic as what we see in *Jim Decker's Party*; the filmmakers rely a bit more heavily on high-angle long shots than the close-ups of *Jim Decker's Party*. But the camera still zooms in and out of interesting compositions; early in the party sequence, the lens zooms in toward and essentially *through* the dancers, to reveal the bride, still wearing her veil, framed between people in motion in a sharply composed and vaguely melancholy image. Furthermore, this greater reliance on high-angle long shots is balanced by the images of the wedding, which feature a number of stunningly composed close-ups, shots that are so close as to become semi-abstract. Close-ups of candles and the cross at the head of the church are relatively short. But a shot of the bride's face, again bathed by the translucent fabric of the drawn veil, is *very* close; on the soundtrack we hear the priest reading the vows, and there is a moment of gentle disconnect between familiar-sounding material on a soundtrack and a more complex, expressionistic image. This is followed by an extreme close-up of the bride and groom's hands as they exchange rings; again the unusual closeness of the image gives it a semi-abstract quality.

Both of these films, then, operate on two levels. In one way their titles truly say it all. But they do not say it all in the same way as do the titles of films like *Thoughts on Fogo and Norway*, *Joe Kinsella on Education*, or, yes, *Billy Crane Moves Away*. Those films do indeed have a sort of zero-degree quality that most observers have ascribed to the series overall, as they use the camera primarily to record people discussing issues important to the island. Instead, films like *Jim Decker's Party* or *A Wedding and a Party* document these communal events with sharp attention to the craft of documentary filmmaking, and are very much part of the vérité lineage that engages with the capturing of musical performance, a lineage that includes such films as the NFB's own *Lonely Boy* (1962), D.A. Pennebaker's *Lambert, Hendricks & Co.* (1964), and Murray Lerner's *Festival* (1967), which features an incredibly visceral sequence with clog-dancers that reminds me very much of what we see in a number of the Fogo films (such as *Children of Fogo*, *The Songs of Chris Cobb*, or *Jim Decker's Party*).

The title of *Dan Roberts on Fishing* might suggest that it is along the lines of *Billy Crane Moves Away* or *Joe Kinsella on Education*, but that is not the case. The opening sequence is a montage of men working on fishing boats, and was clearly shot from other boats or on the boats they document, since the camera sways gently back and forth with the sea; especially when the images are one boat and shot from another boat, the combination of gentle swaying is hypnotic. The next sequence is talking-head footage of Dan Roberts and a few other men (including Fred Earle) discussing the economics of fishing (we can also hear Low's voice asking questions off-screen); in this way the film is indeed *Billy-Crane*-esque. But this sequence is, essentially, the long middle of the film. The end is, like the beginning, devoted to a montage (again with semi-synch sound) of work on these boats and it takes on a rhythmic quality that, frankly, I think Vertov would not find at all unfamiliar. This is especially true of a sequence where men move fish from the lower deck of the boat to the upper; the shot with one worker standing below deck is tight, very high-angle and generally striking. On the soundtrack are the rhythmic sounds of both the shovelling of the fish and the pitter-patter of boat engines. The final sequence of the film (whose soundtrack is comprised of a man singing and playing guitar, recalling *Children of Fogo Island*) features images of fish drying that, like so many other images in the Fogo series, makes keen use of composition in depth to show how this fish-work is inscribed on the landscape of the island.

McGraths at Home and Fishing has a similar duality to it. It opens with a close-up of an old timer in a rocking chair, with Fred Earle offscreen and asking him to sing one of the old songs. The lens zooms in and out, as the old timer recalls a few of the songs he used to sing. After some hemming and hawing, he finally sings "Big Rock Candy Mountain." There follows several minutes of chat with the old timers about fishing, welfare, out-migration, and so on. So far we are pretty squarely in *Billy Crane* territory. But without warning, the film shifts from synch-sound images of old timers sitting around the house to shots of two men working on a small boat. The sound, though, is consistent, as one of the old timers rambles about not wanting to go on welfare and the difficulty of getting the money for a long-liner together. Thus the film shifts into the more complex sound-image relationship so familiar from the other films, and returns to the gentle bobbing rhythms that made *Dan Roberts on Fishing* so hypnotic. And as the film draws to a close it makes this shift wholesale. The voices of the old men are replaced on the soundtrack by guitar music and semi-synch sound of the men on the boat chattering, and there follow some stunningly composed images, including one *very* low-angle and close shot focused between a fisherman's legs as he pulls in a rope on his bobbing boat (a shot that really does seem taken right out of a Vertov film); the next shot retains this framing but moves back slightly; the shot after that re-frames slightly again (although none of these would be characterized as jump cuts). The time is again dusk, and a misty rain appears to be falling, giving all the imagery a certain grey glow. Waugh has zeroed in on this specific sequence as key to understanding *Challenge for Change* and key to its recovery from the historical purgatory in which it now exists. He writes that the film is remarkable for "using the simple, elegant device of cutting back and forth between conversation among family members in their homey kitchen and then action footage of their livelihood on their small vessel bobbing up and down in the swell of the richly luminous ocean," referring to the film as "this modestly confident 16mm black and white masterpiece."[66]

Another masterpiece of mass media that is in conversation with Trudeau-era Canadian nationalism that I earlier evoked as so central to the Fogo films is the radio work that Glenn Gould did for the CBC; it is this radio work which offers the most fruitful point of comparison to the Fogo films. Gould's best-known radio documentary was *The Idea of North* (1967), a meditation on the place of the North in Canadian identity that was mostly in the form of layered voices that move fluidly between signification and semi-abstract musicality (sometimes as many as five people are talking over one another). The fact that this was released in the year of the hundredth anniversary of Confederation, and also the year of Montreal's Expo 67, helps make its connection to an emerging Canadian modernity fairly clear. But two years later Gould broadcast a very similar radio documentary about Newfoundland, called *The Latecomers*. It opens with sounds of the waves washing against the shore, but is otherwise entirely comprised of layered voices. The discussions we hear are *a lot* less economically detailed than what we hear in the Fogo films, and the overall thrust of the piece is much more philosophical. Gould wrote in the liner notes published with the CD release of the programmes that "it was obviously to be about the province-as-island, about the sea which keeps the mainland and the mainlanders at ferry-crossing's-length, about the problems of maintaining a minimally technologized style of life in a maximally technologized age."[67] Early in the programme one of the voices says "Work and duty? Yes, I do think so, very very much. As a matter of fact, I'm not thinking of it so much from the spiritual point of view but from the necessity of doing our best in the material sense. We can't do our best in the material sense unless we are tuned up, on the other side of life." This is a very different way of discussing work and material deprivation to be sure. But in both *The Latecomers* and the Fogo films, there is a pronounced push and pull between degree-zero signification and aesthetics (musical abstraction for Gould via layered voices, photographic or cinematic grace for Low via careful composition and affecting camera movements). They are both works that strongly resist linearity, and are both quite demanding if they are to be understood as wholes. And they are both unmistakably born of an optimism about technology and the way that technology can be used, not simply as an individualist luxury, but as a means of understanding collective identities and landscapes. (Northerners and northern-ness are the unmistakable preoccupations of both Low's most famous film *City of Gold* (1957) and Gould's *Idea of North*, just as Newfoundlanders and the North Atlantic experience are the unmistakable preoccupations of the Fogo films and *The Latecomers*.)

But the modesty that Waugh evokes in *McGraths at Home and Fishing* is not an affliction that Gould ever suffered from; this quality has, I think, been the historical undoing of the Fogo films. Like the *Challenge for Change* programme generally, these films were made by people motivated by an ethic of service, not personal expression. But in the case of the Fogo films, the formal sophistication that had marked all of Colin Low's films was inescapably present. This Newfoundland Project has clearly had considerable impact on less formally adventurous work, most famously on community television projects all over the world. But this really is only *part* of their contribution. By so forcefully disclaiming the aesthetic qualities of these films, a generation of well-intentioned filmmakers and historians have told only part of the cinematic story, and only part of the political story too. It is well past time to look again at these Fogo island films, and perhaps to see them as though for the first time.

NOTES

Bernard Lutz, archivist at the National Film Board of Canada, deserves hearty thanks for his help during my research at the NFB archives. Truly he was my Fred Earle. Thanks also to the Social Sciences and Humanities Research Council of Canada, which supported this research.

1 Colin Low in John Grierson Project, ed., "Grierson and the 'Challenge for Change,'" (Toronto: ECW Press, 1984), 111.

2 Colin Low, Untitled Report on Fogo Island Project, National Film Board of Canada (22 January 1968), p. 1.

3 Gary Evans, *In the National Interest: A Chronicle of the National Film Board of Canada from 1949 to 1989* (Toronto: University of Toronto Press, 1991), 160.

4 Ibid., 163.

5 Ibid., 159.

6 Janine Marchessault, "Reflections on the Dispossessed: Video and the 'Challenge for Change' Experiment," *Screen* 36(2) (Summer 1995): 135.

7 This is part of my book-in-progress on cinema in North Atlantic countries; I also dealt with it briefly in my afterword to David Clandfield's *Pierre Perrault and the Poetic Documentary* (Toronto Film Festival/Indiana University Press, 2004).

8 Pierre Pageau, "Colin Low et Pierre Perrault: Points de convergence," in Pierre Véronneau, Michael Dorland, and Seth Feldman, eds., *Dialogue : Cinéma canadien et québécois / Canadian and Quebec Cinema* (Montreal: Médiatexte / Cinémathèque québécoise, 1986), 139-51.

9 Pierre Pageau, "Colin Low, un anglophone au Québec," in Stéphane-Albert Boulais, ed., *Le cinéma au Québec : Tradition et modernité* (Saint-Laurent: Fides, 2006), 262. My translation.

10 Perrault interview: Léo Bonneville, *Le cinéma québécois par ceux qui le font* (Montréal: Éditions Paulines, 1979), 678. My translation.

11 *Fogo Island Film and Community Development Project*, Report for the National Film Board of Canada (May 1968), 1.

12 Colin Low, *The Fogo Island Communication Experiment*, Report for the National Film Board of Canada (July 5, 1972), 2.

13 Ibid.

14 *Fogo Island Film and Community Development Project*, 5.

15 D.B. Jones, *Movies and Memoranda: An Interpretive History of the National Film Board of Canada* (Ottawa: Deneau-Canadian Film Institute, 1981), 162.

16 Low, *Communication Experiment*, 1.

17 Low, Untitled Report, 3.

18 Donald Snowden, *Film and Community Development*, Report for the Office of Economic Development, Washington, DC (September 1968), 6–7.

19 Low, *Communication Experiment*, 2–3. Crocker, Jones, and Evans all recall that only three minutes were excised, and all three state that this was because islanders objected to the questioner's tone of voice. See Jones, 162, Evans, 164 and Stephen Crocker, "The Fogo Process: Participatory Communication in a Globalizing World," in *Participatory Video: Images that Transform and Empower*, ed. Shirley A. White (London: Sage, 2003), 128.

20 Evans, 164.

21 Low, *Communications Experiment*, 1.

22 Low, Untitled Report, 3.

23 Marchessault, 141.

24 Ibid., 139.

25 Untitled Report on the Film Unit of Memorial University of Newfoundland Extension Service and their involvement with the National Film Board (6 January 1970), 8.

26 Ibid.

27 Sandra Gwyn, *Cinema as Catalyst. Film, Video and Social Change: A Report on the Seminar* (St. John's: Memorial University of Newfoundland Extension Service, 1972), 5.

28 Ibid.

29 Ibid.

30 Colin Low, "*Capitale de l'or* et *Île Fogo*: le documentaire comme outil de communication et catalyseur de changement social," in *Le Documentaire: Contestation et propaganda*, ed. Catherine Saouter (Montréal: XYZ Éditeur, 1996), 70.

31 Thomas Waugh, "Challenging For Change/Société Nouvelle: Two Case Studies in Textual Analysis," paper presented at the annual meeting of the Film Studies Association of Canada (York University, 28–30 May 2006), 11.

32 Jones, 164.

33 Ibid.

34 Evans, 164.

35 Jones, 164.

36 Snowden, 10.

37 Barry de Ville, *Distributive Targets for the Fogo Island Films*, Report for the National Film Board of Canada (August 1972), 2.

38 Colin Low, in John Grierson Project, ed., 114.

39 Crocker, 134. The anonymous booklet *Fogo Process in Communication* recalls how "following the filming of Fogo, the National Film Board, at their Montreal headquarters, undertook the training of a Newfoundland crew to be attached the Extension Services Community Development Division as a permanent film unit.... Subsequently, in the spring of 1968, a workshop was held at Memorial in co-operation with the National Film Board on the use of film in community development which attracted participant from the United States and across Canada. Two southeastern Newfoundland communities Trepassey and St. Shotts were used as locations for practical training" (9). An untitled, anonymous report for MUN's Extension Service, dated 6 January 1970, opens by saying: "Since April 1968, the National Film Board has trained five members of the [Extension Service's] Film Unit, processed film footage shot by us, transferred our sound, cut our negatives when requested to do so, and have made reversal prints of most of our footage. From time to time, the Board has advised us of specific technical problems and has provided further individual training on request" (1). Both the report and the *Fogo Process* booklet detail film projects undertaken by the Extension Service in Port au Choix, the Labrador coast, and projects on successful co-operatives in Prince Edward Island and British Columbia. The anonymous *Fogo Process in Communication* booklet notes that "[a] series of programs called 'Decks Awash' designed to disseminate relevant information on fisheries and related topics, an annual and important project of the film unit, is broadcast over CJON-TV" (16). This work is very different material from the films of the NFB's Newfoundland Project. Films like *Olga Spence: Past, Present and Future* (1969) or *Father McGrath and Students* (1969) are records of conversations about local history or activism, and little more.

40 Crocker, 127.

41 Low, Untitled Report, 8.

42 Low, *Communications Experiment*, 3.

43 Grierson cited in Jones, 159.

44 Ibid., 168.

45 The NFB sent filmmakers to Arctic communities in the 1970s, and trained local people in the use of Super 8 cameras. Some quite lovely work emerged from this project, especially Mosha Michael's short films *Natsik Hunting* (1975), *The Hunters/Asivaqtiin* (1977) and *Whale Hunting/Qilaluqaniatut* (1977).

46 Gwyn, 1.

47 Low, "*Capitale de l'or* et *Île Fogo*," 70.

48 Wells' Newfoundland accent makes this sound indistinguishable from "I like the maple leaf"; the script of the film found in the NFB archives, however, has him saying, "I like to make believe."

49 Roger Riendeau summarizes the history thusly: "After finally rejecting Confederation in 1894, Newfoundland remained a British colony with responsible government until it was granted Dominion status after World War I.... During the great

depression, Newfoundland had to be rescued from bankruptcy by Britain, which suspended responsible government in 1934 and appointed a governor and commissioner to rule the island." In 1946 Britain offered to allow the island to decide its future, and two referenda followed: one that proposed returning to Dominion status, Confederation within Canada, or retaining rule by the commission (the results were 44%–41%–15%, respectively), and a second that proposed either Dominion status or Confederation within Canada (which favoured Confederation, 53% to 47%). Roger Riendeau, *A Brief History of Canada* (Markham: Fitzhenry and Whiteside, 2000), 244. Rawlyk sees the relationship with Britain in similar terms, writing of Britain's role that "[t]hough anxious to be rid of Newfoundland, the Labour government recognized the colony's vulnerability. Of two possibilities opened up by Newfoundland's post-War re-orientation, economic or political union with the United States or with Canada, the British government preferred the latter option and worked assiduously towards achieving that end." See G.A. Rawlyk, *The Atlantic Provinces and the Problems of Confederation: Report to the Task Force on Canadian Unity* (St. John's: Breakwater, 1979), 70

50 Marchessault, 143.

51 G.A. Rawlyk, *The Atlantic Provinces and the Problems of Confederation: Report to the Task Force on Canadian Unity* (St. John's: Breakwater, 1979), 286.

52 Ibid., 282.

53 Ibid., 285.

54 Raymond Blake, *Canadians At Last: Canada Integrates Newfoundland as a Province* (Toronto: University of Toronto Press, 2004), 183.

55 Ibid., 177–78.

56 Marchessault, 135.

57 Waugh, 9.

58 Jones, 168.

59 *Fogo Island Film and Community Development Project* (NFB, 1968), 8.

60 Jones, 162.

61 Jean Pierre Lefebvre, "Colin Low, poète de la survivance," *Objectif* 22–23 (October–November 1963): 34.

62 Crocker, 123.

63 Michael Kernan, "A Way of Social Change Through Film," *Washington Post*, 2 March 1969.

64 Peter Wollen, *Readings and Writings: Semiotic Counter-Strategies* (London: Verso, 1982), 92.

65 Ibid., 95.

66 Waugh, 10.

67 Glenn Gould, *The Latecomers. Glenn Gould's Solitude Trilogy: Three Sound Documentaries* (Toronto: CBC Records, 1992), pp. 6–7. First broadcast November 1969.

7

WHEN THE JIG WAS UP: WHAT DON MESSER'S MARITIME NOSTALGIA MEANT TO THE NATION

JEN VANDERBURGH

English Canada loves to fret about "the state of Canadian television."[1] Whether we're arguing over the dinner table about what is wrong with it, or reading yet another editorial on the subject, it appears to be right up there as one of our favourite "national" pastimes. The state's embeddedness in practices of television production and broadcasting in Canada has meant that we have grown accustomed to thinking that Canadian television is different from "normal" television: that "simple" American entertainment.[2] Historically, we have expected more from national television than entertainment (although entertainment does help). It is a location, we think, that makes our identity observable and tells us who we are.[3] This rhetorical "we" of English Canada refers quite specifically to an understanding of cultural history that is distinct from that of Quebec. It begins with British colonization, ignores First Nations or considers them pre-history, and ends up with immigration and a rather patronizing version of "multiculturalism," as a way to make allowances for "other" cultural practices.[4] In a context such as Canada's, where television shows are expected to commodify ideology as "identity," "entertainment" is considered to be the sugar that makes the medicine go down – useful, but not entirely the point.[5]

While the "hard" regulation of Canadian television makes the industry a ward of the state, the purpose of state-sponsored television is much "softer" and far more elusive. The hope in underwriting television production with public funds is to achieve nationalism by eliciting a perceived shared cultural experience amongst a diverse nation's citizenry. National television, like the nation itself, is less a fixed thing than a representation of complex and highly mutable social relations. Of course, the hegemonic party line argues otherwise, and structures such as the Canadian Broadcasting Corporation (CBC) have been erected as grand metaphors in the service of making the nation appear more solid than it actually is. It bears reminding that national cohesion is the fundamental purpose of the state's interest in cultivating television policy and infrastructure, and producing "Canadian content."[6]

Marc Raboy contends that "the terms *cultural industry* and *public broadcasting industry* are oxymorons"[7] in the sense that there is "inherent conflict between culture and economics."[8] Typically, writing that historicizes CBC television frames its fundamental challenge as negotiating between these two supposedly stable poles. But cultural theory suggests that culture is not stable. Considering also the current knowledge on technological determinism and media effects, the concept that an authentic culture lies in wait for the CBC to "reflect" seems naïve. Even without economics to consider, the CBC has had fundamental challenges with respect to culture. As producer and public broadcaster, its relation with "culture" is inherently dialectical, both reflecting and prescribing what Raymond Williams calls "structures of feeling" – those strains of the collective familiar that others have called (more problematically) "identity."[9] Nebulous as the CBC's ties to the actual cultures of Canada may be, the more it can capitalize on the collective familiar, the more unified and essential the nation appears.

It is now considered contentious to presume that culture naturally stems from national association. The act of conjuring feelings of collective national belonging through programming, more art than science, is a practice that for good reason has often confounded programmers, commissioning editors, and producers at the CBC. Arguably, the institution's policy rhetoric and its bricks-and-mortar presence as a national network have been more effective at symbolically promoting cultural nationalism in Canada than its television content. "Successful" content that has done well to garner a "national" audience, meaning that audience members are spread geographically throughout the country, has come in surprising forms. One example was a program from the Maritimes, *Don Messer's Jubilee* (1959–69), that, popular as it was, was arguably most effective in consolidating a national discourse when it was cancelled.

Don Messer's Jubilee, courtesy of CBC Still Photo Collection.

Produced out of CBC-Halifax, *Jubilee* was a weekly, half-hour national broadcast of "old time" fiddle music performed by Don Messer and his band, the Islanders. Described as straight-laced and folksy, Don Messer personified the depoliticized ideals associated with working-class, white, Anglo-Saxon Protestants, whose numbers at the time represented the largest portion of the national population, particularly in rural Canada. As John Fisher, the Commissioner of Canada's Centennial Commission, said of Messer's Islanders the year of Expo, 1967: "There certainly is no other group who have kept the 'homespun music of the people' alive through TV and radio coast to coast." While the show was called a "Hillbilly Hit" by *Time Magazine*, many of Canada's Toronto-based critics felt that, while Maritimers might like their "hoedown" music, CBC should not "force feed the rest of the country with this corn."[10] But the show's critics had to be careful. After Toronto mayor Philip Givens slighted Messer's show, he had to organize a public apology when 18,000 irate fans complained.[11]

Prior to his regular show on national television, Messer had been seen regionally since 1956 on CHBY-TV, Halifax. From 1944, he also broadcast nationally three times a week on CBC radio, where he had been performing since 1934 (on what was then CRBC) with his band, then known as the New Brunswick Lumberjacks. While Messer was perhaps best loved by his viewers for the performances of what he called "old time favourites," the traditional hornpipes, jigs, reels, and hymns of Scottish and Irish descent, he made his own arrangements and incorporated original compositions of his own and others, earning him the respect of folklorists and musicologists who consider his performances to have contributed to a "distinctly Canadian" synthesis of regional fiddle music, apart from Western, cowboy, or Appalachian varieties.[12]

Although the concept of branding connotes deception, which is antithetical to the transparent, authentic persona that Messer intended to portray, his was deliberately cultivated on the premise that aesthetic "simplicity" and frugality had a hand in maintaining "traditional" values – a coded term invested in the conservation of a particular racialized and religious/ethical cultural standard for the nation. Messer said this to the press, and many other variations on this theme: "I don't have 30 or 40 suits in my wardrobe. I have a small house, no trips to Europe, no fancy car, no place in Greece – but I have a very good life with my family."[13] Although Messer's yearly income was at times more than six times the national median income, Messer's stated priorities heralded fans who equated Puritan simplicity with Godliness. Many fans, particularly those who lived through the Depression, shared Messer's views about "correct lifestyle." Through this lens, the 1960s rock-and-roll years seemed decadent, but this was not the main concern. Messer's conflict with rock culture, as I will argue, is not singularly about class, music, generations, or ideology. It is a conflict about racial, ethnic, and cultural dominance that played out on Canadian televisions in pragmatic and observable ways such as the CBC's programming decisions and viewer responses to that programming. It was disputed, in the case of *Jubilee*, using a value-laden currency of language that rather unproblematically referenced aesthetic understandings of what was connoted by and understood to be "simple."

Intensifying during the run of *Jubilee*, the defining binaries of 1960s Canadian nationalist discourse – traditionalism and modernism, rural and urban, biculture and multiculture – were perceived to be at odds, corrupting the very core of English Canada's so-called "national identity."[14] Abstracted as these debates often were, at times they became grounded in disputes about cultural objects. The flag debate is one notable example from this time (Messer publicly supported keeping the Union Jack as Canada's symbol), bilingual signage another (Messer printed English-only tour posters to protest Festival Canada's bilingual ads), as was debate about the cancellation of Messer's show.[15]

Jubilee was largely perceived, as Li Robbins suggests, as "an antidote – the remedy for rock-'n'-roll."[16] This widespread claim creates the impression that the disputes over music (Messer's "traditional" or 1960s Canadian "rock") are coded disputes about Canadian values, and which version should be dominant. While no doubt there is truth to this, there was also much more than morality at stake. Adding yet another layer of meaning to the Messer debate, outspoken lead singer Charlie Chamberlain, who pumped gas to supplement his *Jubilee* salary, publicly referred to Messer as "tight as me own arse. He wouldn't pay five cents to see the Pope do the shimmy."[17] Chamberlain's statement speaks to how ideology and political economy are enmeshed. Just as Messer's image and popularity relied on the impression that he was a man of the ("simple") people, among the nation's economically oppressed, the currency of his folksy image was also endangered at the CBC, placing *Jubilee* and "youthful," "urban" programming in direct competition for production money, jobs, and access to the "national audience."[18] As Messer was fond of saying, "We live what we play."[19]

Li Robbins describes the opening strains of *Jubilee's* theme, "Got my dancin' boots on, got my Sunday best" as "an invitation to a *world* [my emphasis] of old-time music and values."[20] The placefulness of this "world" relies on a particular notion of the Maritimes as the original location of English Canada's oldest, most traditional music. Messer took pains to distinguish his music from newer forms of "Western or cowboy [fiddle] music." "Our tunes," said Messer, "have been around for two or three hundred years. They're folk tunes passed from generation to generation."[21] Messer's performances were dialectically considered "wholesome" (read: innocuous) fun "as clean, straight-ahead and neat as a well-tended farm,"[22] and important re-enactments of the nation's foundational oral culture.[23] As an informal folk archivist in the public eye, Messer became a significant ambassador of this cultural "place" rooted in the Maritimes, both actual and fictional, the perception of which has so inspired notions of an historical, naturalized, and place-specific derivation of "national culture." Richard Green points out that, from 1949 to 1969, Messer completed eighteen formal performance tours, including an extensive three-month, sixty-one-stop national centennial tour in 1967.[24] These tours were a way for Messer to bear witness with fans who spanned the country, to earn performer's wages, and to promote his musical recordings, which he personally facilitated and sold through the mail. This was a way to augment his contract with the CBC, which, despite his show's consistent national popularity, reached only $25,000 at its peak year.[25]

Masterful at creating and maintaining a perceived tension between the distinctiveness and timelessness of his music, Messer endures as an emblem of what is considered to be Canada's "national" legacy. In recent years, two musicals based on Messer's music and his life have toured across Canada, and a lengthy court battle between them, based on the rights to Messer's name, indicates that the Messer name is still big business.[26] Ontario fiddler Frank Leahy has built a career performing with Messer's violin,[27] and in April of 2006, psychic Alan Hatfield's attempts to record Messer with a microphone at his gravesite made the national news, suggesting that over thirty years after his death in 1973, the Messer name still has significant cultural capital and national resonance.[28]

For most of 1960–63, *Don Messer's Jubilee* was the top-rated television show in Canada. At times, more Canadians watched *Jubilee* than Ed Sullivan and NHL Hockey.[29] Even after its heyday, *Jubilee* rarely dipped below eighth in the national ratings, which included American-made shows.

And yet, despite the popularity of this program that was inexpensive to produce (one quarter the average for a CBC variety show at the time)[30] and provided valuable "regional representation" for the centrist CBC national network (one of its institutional bête noirs), it was cancelled abruptly, for no immediately apparent reason, in the spring of 1969.[31] Johanne Trew locates the cancellation of *Jubilee* within a broader shift in articulations of Canadian cultural identity in the 1960s, literally, in this case, a change in the performance of nationalism.[32] In a "rush to establish new Canadian symbols," she argues, within the context of an "emerging liberal nationalism," Messer's dismissal was in keeping with "the abrupt disposal of British symbols and the removal of established media icons from the airwaves."[33] The cancellation of the show can also be read as a continuation of the historical narrative of centrist national policy decisions that has affected the Maritimes. The way that Messer found out about the cancellation, second hand, in a telegram from Toronto, effectively elevated him to martyrdom in his public's eye.[34]

Canadian television viewers have never been more irate about the cancellation of a television show than they were with *Jubilee*. The CBC received 21,000 pieces of protest mail[35] and 1,500 phone calls within a month of announcing the cancellation.[36] And while two protests on Parliament Hill, one numbering upwards of 300 people, did not reverse the CBC's decision, it did force journalists and fans to articulate their support of *Jubilee* and Don Messer in a way that has been archived for study, a rare occurrence indeed for Canadian television.[37] That newspapers archived the debates amongst journalists is self-evident, but that an archive exists which consolidates a particular nationalist sentiment of a moment is directly due to Messer's popular image as the approachable folklorist of Canada's national heritage. Many of the outraged fans who protested the CBC sent copies of their letters directly to Messer. These letters remained in his personal files, and today they reside, available to the public, at the Public Archives of Nova Scotia. Many of these protest letters are prefaced with a short personal note to Messer, stating support for his "cause," suggesting that he was a rallying point that consolidated debate about issues larger than the show.

Television, as McLuhan first told us in Canada, is as ephemeral as the electricity on which it relies.[38] But since such a large portion of our lives is spent in its presence, we must presume that the effects of its content have been profound. By one account, *Jubilee* was watched in 50 per cent of rural Canadian households with televisions and 25 per cent of urban Canadian households.[39] Ironically, the matter-of-factness of its presence rendered it rather invisible, like breathing or wallpaper. Archival evidence of Canadian television content is sparse, which has made the study of the effects of this content impossible. Herein lies the challenge: how can we study that which is thought so innocuous that it cannot be seen?

Rebecca Sullivan and Bart Beaty recently point out that more ink has been spilled over the *concept* of Canadian television than its content perhaps because of the widespread assumption that debate about the cultural industries is coded talk about who "we" (as *a people*) are.[40] It is instructive, then, that the documents made available for historical research into Canadian television, those that we consider to speak of "the people," are most often those wherein the state features prominently. In large part this is due to the available materials for historical research into Canadian television, which tend to be state-sponsored documents written as policies or assessments, and national newspapers, whose business depends upon naturalizing the nation, thereby reinforcing the state.[41] The (archival) accessibility of newspapers and public records such as policy documents and reviews, versus the (ephemeral) inaccessibility of animated dinner-table debates (oral histories) have shaped our "knowledge" of what "the people's" opinion of television has been over time. Partly this is a practical problem of research methods that I will only allude to here, but should we need to be convinced of its importance, Eva Mackey's *The House of Difference: Cultural Politics and National Identity in Canada* (1999), for one, offers compelling evidence that official articulations of identity found in state-sanctioned expressions, whether policies or celebrations of "cultural identity" systematically belie the multiple, often discordant voices of the state's "people."

While the antidote might appear to seek out moments where "the people" speak for themselves, cultural studies warns us that the act of expression is cultivated and not a reliable measure of authenticity. Such is the case with folklore. Ian McKay, in *Quest of the Folk*, charges folklorists with deriving essentialist claims from notions of authentic speech or "lore"[42] as a way of demonstrating "organic, natural ties ... between the Folk and the Nation [that] were far more essential than the superficial and transitory divisions of ethnicity, gender, or class."[43] Though the speech/lore of the folk is considered to have superseded the state, its record and preservation serves a national interest, wherein folk "speakers" become "mere vessels of national essence, bearers of cultural treasures whose value they themselves could never understand."[44] There is much at stake for the nation, McKay goes on to argue, in seeing "a *bricolage* of unrelated cultural artifacts ... as whole and traditional."[45] Don Messer, upon the cancellation of his show, became a figure whose function within 1960s Canadian pop culture was to unify a "bricolage" to which McKay refers and make it appear "traditional." This synergy between changes within the nation and the lore of the people is, argues McKay, at once cultivated and not inauthentic. Such is the case with national television.

We doth protest too much, methinks

The following letter was addressed to the President of the CBC, June 26, 1969:

> I know that many letters, petitions of protest have already arrived at your office expressing disapproval of the dropping of the Don Messer Jubilee show. I also know that I will always have a guilty feeling if I do not also add my protest, and I sincerely hope that enough other Canadians are at this time continuing to express protest.... Don Messer's program represents a way of life to Canadians, one we should not lose sight of and cannot afford to permit to go into disregard. He gave us good, clean, wholesome entertainment, which we in our home, along with the many thousands of other Canadians who are protesting, looked forward to weekly with great anticipation. We feel that we have lost something for which there is no acceptable replacement, and, something we did not want to lose.

Another letter addressed to "CBC Toronto" reads:

> Don Messer is a God fearing man.... When we have to turn our dial and find African Jungle type of music with yelling and screaming and head nodding and hip shaking then we have nothing to do but turn it off.... Liberal Society at Present by their attitude toward this Don Messer Program has surely caused a fervor down here and believe me when election time rolls around we down-easters and a lot of people from all over Canada will cast a vote in the opposite direction.

These excerpts are representative of two approaches found in the collection of letters that protested *Jubilee's* cancellation. Differences are found in their use of language. The first letter is more cryptic, and vaguely justifies the need for protest based on the loss of a "way of life," signified in the author's estimation by Messer's "good, clean, wholesome" entertainment. The language of the second letter is more to the point and decodes, in relation to what the terms "clean" and "wholesome" implicitly reference, and defines precisely how "loss" is determined. The presence of "Jungle music" on the nation's airwaves, endorsed by what the author characterizes, in fact, personifies in capital letters as "Liberal Society at Present," is considered to be evidence jeopardizing Messer's "God fearing" dominance. In these letters, *Jubilee's* cancellation is perceived to be emblematic of a larger cultural slippage away from the primacy of the white "race," Anglo-Saxon culture and its religions, and rural/regional working-class values, as defining features of the nation's dominant performance of "identity." In keeping with Richard Dyer's claim that the dominance of the ruling "race" renders it "invisible," Messer's "whiteness" functions here as the naturalized standard against which the potentially disruptive "otherness" of the encroaching "Jungle music" is defined.[46] This discourse also obliterates the African-Canadian presence and culture in the Maritimes.

The letters protesting the cancellation of *Jubilee* suggest that Messer's performance of nostalgia for a national narrative rooted in ethnicity was dependent upon an economy that conflates race, class, region, and age. Their authors provide us with articulate evidence. "Nostalgic purity is a rare quality on television," says one. "Perhaps the CBC should stop and think," says another. "It might realize that millions of Canadians live beyond the cocktail set of Toronto and Montreal." One fan writes, "I can't see why elderly people can't have one program that they enjoy without being criticized by snobs like this." Another writes, "Morality, principle, dignity, old institutions, traditions must go, and so goes the Don Messer show." "Don Messer," says one viewer, "is one of God's special people." "Apparently," says another, "the only type of protest to which the CBC pays any attention is that coming from bewhiskered and dirty-looking bums who call themselves hippies. Let a hippy [*sic*] protest anything and he gets all kinds of attention from the CBC. If a man is too lazy to wash or comb his hair, or too uncaring to dress decently, too indolent to work, he can spout off on any subject ... and he gets all sorts of publicity from the CBC and plenty of crocodile tears for his 'cause.'"

As ludicrous as the rhetoric of these letters might seem, it is not surprising that they considered television to be a location wherein changes in national identity were rendered visible, and that the (supposedly youth-oriented, multiculture-supporting, Toronto-centric) CBC was accused of tampering with "tradition." As a "new" technology, television was understandably viewed with some suspicion. Canada was relatively late to television when the CBC began broadcasting in 1952. It was adopted quickly and by 1963, 90 per cent of Canadian households owned a TV.[47] Although many Canadians within range of the U.S. border had been watching American television signals for years, the CBC was the only Canadian network broadcasting Canadian programming until the CTV received the first broadcast licence for a private network in 1960. Understandably, Messer's devotees considered the CBC to be synonymous with Canadian television due to its prominence during these years.

The "new" (to Canada) technology offered up nationally regulated airwaves as a fresh "landscape," and as with new lands, opportunities for colonization. Expectations that CBC should patriate this new media "space" feature prominently in *Jubilee's* protest letters. Consistently, the CBC is charged with wanton neglect of the "tradition" that Messer represented on Canadian airwaves, and abuse of its privileged access into Canadian homes for the purpose of conducting revisionist cultural history. This, says one letter, at the expense of Messer's "ablest, undemented talents." Entire communities, particularly in rural areas, organized lengthy petitions, newspapers printed protest coupons in effort to expedite complaints to Members of Parliament, and in the House of Commons the suggestion to pull rank and reverse the CBC's decision to cancel the *Jubilee* was debated multiple times. One letter calls for a "good house cleaning" at the CBC. Says another, "Let [the CBC] not be used as a media to defile and debauch the broadest standards of social and cultural decency." In reference to the cancellation, Former Prime Minister John Diefenbaker raged in question period that "the Black Panthers and the like [had] an inside track at the CBC."[48] While alarming, Diefenbaker's comment is instructive and, I have found, representative of the kind of coded rhetoric that was levelled at the CBC's "politics" and "classism," and that defended Messer's "popularism," "clean entertainment," and "simplicity" in so-called "complicated times." What people seem to have been reacting to in these protest letters, what they consider to be under siege, is not just Messer's show. Their anxiety reflects the perception that the ethnic primacy of their particular national

Don Messer's Jubilee, courtesy of CBC Still Photo Collection.

narrative was under threat. Fiddler Graham Townsend blatantly associates Messer with a Canadian ethnic narrative. He was quoted in the *Globe and Mail* saying, "The Negroes in the United States fight for their rights. We in Canada must fight for the Don Messer show."[49]

We must question, I believe, the transparency of Messer's "simplicity." It is found in the language that frames him. A "simple" fiddler who began on radio, Messer "simply" made the transition to television, and, as the story goes, did not forget his roots, or lose his common sense in the process. Lurking in the discourse that surrounds the show and its cancellation is the assumption that the CBC, the medium of television, and sixties youth culture were considered to be "complex" and "political," while the *Jubilee* and Messer were (and are) not.

As a result, Messer's "simplicity" should be viewed in context of the norms of 1960s television aesthetics. Considering the standard, *Jubilee*'s format and style were clearly out of step, which is why the CBC repeatedly justified its decision to cancel *Jubilee* in favour of a "fresh new element" in the schedule.[50] Doubtful as it is that the CBC would consider "freshness" a compelling enough reason to cancel one of its most popular programs, when considering the show's ratio of jolts per minute, the point is well taken.[51] Aside from guest artists, who still fell within the bounds of the show's musical genre, the format and aesthetic of *Jubilee* was, as one reporter described, "monotonously familiar."[52]

If you have seen excerpts of *Jubilee* (and I invite you to view them online at the Public Archives of Nova Scotia's Web site), you are apt to find its popularity shocking.[53] A fair description of *Jubilee* might be to say that it was a variety show without the variety. Messer changed very little of the show's format in making the transition from radio to television. The musicians usually stood still in front of the camera, while the small Halifax studio offered little in the way of opportunities for camera movement. In relation to glamorous performers showcased on U.S. and other Canadian variety shows of the 1960s, Messer's lead singers, Marg Osburne and Charlie Chamberlain, were comparatively "plain," described by one journalist as "everyday folksy people who don't pretend to have perfect teeth or perfect figures."[54] Contributing visual interest, the Buchta dancers, a popular east coast dance troupe led by Gunter Buchta, were added to the program. As one journalist noted, Messer's one concession to television was that he learned how to smile and play the fiddle at the same time; a skill that was, of course, less important on radio.[55]

Ironically, it was *Jubilee's* decidedly anti-televisual aesthetic that accounted for its popularity with fans, which, as previously discussed, was mainly comprised of a conservative demographic, resistant to the "youthful" and "urban" (read: racialized) cultures gaining predominance in 1960s Canada. To write off Messer's *Jubilee* as boring television is to underestimate the importance of its "simplicity" in consolidating a popular structure of feeling. For its four million viewers, the predictable format and content of the show became a rehearsal of identity, a coded defence, as I have argued, opposed to social changes that were considered to be undermining Canada's dominant narrative of national identity.

As Johanne Trew contends in an article in the *International Journal of Canadian Studies*:

> [Messer's] views and the image of Canadian life which his programmes projected and, arguably, helped to reinforce, were … in direct conflict with the new liberal nationalism emerging both in Quebec and the Canadian federal government and its agencies, including the CBC. In short, I believe his popular programme, *Don Messer's Jubilee*, did not project (or perform) the new image of Canada … Viewed from this perspective it begins to look as though Messer's tremendous popularity may in fact, have worked against him and led to the cancellation of his programme.[56]

Trew's assessment certainly reflects the popular discourse held by fans of the show and critics of the CBC in the 1960s, the anxiety that Canada's narrative was changing, moving from "simple" to "complex." But the rhetoric that is used to defend Messer here is instructive. Insisting that *Jubilee's* representation of Canada became outdated tends to presume that it was agreed upon in the first place. It also reifies the belief that the Anglo-Canadian folk tradition out of the Maritimes is a privileged seat of the nation's "original" culture. This is the basis on which the national narrative associated with *Jubilee's* demise receives support and promotion. As a discourse for a nation that now iterates an identity based on multiculturalism, it is obviously highly problematic. Yet the language of "simple" traditionalism continues to circulate in debates about the cultural identity of "the nation," and still Messer presents as a central figure. Trew, for example, offers this by way of conclusion: "Despite the continued lack of official recognition and support, and perhaps even because of it, traditional culture in Canada continues to thrive due to the meaning it holds for ordinary people. Nonetheless, this does not relieve the various levels of government in the country of their responsibility to preserve, protect and promote it (e.g., via the public broadcasting system)."[57]

As with Trew's support for "ordinary people," the limited critical writing on *Jubilee*'s cancellation sees it as a challenge to the Massey Report's prescriptive call to develop national culture as high culture.[58] But it is instructive to probe the implications of framing *Jubilee* as "simple," "ordinary," or even as "popular" culture. At what price was the show popular, we should ask, since not only does the response to the show express a shared cultural feeling, it also expresses xenophobia and racism.

Messer continues to signify as a folk hero for a "simple" national culture. The worst thing that has been written about him is that he was boring. Perhaps ironically, what the CBC learned from *Jubilee* is that there is a market for narratives that depict nostalgia for "pure" or "authentic" ethnicity. The organization has evaded accusations of racism or ethnocentricity by strategically locating these narratives in the Maritimes, making them "regional," not blatantly national stories. The CBC broadcasts of the dramatic series *Road to Avonlea* (1990–96), *Pit Pony* (1998–2000), *Wind at My Back* (1996–2001), and the annual *East Coast Music Awards* (1989 – present), operate within an understanding of a national narrative that is in line with Messer's, but as they are specifically situated as regional material, they have enabled a problematic nostalgia for ethnic "simplicity" (read: purity) to continue.

Although fans of the show might disagree, it seems that the legacy of *Jubilee* is not the show itself, but rather how the cancellation of the show consolidated disputes about the purpose of national television in English-Canada. At the same time that I am advocating recognition of the way in which the protest letters conflate race and ethnicity with national origin, "purity," and "simplicity," I do not want to suggest that the connection that people felt with Messer, and with each other through the act of watching *Jubilee* as a community of viewers, was somehow invalid.[59] Messer's letters of support demonstrate that fans felt useful, personal connections with Messer, which were often therapeutic and cathartic. While no doubt there is evidence of this in any kind of fan mail, the difference with Messer's fans is that they considered him to be not only an entertainer, but also a like-minded authority on the language that defined their perspective of national culture. Writing to Messer was like going to the national confessional, sharing personal news, as well as social opinion. Fan letters like this one are typical, where the writer complains of personal aches and pains, the rise in the cost of living, along with the decline of the state of the nation:

> Dear Don ... I took this Burcitis in the right shoulder joint and every time I'd move my arm it would crack and send a pain right down in my hand.... We are hoping there will be a great change in the government soon; lower taxes and the cost of living. I hear the Hydro is raising up again and I think this makes the third raise. We own our house and believe me I do hope we won't have to sell it and go to the Citizen's home.

This chapter has contended that the language of Messer's letters of support are symptomatic of conflicting discourses in Canada over television and nationhood; attendant disputes over race, ethnicity, class, gender; and concepts of culture, community, and belonging, at the time that *Jubilee* was on the air, and then cancelled. Further to this, I make the methodological point that the contribution of Messer's archive of letters demonstrates a link between television content and ideas of nationhood in a way that is not usually so readily observable for those of us who study Canadian television. The language of the letters show how arguments over national television content reveal themselves to be thinly veiled disputes about the nation.

One of the CBC's greatest contributions, it seems to me, is that its institutional presence is a rich, living archive of ways in which "culture" is perceived and performed within nations. While there has historically existed a synergy between the institution of the CBC, the consideration of state interests, and those of audiences within "the nation," the example of *Don Messer's Jubilee* demonstrates that the institution has, at times, acted independently of public opinion in articulating definitions of "national identity." We might want to ask what this practice could be in service of. Strangely, *Don Messer's Jubilee* was replaced with another similar musical variety show, also produced out of Halifax, called *Singalong Jubilee* (1961–74).[60] Emphasizing choral arrangements, *Singalong Jubilee* continued Messer's performance of nostalgia for a colonial, national narrative derived from the Maritimes, an alternate staging of the nationalism being performed in 1960s Toronto.[61]

NOTES

1 I am referring to English Canada throughout as a problematic term that is used colloquially and strategically to exclude Quebec in order to make possible discussions of national culture. The implicit assumption is that Canada would be easier to identity if not for Quebec, whose differences are presumed to be cultural, not national, and therefore, less threatening to the concept of a singular nation. The term is obviously contentious for many reasons, not the least of which is that it conflates British colonialism and language, both of which are slippery reference points when describing the citizens of the country.

2 For an excellent backgrounder on and chronology of the state's role in Canadian broadcasting, see Marc Raboy's "Public Television," in *The Cultural Industries in Canada: Problems, Policies and Prospects*, ed. Michael Dorland (Toronto: Lorimer, 1996), 178–202. Raboy outlines Canada's history of state involvement in television production and broadcasting, and suggests that the lines between the public and private sectors have always been blurred. Methods of regulating broadcast licences and issuing public funds for the production of content even in the private sector results in a culture of vetting by the state that Raboy calls "public-ization."

3 For a useful chronology of Canada's federal strategy to develop identity through broadcasting and Canadian television production see Culturescope.ca Canadian Cultural Observatory, "Timeline of Canadian Federal Cultural Policy Milestones 1849 to 2005," Department of Canadian Heritage, http://www.culturescope.ca/policy-timeline/timeline-1970_en.htm.

4 This is the subject of Eva Mackey's *The House of Difference: Cultural Politics and National Identity in Canada* (London: Routledge, 1999). She argues that Western exclusionary identities of power are often constructed using "liberal con-

cepts and practices of pluralism, diversity and tolerance" (5). "Multiculturalism," she says, "has as much to do with the construction of identity for those Canadians who do not conceive of themselves as 'multicultural', as for those who do" (3).

5 The hope that federal support for cultural production will produce national identity underwrites the objectives of any federal funding agency. Telefilm Canada, for example, defines as its "mission," "to foster the production of films, television programs and cultural products that reflect Canadian society." Telefilm Canada, "Mission: Telefilm Canada – Developing and promoting the Canadian audiovisual industry." http://www.telefilm.gc.ca/01/11.asp.

6 One of the peculiarities of Cancon is that while its intention is nationalist, the rhetoric of Canada as a pluralistic nation has prevented the Canadian Audio-Visual Certification Office (CAVCO) from developing criteria to assess a project's "Canadianness" based on theme or subject. Instead, projects are determined to be Canadian by accumulating "points" that are awarded for key positions that are held by Canadian citizens. It is a quantitative, not qualitative assessment. See "Canadian Content Rules," Department of Canadian Heritage, http://www.pch.gc.ca/progs/ac-ca/pubs/can-con/can_con.html.

7 Raboy, 178.

8 Ibid.

9 Raymond Williams, *The Country and the City* (New York: Oxford University Press, 1973).

10 Anonymous TV critic, *Globe and Mail* (September 1959) as quoted in Liv Robbins, *Don Messer's Violin: Canada's Fiddle* (Toronto: CBC, 2005), 47.

11 "It's 2:55 – and the Yawn's in order," *Toronto Star*, 25 March 25, 1964, 1.

12 Richard Green mentions Al Cherny, Andy DeJarlis, Jim Magill, and Graham

Townsend in particular. See Green's "Don Messer," *The Canadian Encyclopedia*, www.thecanadianencyclopedia.com/index.cfm?PgNm=TCE&P.

13 *Toronto Star* (27 March 1973), quoted in "On this Day" May 9, 1909 – The World of Don Messer," *CBC Archives*, http://archives.cbc.ca/IDC-1-68-2224-13353-10/on_this_day/arts_entertainment/twt.

14 See Johanne Devlin Trew, "Conflicting Visions: Don Messer, Liberal Nationalism and the Canadian Unity Debate," *International Journal of Canadian Studies* 26 (2002): 41–57.

15 Ken Reynolds as quoted in Trew, 41. Interview by Trew, Tape recording Ottawa, November 1995.

16 Robbins, 48.

17 Stephen Cole, *Here's Looking at Us: Celebrating 50 Years of CBC TV* (Toronto: McClelland and Stewart, 2002), 76.

18 To be fair, although Messer's income was well above the national average, his earnings were less that one might expect considering both his popularity and what rock stars were earning for comparable work.

19 Robbins, 67.

20 Robbins, 46.

21 *CBC Times* (11–17 April 1964), quoted in Green.

22 Dorothy and Homer Hogan's notes in Graham Townsend's LP *The Great Canadian Fiddle*, quoted in Green.

23 It begs mention that while Messer's practice of oral culture was considered of cultural importance to national 'identity,' for obvious reasons, First Nations' tradition of oral culture was considered 'unreliable,' or of lesser 'national' significance.

24 Green.

25 Although Messer had various recording arrangements throughout his career, the sale of recordings was not lucrative on its own. Robbins notes that Messer received a quarterly royalty cheque for $3.48 in 1939 (23).

26 The court battle between Ontario fiddler Frank Leahy and Grayec Management Ltd. found in favour of Grayec in June 2005. "On this Day," CBC Archives, http://archives.cbc.ca/IDC-1-68-2224-13353-10/on_this_day/arts_entertainment.

27 In 2006, a Messer fiddle sold for over $11,000 at auction. *Globe and Mail*, 24 July 2006, A5.

28 Jane Armstrong, "Hoping for a song from beyond," *Globe and Mail*, 28 April 2006, A3.

29 A sample of copies of Bureau of Broadcast Measurement ratings reports are available to view in the Messer files at the Nova Scotia Archives. Robbins cites one from 10 June 1960 where *Jubilee* reached 1,706,900 households, the *Ed Sullivan Show* 1,685,200, and *NHL Hockey* 1,549,400 (53).

30 Paul Rutherford in Robbins, 55.

31 See Mary Jane Miller, "Regional or 'What Toronto Doesn't Know,'" in *Turn Up the Contrast: CBC Drama Since 1952* (Vancouver: University of British Columbia Press, 1987), 325–56.

32 Trew, 41–58.

33 Trew, 41.

34 Robbins, 81. The telegram was sent 14 April by Doug Nixon, CBC's Director of Entertainment to Keith Barry, CBC Halifax.

35 Lester B. Sellick, *Canada's Don Messer* (Kentville, NS: Kentville Publishing Company, 1969). Quoted in Trew, 46.

36 Robbins, 83.

37 Robbins, 83.

38 Marshall McLuhan, "Television: the Timid Giant," in *Understanding Media: The Extensions of Man* (Cambridge, MA: MIT Press, 1994), 308–37.

39 Robbins, 66.

40 See Bart Beaty and Rebecca Sullivan, *Canadian Television Today* (Calgary: University of Calgary Press, 2006), 1–2, 9–11.

41 For a good chronology of some of these documents see Raboy.

42 Ian McKay, *The Quest of the Folk: Antimodernism and Cultural Selection in Twentieth-Century Nova Scotia* (Montreal: McGill-Queen's University Press, 1994). McKay defines the "lore" of the folk as "their ballads, songs, games, proverbs, sayings, curses, magical beliefs, myths, and superstitions" (13).

43 McKay, 13.

44 McKay, 15.

45 McKay, 17.

46 Richard Dyer, *White: Essays on Race and Culture* (London: Routledge, 1997).

47 Robbins, 65.

48 Paul Rutherford, *When Television Was Young: Primetime Canada 1952–1967* (Toronto: University of Toronto Press, 1990), 218.

49 Quoted in Robbins, 83.

50 Robbins, 81.

51 Morris Wolfe, *Jolts: The TV Wasteland and the Canadian Oasis* (Toronto: Lorimer, 1985).

52 Bob Burgess, "TV and Radio," *The Journal*, August 1959.

53 Segments of the show can be viewed, along with photographs and other materials, in an online exhibit at the website of the Public Archives of Nova Scotia, http://www.gov.ns.ca/nsarm/virtual/messer/album.asp. This archive also holds the Messer fan letters discussed in this chapter.

54 "More Glamorous Singers Needed?" *Halifax Chronicle Herald*, 19 November 1960.

55 Robbins, 51.

56 Trew, 48–49.

57 Trew, 51.

58 For a discussion of the Massey' Commission's desire for "high" culture, see Paul Litt, *The Muses, the Masses, and the Massey Commission* (Toronto: University of Toronto Press, 1992).

59 Trew expands on this "sense of community" or "communitas" across space and time that was achieved by watching Messer (43–44).

60 From 1961 to 1969, *Singalong Jubilee* was the summer replacement show of *Messer's Jubilee* and, with the cancellation of Messer's show, subsequently became the regular season replacement.

61 Giving some currency to the Messer fan conspiracy theories, Knowlton Nash quotes Doug Nixon, the CBC executive who ordered the show's cancellation, as saying: "I am bloody-well going to kill the geriatric fiddlers" (388). Nixon is also cited in Robbins, p. 86. Nash quotes Messer's response, upon hearing the news of his cancellation, as "Tarnation poop!" (389). Knowlton Nash, *The Microphone Wars: A History of Triumph and Betrayal at the CBC* (Toronto: McClelland and Stewart, 1994).

8

IMPERIALISM, REGIONALISM, HUMANISM: *GULLAGE'S, TRAILER PARK BOYS,* AND REPRESENTATIONS OF CANADIAN SPACE IN GLOBAL HOLLYWOOD

JOHN MCCULLOUGH

In this chapter, I discuss the conditions of regional Canadian television production in the context of contemporary thinking about space and globalization. This approach has the advantage of seeing such production in the context of global flows of capital, technology, entertainment, and cultural labour; a perspective that is not only relevant to Canadian culture but is also revealing about other national cultural contexts. In Global Hollywood, almost all the world's regions compete for limited numbers of media productions, so that even though their national political contexts may be quite distinct from our own, there is a strong correspondence between various state-sponsored attempts to attract media work. For example, tax rebates, labour cost reductions, ease of permitting, and studio construction are strategies common to an international array of regional jurisdictions vying for film and television production. Studying the Canadian context illustrates crucial themes in contemporary international media production, encouraging us to think about the relationship between labour and culture. Additionally, this approach encourages us to think about the space of the world and how, in national and regional attempts to attract media work, there is competition organized around space. In "media culture," we see that regional jurisdictions promote and sell their space and labour to a global media economy that consumes both at an ever-increasing pace.[1]

Regionalism plays an important role in global media economies to the extent that regions provide cost benefits in terms of both labour and space. As much as this is true of the media industries, it can also be seen to operate in the realm of other industries in globalization. For instance, the call centre industry and the prison and security industry are also globalized industries that require cost benefits in terms of land, access to services, and access to labour cost reductions. It is not surprising that such "growth" industries as media, prisons, and call centres have all recently taken up stakes in Canadian regions, including the Atlantic provinces. The region has used the expansion of service industries in the period of globalization as a way of responding to devastating changes to the region's traditional economies that were organized around natural resource extraction and development.[2] I use *Gullage's* (Dir: Bill MacGillivray, series, 1996–98) and *Trailer Park Boys* (Dir: Mike Clattenberg, series, 2001 – present and feature film, 2006)[3] as illustrative examples of how Atlantic Canadian space, labour, and culture have been developed in the last ten years. One could even say the last twenty years to include the neo-liberal economic reforms beginning in the mid-1980s (as discussed in Malek Khouri's chapter) and subsequently influencing cultural policy and the economic framework through which regional production takes place. These two television shows mark the shift toward an industrialization of regional production under conditions of Global Hollywood, a drift likewise mapped in Darrell Varga's chapter of this book. I conclude by commenting on the tone and meanings of these works and, ultimately, the central role that humanist ideology plays in global media culture.

It is necessary to insist that whatever else globalization may mean, it is fundamentally the contemporary formation of capitalism – a structure that determines, and I use the term provisionally, the conditions and prospects of human experience. I mention this because, in the midst of all the various celebrations of global culture, it is tempting to think of globalization as a neutral phenomenon, sometimes even rational or natural, and sometimes, from a culturalist perspective, globalization has been argued to be progressive and inevitable. For instance, Tomlinson has argued that the global expansion of capital perpetuates interconnections and networks, which he sees in positive terms.[4] The multiculturalism that emerges in globalization is often celebrated as unequivocally progressive in the context of various stripes of liberal humanism. The idea that multiculturalist media is a positive and emancipatory response to globalization, though, seems a droll observation when contrasted to the types of aggravated conflicts that have accompanied both political and cultural globalization.

Nonetheless, in the context of globalization, films and television and entertainment, generally, are often promoted as capable of transcending the shortcomings of the economic and political spheres. In the "export processing zones" of media culture, in Canada for instance, there is a sense that this will now be an opportunity to tell "our" stories. Setting aside the issue of what would constitute a Canadian alterity in "our" stories versus Hollywood stories, it is initially important to recognize that images are not independent of political economy. Nonetheless, although we have two decades of images and accounts of resistance to globalization (from farmers in France and young workers in Indonesia, to WTO protests around the world), it is still quite common to read culturalist accounts of globalization that characterize this conjuncture as being principally about "increased connectivity" or "hybridity" or equally neutral and apoliticized designations. In film studies, one of the tiresome points that is regularly made, almost as an apology for globalization, is that film culture has always been global, and this precedent is meant to justify ignoring the specific ways in which "Global Hollywood" is substantially different from Old Hollywood and even New Hollywood. As Toby Miller et al. make clear, contemporary Hollywood is a significantly unique model of cultural production – one that requires an international rearrangement of labour relations in media industries and the creation of what the authors call the NICL – "the new international division of cultural labour."[5]

I see contemporary Canadian television as a symptom of contemporary capitalism, and I want to point out some of the ways in which globalization can be discerned within the aesthetic structure and affect of regional Canadian television. Although much Canadian television production (and even more of its film production) is the result of "contracting out Hollywood," I argue that Canadian television culture is not necessarily organized around hiding itself as a "runaway production."[6] Where the claim was previously made that Canada was consistently obscured or hidden by Hollywood, the current globalized media industries are just as likely to foreground Canadian and international localism. How can we explain this change in strategy? The short answer is that Global Hollywood represents a particular conjuncture in which the perpetuation of "runaways" has resulted in Hollywood becoming the hidden country. Beyond this, the use of localism and regionalism tends to blunt any criticisms of globalization by redirecting our attention toward tales of what are presented as common (and universal) human experiences. One of the achievements of localism and regionalism in this conjuncture is the effective transposition of an international economic structural crisis into local cultural 'solutions.' This is achieved by developing a series of portraits that are, by turns, emphatically sentimental, flippantly derisive, and "human, all too human," as Nietzsche would have it. In my formulation of this history, we no longer live with a "cultural discount" in Canada, but a "cultural bonus" built on the back of regionalism and humanism.

For instance, if *Trailer Park Boys* has become popular because of its portrayal of the main characters' "grace under fire," as they wallow in regional underdevelopment, dysfunctional domestic relations, and generalized social devolution, it does not do this in order to generate a coherent critique of the effects of globalization that have left the Maritimes, for instance, as part of the network of de-industrialized, service-oriented "processing zones" that now characterize the industrial frontline of globalization. As the regions in Canada have adjusted to the neo-liberal economic changes that were ushered in throughout the Free Trade initiatives of the 1980s, and then full-blown globalization and the entrenchment of "the new imperialism" from the time of the first Gulf War in 1991, the Canadian television industry (assisted by many offices in provincial and federal governments) has prepared itself to be a prime player in Global Hollywood. As neo-liberal economic reform led to shrinkages of services in the regions, and the loss of industries and work that had maintained the workforce (usually organized around natural resource industries), programming that depicted the regions, and were made there, became a regular diet on Canadian television (e.g., *Black Harbour, Pit Pony, Emily of New Moon, Anne of Green Gables, This Hour Has 22 Minutes*). Additionally, with the expansion of demand for programming due to the proliferation of cable television (and "CanCon" regulations), regional shows were able to find a consistent source of funding and access to national broadcasters. This regionalism was different from earlier forms, which had been typically produced in line with federal government support for regionalism in the specific context of nation-building.[7] Canadian television has often been discussed by scholars as a consequence of federal cultural policy initiatives, an approach that emphasizes the role of governance and discursive power. Such an emphasis on policy leads Beaty and Sullivan, for instance, to claim that "television is controlled by the state in order to promote a unified sense of national identity that will in turn justify the state's continued authority."[8] In this chapter, I attempt to broaden the appreciation of the various pressures that give rise to Canadian regional television, and I especially emphasize the role of global capitalism in this process. I argue that contemporary regionalist representation is a direct result of market logic, not nation building. The portrayal of the Maritimes in *Gullage's* and TPB is consistent with the structural changes in television culture in Canada, and their representations of Canadian space and characters are also directly related to the larger structural changes taking place in global capitalism.

Gullage's and *Trailer Park Boys* offer us a case study in the ramifications of globalization and neo-liberal economic reform as these impact on Canadian television production. In particular, their similarities point to a shared strategy of "regional commoditization," something that accompanies global exchange. The differences between the shows, and their different receptions, are also an indication of the different time periods in which these television shows entered the global image market. This chapter serves as a cautious introduction to this case study, and will broadly consider institutional elements such as trade agreements, institutional mandates and policies, state policies, international television culture, U.S. television culture, trends in popular culture, and niche/exploitation markets in popular culture. I approach these television shows as popular cultural artefacts containing or being symptomatic of their "conditions of practice," a concept which Raymond Williams used in analyzing culture. His materialist approach to literary and cultural criticism argued, for instance, that the realist novel emerged as a cultural form with the rise of the bourgeoisie and its form is such that a motivated critic could tease out the traces of industrial capitalism in the phrasing, style, and structure of the written passages. In this, he borrowed significantly from Lukács, whose theory of the realist novel presented the case that what realism really depended upon was the realization of characters who presented a totality – a reification of the society which gave rise to the cultural form. Williams, following this strand of reasoning in Lukács, argued that cultural forms represented a "structure of feeling," something that suggested lived ideology. We see the genealogy of this idea continued in the work of Fredric Jameson, who has provided a model of this critical approach as it applies to cinema. He uses terms such as "cognitive mapping" or the "geopolitical aesthetic," which have proven useful in film studies to understand the ways in which ideological positions and discursive "worlds," are manifest in cultural form.[9] To the extent that I foreground this critical approach, I am also involved in ideological analysis. As ideologies are bolstered and contained within different regimes of discourses, policies, institutions, and various social agents, the question would be, in looking at such highly collaborative cultural productions as television: can we discern specific traces of these discourses, policies, institutions, and social agents in a particular artefact? As an aesthetic affect? And what would count as relevant in such a reading? In short, the goal of this chapter is to suggest that the globalization of media production is discernible in regionalist television, and regionalism and humanism in these shows serve to mask the imperialism and pointedly anti-humane character of globalization.

Particularly germane to my discussion is Jameson's elaboration of cognitive mapping in his later writing on the concept of the "geopolitical aesthetic." His work and the concept encourage us to read spaces of production, and spaces of capital, in cultural artefacts themselves by reading the operations of capitalism in the representations produced in media culture. Because the world exists in large part as mediated images (e.g., we 'know' things about the world – its fashions and currency, its discourses, its norms and codes of social and personal behaviour – because we see them on-screen), the role of film and television production is central to the meaning of contemporary social relations. In a way, the media reifies these relations, and this provides the opportunity to read, following Jameson, cultural forms as cognitive maps. In a sense, I consider *Gullage's* and *Trailer Park Boys* as negotiating the social and power relations which were operational during their production. In this sense, I consider them to be crystallizations of the structures of dominance *and* expressions of utopian desires of this particular historical conjuncture. One of the advantages of this approach is that it encourages us to ask: if it were the case that we could see the structures that give our world shape by enjoying popular regionalist culture, is there still the possibility of imagining local cultures that would effectively resist global hegemonies as well as regional backwardness?

On both an explicit level and the level of allegory, television shows like *TPB* reproduce the geopolitics of globalization. This includes, in telling ways, an emphasis on representing the narrative of globalization in various forms of popular comedy, typically, with large doses of sentimentality, derision, indifference, aggression, criminality, and profanity. In short, there is an aspect of the *carnivalesque* in these shows, and they are often celebrated as regional triumphs largely on the basis of what is argued to be their subversion of codes and conventions of typical bourgeois and national culture (i.e., content which is sanctioned by middle-class morality and government regulation). To achieve this aesthetic end, the producers foreground those aspects of regional life that are understood as unique to the region – in effect, over-exposing life in the regions. In *TPB* this includes themes of unemployment, crime, poverty, promiscuity, and the aesthetics of "white trash" culture. These threats to human "progress," easily understood in the context of historical regional underdevelopment that characterizes Canadian federalism, often skewer bourgeois ideologies in rich satirical sketches but, ultimately, the stories tend to be played out as a comedy of errors, becoming quite ideologically harmless. Similarly, but in a much more ingratiating and highly moralized manner, *Corner Gas*, about contemporary life on the Canadian prairies, reproduces the self-deprecating tone of *Gullage's* and TPB , so that part of its humour lies in taking shots at crude stereotypes of regional culture. For instance, the regular cast includes the old-timer (Eric Petersen) who is crabby and backwards, his long-suffering wife (Janet Wright), the recently arrived Toronto snob (Gabrielle Miller) who is embarrassingly pretentious, and the "village idiot" character (Fred Ewanuick). A similar range of character types can be found in the Newfoundland feature film *Young Triffie's Been Made Away With* (Dir: Mary Walsh, 2006), with the actor Fred Ewanuick cast as the bug-eyed and hapless lead. One of the strategies in *Corner Gas* for dealing with the contradiction of such hyper-regionalism in the context of Global Hollywood is its overwhelmingly derisive attitude toward all its characters. In a sense, the show winks at the global audience, by taking the piss out of the regions – but this is also another way of covering over the structure of globalization that gives contour to life in the provinces, all around the world.

It is notable that these provincial stories have the popularity they do, and this suggests that there is a utopian dimension to their appeal. In an obvious sense, they seem to offer a respite from the workings of globalization, as they are removed from the metropolis, immersed in bucolic landscapes and backwoods dramas. On another level, we might also think that their utopian appeal is connected to their subversive potential, which is connected to their acknowledgment, and then denial through narrative deflection, of the role of the regions in the structure of globalization. While this version of the utopian appeal of the shows is only fully worked out in less popular and less well-known shows, such as *Gullage's* and especially the first season of *Moccasin Flats*, there are two things worth noting: 1) in this conjuncture, regional stories have potential international appeal on the basis of shared human experiences in global capitalism; and 2) liberal-humanism has re-emerged, in a time when human life is actually substantially devalued, as a cultural value that disguises itself as regional survivalism in underdevelopment. In these comedies and dramas about human struggles, it is not the Canadian region that disappears. In fact, it is the region, underdeveloped as it is, that perpetuates the principle that human survival alone is a sign of progress. In this sense, popular contemporary Canadian television, like *TPB*, is a clever cover for globalization, muzzling any criticism of the geopolitics that give rise to the human crises that we see represented in the show. In *TPB*, there is a bold normalizing of underdevelopment: the show is so equivocal that it treats the "new imperialism" as both something to celebrate and something to be afraid of, particularly the extraordinary gaps between the wealthy and the poor, between the centre and the regions. Nonetheless, while we recognize that we live in a "planet of slums," we agree with Ricky's dad Ray (played by Barrie Dunn, one of the show's producers) that we just don't want anyone knowing that we're living at the dump.[10]

In what follows I will discuss the period 1995–2000 as a significant period in Maritime film and television production, and then I will provide some readings of *Gullage's* and *TPB* which are usefully understood as 'cognitive maps' of the contemporary (2000–2005) period. Initially, it is useful to think of the way that ideas about globalization have changed over time, and it reminds us that what we know about this stage of capital development is always conditional, theorized through a series of abstractions that attempt to represent the totality of globalization. For instance, on the one hand, theorists up to the mid-1990s often bemoaned globalization as a "McDonalds-ization" of cultural experiences. The argument was that global culture was too generic and could never respect regional specificities and differences. In these arguments, there are clear distinctions drawn between centre and margin, and this position proposed global culture as a vehicle for U.S. cultural imperialism. A bit later (~2000) another level of abstraction emerges as influential: it recognizes that, contrary to the earlier view, certain types of regionalism have actually thrived in the period of globalization. Furthermore, within the context of globalization, Canadian regional television production became financially viable and, in this way, globalization was often perceived as a way of telling our own stories, from the margins. In this formulation, the centre and margin are dialectically

Trailer Park Boys, courtesy TPB Productions.

related and this is captured in the neologism "glocalism." But the more relevant term is the new acronym NICL, which is used to designate the emergence of a globalized division of labour in contemporary cultural production. We might want to hope that there is another level of abstraction about globalization that could lead Canadian television producers, for instance, to create not only regional work, but work that expresses the frustrations of, and resistance to, regional underdevelopment in global capitalism. In *Gullage's*, this possibility suggests itself, and sometimes this strategy also influences *Trailer Park Boys*. In large part, this depends on location shooting and the representation of local social relations. Not surprisingly, these are also consistent with some of the aspects of film movements previously identified as progressive – for instance, neo-realism and third cinema. In the context of this aesthetic, spatially specific culture seems to have an advantage in articulating the social relations in the area and in the period depicted. This tends not to be the case with regionalisms that are vague about their locations – they tend to be toothless as forms of critical commentary. Nonetheless, even uncritical cultural forms represent their geopolitical aesthetic, and it is not without interest that those forms that tend to be without specific reference to a specific place in the world also speak more generally (and more favourably) about humans in the world.

In looking at Atlantic Canadian regional television culture in the years 1995–2000, the period in which the first abstraction about globalization starts to be reformulated into the second abstraction, several significant elements emerge as influential in the development of *Gullage's*, an early example of adult-oriented regional television comedy produced in this context (it is the first CBC national TV series made in Newfoundland). The show was produced for two seasons, 1996–1998, approximately at the same time that the characters that would become the "trailer park boys" were being developed in Nova Scotia in short films by Mike Clattenburg, *The Cart Boy* (1995) and *One Last Shot* (1998). In 1999, a third short film, *Trailer Park Boys*, was released and its popularity at film festivals generated a television production deal, with the first episodes telecast on specialty channels in 2001. Not surprisingly, the dates of this history reflect key industry developments. In particular, the establishment of the Canada Television and Cable Production Fund in September 1996 encouraged independent writers and producers to propose and develop a wide variety of television products. In this, the producers were influenced by a variety of forces, including:

Gullage's, courtesy of Picture Plant.

John McCullough

the appeals of regions offering low production costs; global media markets demanding new product; and the influence of American popular culture.

Given that the production of *Gullage's* and *Trailer Park Boys* correspond to each other in a variety of ways, it is not surprising to see that they have several formal, aesthetic, and thematic similarities. For instance, they each have abbreviated seasons (usually six episodes) and they are comedies – both of these elements suggest themselves as attempts to reduce the economic risk of the projects. They each feature a decidedly warm attitude to their characters, and this suggests their common humanist predisposition, which is emphasized in, and linked to, the representations of regionalism (e.g., dialects, word play, fashion, lifestyles, cultural talent). The minimal production values of *Gullage's*, in particular, provide a sense of negotiating with regional underdevelopment. The interior shots all evoke a sense of cramped old city building construction, but they also contribute to a sense that this is an underfunded Canadian regionalist television program. There are notable differences between the shows, as well, and these include their attitudes toward spatial specificity and the goal of their comedy. *Gullage's* is absurd but notably reverential in its attitude to its characters. It contributes several minutes per episode to cultural performances and weaves art forms and practices through the narrative and the lives of the characters.

For example, two characters, Bert and Russell, recite their lines as couplets and they mimic not only each other's speech but also their appearance. This absurdity is heightened by the fact that their names, when pronounced fast and by someone from the town, sounds like "Bertrand Russell," a British rationalist philosopher who would not normally be associated with such an assault on common sense. In *Gullage's* such characterization is linked to the narrative's specific geographical location, St. John's, Newfoundland. It is as though the reference to a philosopher in a television comedy is as misplaced as referring to Newfoundland as part of Canada. Given the history of Newfoundland's late entry into Canadian federalism and the perception outside the province of its marginality to Canadian national identity, the show's attention to the details of location cannot help but encourage a range of rich associations for viewers. As to the matter of viewership for the show, CBC regularly scheduled it with *Coronation Street*, and one of its broadcast times was Sunday morning, which suggests a demographic that skews upward. By contrast, *TPB* is raunchy and aggressive, featuring broad humour. For instance, some of the more popular comic routines from the show include park supervisor Jim Lahey's scatological fits, the size

On the left: Bert and Russell (Philip Dunn and Brian Best) in *Gullage's*, courtesy of Picture Plant.

of his partner Randy's gut, and Ricky's mispronunciation and mangling of common words and phrases – all examples of low-brow North American humour also found in such popular American sit-coms as *Married ... with Children* (U.S., 1987–97, Fox Broadcasting). The general appeal of the show is also reflected in its attitude to location and spatial specificity. Located somewhere "in the vicinity of Halifax," the narrative unfolds against a vague social background. Additionally, *Gullage's* emphasizes its geographical specificity by shooting *in* the winter; not so *TPB*.

The comedy of *TPB* diverges from specifically regionalist humour and locates itself comfortably within modes of presentation that are popular across the Americas. Specifically, the show is an early example of the exploitation of the "reali-tv" aesthetic, including hand-held camera, which has been used in recent television programming (e.g., *The Office*). *TPB* also specifically identifies itself with "white trash culture," and media fascination

Ricky (Robb Wells), Julian (John Paul Tremblay), and Bubbles (Mike Smith) in the Shitmobile, courtesy of TPB Productions.

IMPERIALISM, REGIONALISM, HUMANISM

with the bad taste and manners of North Americans living in poverty. A good example of this type of cross-reference is the park's rapper J-Roc, who corresponds to a 'real' rapper like Eminem, whose biography and hit film *8 Mile* (US, 2002, Curtis Hanson) are narratives of white trash and trailer park redemption. In this context, *TPB* finds favour not by being regionalist but by playing to modes of entertainment that have a powerful connection to contemporary North American lifestyles and social relations. One popular example of this is the phenomenon of celebrity talk shows associated with the atrocity exhibit that is "trash TV," in particular *The Jerry Springer Show* (U.S., 1991–, NBC Universal). That *Springer* is as popular as it is suggests that the show successfully captures our fascination with the spectacle of devolved American social relations. On the one hand, this is an example of popular culture as populist revenge in which the whole continent shares a standardized experience of global capitalism that is defined by intolerance, violence, ignorance, racism, sexism, homophobia, vengeance, duplicity, and fear. Looked at from this perspective, trash TV seems to offer a critical vantage point from which to view official ideologies of globalization which unapologetically celebrate capital. Unfortunately, with the official party line of globalization more and more resembling the diatribes of hate that manifest themselves on *Springer*, it seems that a truly critical perspective would likely have to *trash* trash culture rather than appropriate it. Caught in this dilemma, *TPB* normalizes the idea of living in a dump and finds it difficult to develop a critique of the social relations that lead to a planet of slums.

In spatial studies and spatial theory, the specificity of location is often considered to be a significant element in the perceived authenticity of any space.[11] In these studies, authentic spaces are usually referred to as places; this differentiates between space as a generalized and measurable geography and place that is experienced as a lived environment with immeasurable layers of history, memory, and socio-cultural practice. For these theorists, though, place is not disconnected from the global but is, in fact, thoroughly reflective of the dialectic that binds the local to the global in contemporary social relations. Seen from this perspective, places in the world can be "read" and "interpreted" as embodying the contradictions of capitalist relations. In what I have provided as a broad overview of *Gullage's* and *Trailer Park Boys*, we can see that the former would be an example of regional television production that strongly evokes place. At the time of its production, the head of CBC's drama/comedy area, Phyllis Platt, was astute to understand that global markets were impacting on the public broadcaster in unpredictable ways. Her response to this crisis-oriented scenario was to encourage a wide range of regional co-productions using Television Fund support to create CBC shows that would counter the homogenizing effect of Global Hollywood. Global television production became the context that encouraged film auteur Bill MacGillivray to make regional television. His show had a limited run and it fell to *Trailer Park Boys* to inherit *Gullage's* structure and regionalist flavour. Like a lot of product that is successful in Global Hollywood, though, *TPB* finds it difficult to consistently evoke place as a site of local resistance. This may partially explain its popularity and it is useful to compare it to global television product that has similarly found favour in America on specialty channels dedicated to international product. For instance, *TPB* was sold to BBC America, and this parallels the success of shows like the New Zealand–themed *Flight of the Conchords* (2007) (which was bought by HBO), It is significant that these shows evoke a specific regionalism that nonetheless is smoothly integrated with American "boutique television." Since 2000, Canadian television has, in general, responded to Global Hollywood by marshalling regional labour, humanist narratives, and multicultural marketing into product that is both nationally and internationally successful, seemingly at home everywhere. In doing this, popular Canadian television production completes a process of reification that provides a cognitive map of contemporary Canadian social relations – a space in which jail and trash dominate as figures in the local landscape, ignorance and silliness abound in the citizenry, and a "shit-storm" threatens to blow away all our pretensions about the myth of progress (but sadly never does).

It would be unfair and inaccurate to leave the impression that *Gullage's* and *Trailer Park Boys* are worthwhile only as criticisms of neo-liberalism or that they only serve to normalize poverty and social devolution in the context of globalization by trading in excessive humanist sentiment. In their own ways, it has to be said that the shows are also pregnant with the progressive possibilities of cultural production that is recognizably locally made and politically resistant. The depictions of regional spaces as settings for the stories; the use of a rich regional talent pool; and the development of characters and themes that are contemporary all lend a degree of modest detail that impresses the viewer as authentic (but not nostalgic) regional culture. In this, it is hard to ignore the allegorical meanings of a show like *TPB*. Here, the criminality of the poor is directly connected to the oppressive social relations they encounter daily, and the power of the local authorities is consistently undermined in acknowledgment of the larger geopolitical forces which transcend even the power of the local cops and trailer park supervisors. In fact, one of the show's extraordinary action-comedy sequences, which features an armed stand-off in the streets of Dartmouth, seems to address specifically the theme of impotence which pervades the show's overall tone. The scene seems to suggest that, in the regions, the criminals and the law are equally powerless to effect change given the larger geopolitics of globalization which organize everyday life.

At the same time, Ricky and Julian's pot-growing operation and trade in hashish are emblematic of the spaces of regional production that emerge in contemporary capitalism. Part of the pleasure in encountering their specific activities on Canadian television is triggered by Canadian audiences' understanding that Canadian weed is internationally recognized as a top grade product and that importing and distributing hash is an illegal activity associated with maritime culture (because it is typically imported through ports). When we look at elements of the show this way, the location becomes a powerful point of audience self-recognition and regional/national identity. It is crucial to recognize, though, that this affect is not achieved through adherence to a nationalist or social ideal but through a deft recognition of the place of the local and the region within the context of global relations and networks. The feeling of recognition for Canadians watching *TPB*, then, is not a result of federalist policy or even regional boosterism, but is crucially connected to ways that Canadians understand what it means for Canadians to "get away with something" in the context of being an underdog in global capital. This is a more complex affect than simply feeling a shared identity with losers, a trope that has been identified as quintessentially Canadian, and it is not simply restricted to Canadians who have an affinity with drug subcultures. By contrast, when ex-pat Ivan Reitman produced the movie version of the show, he imported a specifically Hollywood aesthetic that downplayed these regional micro-industries and amplified the sex and violence that is often associated with American popular entertainment. To read the allegory of *TPB* explicity it could be argued that Ricky and Julian's drug dealing represents Clattenburg's own development of regional cultural production that attempts to exploit a niche market in global commodity trade. The mediocre international success of the movie (by contrast to Hollywood hits) suggests that the very tactics that got Reitman out of Canada and into Hollywood, with teen sex comedies such as *National Lampoon's*

Animal House (1978) and *Meatballs* (1979), not only watered down the original *TPB* concept of resistance but also made the movie a generic commodity with limited appeal for international audiences.

The two categories of analysis that have substantially shaped my approach to studying Atlantic television culture in this chapter are space and labour. On the one hand, regional space offers a cost-benefit for many in- and out-of-region producers (through state sponsored subsidies and tax relief programs), but the space, in the form of location shooting, also offers the possibility of representing history as allegory. For its part, labour (i.e., in front of and behind the camera) is also present in the product as the cultural force that imagines and represents the region. While it is true that much cultural labour is "immaterial" and it is equally true that many of the locations in regional television are staged or virtual, there is nonetheless a vital trace of the socio-historical context from which the work emerges. Among other things, it is this utopian promise of representing the Real that continues to fire the imagination of Canadian producers and audiences alike when they recognize the global contest of capital in stories about local people and places.

It is clear that such a utopian desire can only be fulfilled when a significant pool of cultural labour is present in the region. This means that regions that are successfully situated to attract media work not only provide the region with revenues derived from the television industry but also provide the infrastructure (capital and training) for a homegrown pool of talent that is prepared to do strong work based on regional stories. Consequently, the product which is developed, Canadian regional television, tends to have a good chance of being both a domestic hit (because it is 'true' to the idea that Canadians have of the region) and a strong international seller (because it is made in the context of state-of-the-art technology and highly trained labour that is typical of Canadian regional media production). From this perspective, it is not possible to unconditionally argue that the commercial media in Canada is aligned against politically motivated media or culturally elevated artistic practice, and it is useful to see that popular culture, as in the case of *Gullage's* and *Trailer Park Boys*, also contains the ingredients for resistant national and regional cultural production.

NOTES

1   The term "media culture" is derived from the work of Douglas Kellner. See, for instance, *Media Culture: Cultural Studies, Identity and Politics Between the Modern and the Postmodern* (New York: Routledge, 1995), 34.

2   Tom Good and Joan MacFarland, "Call Centres: A New Solution to an Old Problem?," *From the Net to the Net: Atlantic Canada and the Global Economy*, ed. James Sacouman and Henry Veltmeyer (Aurora, ON: Garamond Press, 2005), 99–113.

3   As this book goes to press, industry speculation says that the producers are not continuing the series, but that another movie or special episode is possible.

4   John Tomlinson, *Globalization and Culture* (Chicago: University of Chicago Press, 1999).

5   Toby Miller et al., *Global Hollywood* 2nd Revised ed. (London: BFI, 2005), 3.

6   For a series of informative discussions about these distinctions see Greg Elmer and Mike Gasher, *Contracting Out Hollywood: Runaway Productions and Foreign Location Shooting* (Lanham, MD: Rowman & Littlefield, 2005); and Serra Tinic, *On Location: Canada's Television Industry in a Global Market* (Toronto: University of Toronto Press, 2005).

7   Zoë Druick, "Framing the Local: Canadian Film Policy and the Problem of Place," *Canadian Cultural Poesis: Essays on Canadian Culture*, ed. Garry Sherbert, Annie Gerin, and Sheila Petty (Waterloo: Wilfrid Laurier University Press, 2006), 85–98.

8   Bart Beaty and Rebecca Sullivan, *Canadian Television Today* (Calgary: University of Calgary Press, 2006), 50.

9   See, for instance: *The Cultural Turn: Selected Writings on the Postmodern, 1983–1998* (New York: Verso, 1998); *The Geopolitical Aesthetic: Cinema and Space in the World System* (Bloomington: Indiana University Press, 1992); *Postmodernism, or, The Cultural Logic of Late Capitalism* (Durham, NC: Duke University Press, 1991).

10 Mike Davis, *Planet of Slums* (London and New York: Verso, 2006).

11 Some of the key texts in spatial studies include: Don Mitchell, *Culture Geography: A Critical Introduction* (Malden, MA: Blackwell, 2000); Kevin Cox, ed., *Spaces of Globalization: Reasserting the Power of the Local* (New York: Guilford Press, 1997); Michael Hardt and Antonio Negri, *Empire* (Cambridge, MA: Harvard University Press, 2000); David Harvey, *Spaces of Capital: Toward a Critical Geography* (New York: Routledge, 2001); and by Doreen Massey: *For Space* (Thousand Oaks, CA: Sage, 2005); *Space, Place, and Gender* (Minneapolis: University of Minnesota Press, 1994); *Rethinking the Region* (New York: Routledge, 1998); and with Pat Jess, eds., *A Place In The World? Places, Cultures, and Globalization* (New York: Oxford University Press, 1995).

9

ON THE FRINGE OF THE "CANADIAN STATE": GRASSROOTS FILM AND VIDEO MOVEMENTS IN HALIFAX, 1960S-1980S

TRACY Y. ZHANG

The marginal status of artist-run media centres in Canada has been described by artists and critics as self-styled "utopian spaces." In opposition to the corporate media, established arts institutions, the state censorship of media, and the local authorities of all sorts, grassroots media organizations have been mandated to nurture an independent and collective spirit of making and disseminating media artworks.[1] While imagining a network of coast-to-coast Canadian media artists, the scholarly examination on artist-run centres in English Canada tends to focus on Vancouver media arts groups,[2] with a few Toronto-based media centres often made to represent all the eastern media arts organizations.[3] If celebrating one 'authentic' (or popular nationalist) media sector is a tactic to battle against American cultural imperialism, then the literature of grassroots media in English Canada unconsciously overlooks the regional-local diversity of the country and the complex (and often contradictory) process of declaring media independence.

In this understudied area, there is limited understanding of the relationship between the local knowledge that video and film artists possess about the politics of media production and the historical development of Canadian cultural policy. Drawing from feminist cultural policy studies, I examine changes in federal cultural institutions in relation to artists' experiences of film and video production.[4] Focusing on a regionally specific media arts community, I explore the early movements of the Atlantic Filmmaker's Co-operative (AFCOOP) and the Centre for Art Tapes (CFAT) with the aim of making analytical linkages between cultural policy practices[5] and Halifax grassroots media production.

In the first section, I draw on archival and interview materials to demonstrate the ways in which the National Film Board of Canada (NFB) and the Canada Council influenced Canadian media production in general and the Halifax grassroots media movement in particular. This analysis focuses our attention on the various ways the NFB and the Canada Council both exemplify and extend governmental involvement in the making of the Canadian grassroots media sector. The second section supplements this historical analysis by drawing on interviews with several former members of AFCOOP and CFAT. I focus on how Halifax film and video artists came to work with the federal cultural institutions to secure their artistic production even while disobeying the principles of media industries and arts institutions. In particular, I look at different discourses of "media independence" that emerge from the policy documents and artists' recollections of the time they got involved in AFCOOP or CFAT. These narratives of "independent film and video" articulate a particular identity politics and respond to the political economy of media art production in 1970s and '80s Canada.

Technology, Political Economy, and the Canadian State

Canadian political economist Harold Innis long ago observed that the Canadian state emerged from the interaction of technology, geography, and political economy.[6] In his sense, the idea of 'the Canadian state' is not fixed and stable but continues to evolve, as changing economic systems and communication technology create new room for political imagination. In the context of the literature on Canadian cultural policy, many observe that in post–World War II Canada, the federal government began to actively invest in constructing social realities of Canada by using and regulating media technologies to educate immigrants about Canadian citizenship, to accommodate foreign policies, and to boost Canadian economy in an increasingly media-saturated world.[7] The late 1960s saw multidirectional assaults on the Euro-centric elitist assumptions of Canadian arts programs originally drawn from the British system in the 1950s.[8] At this time, Canada's flagship cultural agencies, the National Film Board of Canada and the Canada Council, underwent significant adjustments in terms of their objectives, programs, and institutional arrangements. The revised policy orientation and implementations enabled the federal cultural agencies to reach an emerging spectrum of 'cultural producers,' who began applying varied new media technologies to pursue their artistic or activist ambitions. In this section, I discuss the policies associated with artist-run media centres to demonstrate how these institutional actors, through varied policy mechanisms, had contributed to forming a Canadian grassroots media sector and strategically introduced government visions to the media organizations growing on the fringe of the Canadian state.

Social Animator, the National Film Board of Canada

In her historical assessment on the National Film Board of Canada (NFB), Zoë Druick emphasizes that cultural institutions such as the NFB are important parts of Canada's symbolic environment as they produce the "official" frames in which cultural products are made and disseminated.[9] By looking at the linkages between the NFB documentary films and the policy mandate given to the NFB, Druick describes NFB endeavours in the 1960s and 1970s as responses to the concept of participatory citizenship and the new social politics, infiltrated by discussions on gender, class, and race in Canadian society.[10] Documented in other sources, the criticisms against the NFB characterized the film board as having an "unhealthy" elitist atmosphere, insufficient production budget, and discordant headquarter-regional relations.[11] This hostile socio-political environment in fact catalyzed the changes in the NFB; the unionized filmmakers were compelled to cope with organizational stress and a philosophical dilemma. Gradually departing from the centralized production structure, the NFB officials began to deploy the social animator approach that ostensibly promoted a democratic culture, while its real aim was to usher in the agendas of a federal cultural agency in the arts communities of provincial metropolises.

The first strategy was massaging a rigid bureaucratic body by decentralizing the concentration of power in the Montreal headquarters. In the mid-1960s, several NFB representatives arrived in the cultural centres of different regions, including Halifax, Vancouver, and Toronto. They initially served as investigators and supporters for local artists and writers.[12] In Halifax, several senior executives from Montreal came to build a regional office in the spring of 1973 with distribution and production facilities. The leading producer Rex Tasker stated that the main objectives of the regional studio were threefold: "To make good films about or relevant to the four [Atlantic] provinces; to provide an opportunity for local filmmakers to develop and work without leaving their home provinces; to do whatever possible to create a vigorous film/video community."[13] This statement indicates the ways in which NFB producers defined their relationship with Halifax film and video makers. It portrays the NFB as a combination of the spokesperson for the Atlantic Provinces, a generous employer, and an enthusiastic trainer. These self-identified multiple roles suggest an attempt at reconciling the local interests with the NFB mandates. While Tasker's statement omits Halifax's indigenous film and video history that predates the Halifax NFB office,[14] the government representatives deliberately labelled themselves as the 'creators' of a genuine film/video culture to legitimatize their intervention and superior position in the local affairs. For the NFB officers, such ways of self-positioning and defining "film/video community" are not only important to reinstating the agency's function in the federal cultural policy scheme, but also critical to setting up practice standards and assumptions that would affect how local media producers perceive themselves. I revisit this point in the second section of the paper.

Secondly, the NFB's elitist mode of film production was also under critical scrutiny. Several director-driven NFB films failed to serve their intended objective, which was to placate the socio-economic unrest at that time.[15] Around 1967, the NFB incubated new programs, the *Challenge for Change* (the English version) and the *Société Nouvelle* (the French version) to solve problems in the NFB filmmaking style as well as to fulfill its commitment to the federal government's anti-poverty campaign.[16] The mandate of the *Challenge for Change* program was to "give the disenfranchised and marginal communities of Canada a voice by giving them access to the media ... [and discuss issues] of poverty."[17] Motivated by such notion of participatory democracy and a fascination of new portable equipment, some NFB filmmakers went on a journey to experiment with video technology in their subject communities.[18]

By the end of the 1970s, in addition to eighty-three documentary films produced to meet the objective of *Challenge for Change*,[19] these projects gave rise to the development of production facilities and the cultivation of a coalition of video artists, educators, and social activists who gradually established video access centres in major cities, such as *Metro Media* in Vancouver and *Vidéograph* in Montreal from the late 1960s to the early 1970s. *Tel-Ed* was the brainchild of the *Challenge for Change* program in Halifax. It was the first community-based organization with video production facilities. The NFB's involvement and efforts left clear ideological marks on these video access centres concerning social activism, feminism, and minority politics.[20]

The Cultural Engineer,[21]
the Canada Council

Funding arts organizations

The mandate of the Canada Council for the Arts is to design and implement grant programs by which the agency can orchestrate and facilitate a range of officially recognized artistic activities from coast to coast. As it was an important gadget in the governmental toolbox, translating federal cultural policies into local activities, the chief officials of the Canada Council were also urged to pursue principles of "democratization and de-centralization"[22] in the early 1970s. On March 28, 1972, Gérard Pelletier, then secretary of state (1968–72) and minister of communications (1972–75), delivered his famous speech at the Canadian Club in Calgary:

> Democratization means increasing access to the products of cultural activity for all taxpayers, not only for a select group as has been the case in the past. Since this concerns the use of public funds, it would be unfair to promote cultural activities that are reserved for the happy few.... Decentralization, in a country such as Canada, signifies an active battle against vast distances in order to make our cultural symbols available to all Canadians, no matter where they live.[23]

Given the rubric of "democratization" and "decentralization," the Canada Council began conceiving several programs that made the expenditure structure change from individual-based grant programs into more dispersed forms. In addition, Kevin Dowler points out that interdepartmental politics influenced the Council's policy, and encouraged the Council to take over the community organizations created by federal projects such as *Challenge for Change*, *Opportunity for Youth* (OFY), and *Local Initiative Program* (LIP). Political pressure from the prime minister's office was exerted on the Canada Council to redirect arts funding toward social needs and federal government objectives.[24]

Sponsoring community-based arts organizations eventually became one of the major socio-cultural engineering endeavours of the Council. In the early 1970s, the Council started to fund the co-operative movement, in particular, to finance the film co-ops across Canada. Halifax's Atlantic Filmmaker's Cooperative obtained seed money from such programs in 1974. Many video access centres, which had been affiliated with the NFB, turned to the Council for financial support as well. In Halifax, when the first community-based media organization *Tel-Ed* folded, a new video organization, *Video Theatre*, inherited *Tel-Ed*'s equipment and deliberately mixed artistic interests with social development goals so that *Video Theatre* could receive funds from both the Council and the NFB.

Establishing "media arts" as a discipline in the Canada Council

The arrival of the Sony Portapak in the mid-1960s brought different opportunities to the NFB and to the Canada Council. For the NFB, the portable media technology was instrumental in creating the philosophy and aesthetics of so-called "process films" that could be carried out in rural and isolated communities.[25] When the portable video camera appeared in the market, Canadian "media art" began, and a number of visual artists first sought financial support through various visual arts programs. For example, on the west coast, *Intermedia*, an artist-run video centre in Vancouver, was awarded a one-off Canada Council visual arts grant in 1967.[26] In Toronto, like-minded visual artists created a production/exhibition centre, *A Space*. Others funded *Video Ring*, a mobile video editing suite, with borrowed cameras from Sony Canada and some visual arts funds from the Canada Council. NSCAD University pioneered the east coast school of video art "in the performance/document vein."[27] The growing interests in creating a novel discipline within the established visual arts institutions appealed to the Canada Council.

In the mid-1970s, Dale McConathy observed that artists did not enter into an effective dialogue with the institutions that possessed numerous resources critical to their careers and their work.[28] The Canada Council actually began to recruit media artists and curators, such as Peggy Gale (1974), Michael Goldberg (1975), Renee Baert (1977), and Tom Sherman (1981). These artist video officers took short-term posts, and their experiences helped the Council build and facilitate the relationships between scattered media practitioners and the governmental cultural agency in Ottawa. Moreover, their first-hand knowledge of the early Canadian media art movement was critical to defining "independent media" in the subsequent policy documents.

In the spring of 1983, video artist and then video officer, Tom Sherman, proposed to establish a separate Media Arts Section that eventually consolidated many grant programs and created new juries for three subdivisions focusing on the new media: the Film and Holography, the Video and Audio Art, and the Computer-Integrated Media. In a Canada Council document (1982), Sherman described a political-economic rationale behind this organizational change:

> Artists functioning within the independent film and video communities are engaged in a constant struggle to survive in a media environment dominated by the cultural industrial complex. Mass media conglomerates consume vast technological and human resources.
>
> Film and video artists have continually been denied access to the means of production and distribution of their media art. When it is admitted that most of the financial support for independent film and video activity comes from the Canada Council … the independent media sector is left severely underfunded.[29]

Not only did this document assume an irresolvable contradiction between the commercial interest and artists' needs, but Sherman also depicted the media industry as a threat to a class of "independent film and video communities" that would depend on the Council to prosper. With this paradoxical interpretation of "independent" media, the document concluded that the Council takes on the responsibility of empowering the arts communities by putting the means of production back into the hands of artists. After nearly twenty-four years, Sherman recalled in an interview: "This was a very interesting period as digital technologies were transforming the managerial and creative landscape. It was clear that the Council had to be involved, and part of this involvement would be to support artists and organizations wishing to work with the then very new digital technologies."[30] Sherman's reflection suggests that supporting artists and organizations is a significant governmental intervention in a transforming economic and technological environment. The late 1970s saw the plethora of media capitalism and mixed activities of media producers, who worked within traditional arts institutions, vanguard organizations, or private media companies. In reality, many media producers frequently crossed the borders of these sectors. The Council officers acknowledged the limits in the official definition of "Canadian art," not so much in the light of democratizing Canadian art, but rather in looking for ways to expand the Council's jurisdiction over the broadened "managerial and creative landscape."

As the Council needed to justify a governmental intervention in a new cultural field, it projected an image of the decadent (presumably American) cultural industry, in contrast to the so-called Canadian "independent" media communities. If a direct state sponsorship toward media artists contradicts the notion of "independent media art," the Council's involvement in the artist-run media centres came to be an effective solution for both the state sponsors and the recipients. Despite their different histories, memberships, and mandates, a variety of arts organizations gradually became subject to the funding structure of the Council. In one way or another, these organizations depend on the Council for financial resources and for their survival. Moreover, these media centres became self-governing gadgets themselves that administer allocation of equipment and their members' artistic production and personal information.

Discussion

Federal cultural reports such as the Massey Report (1951) and the Applebaum-Hébert Report (1981) have reiterated cultural policy principles over the years. Canadian cultural agencies have a mandate to assist Canadian cultural development, including the psychological instillation of Canadian consciousness and strengthening a Canadian-content based infrastructure. Millions of federal tax dollars have been spent on the media sector to influence the cognitive and semiotic dimension of Canadian society. In the historical process of building Canada, the participating agencies and social actors have been acquiring skills to cope with technological challenges and the political-economic transformation. From the late 1960s to the mid-1980s, as the state-supported commercial film industry grew exponentially, the NFB and the Canada Council spread the seed money and laid down infrastructures for the growth of grassroots media organizations.[31] These policy reforms strategically keep the ghost of government in the theatre of "cultural development" through decentralization and proliferation of its functions. The governmental power took a different shape and retained influence on regional and local cultural production, through these seemingly independent, arm's length cultural agencies. In Halifax, the NFB senior officers sought to consolidate their grip on the making of regional identities and the production of media products. They built a nicely furnished studio and invited people to participate. In contrast, the Council has adopted a self-disciplinary method to manage an artist-run system that came to be a form of both autonomy and social control.[32] In the next section, I turn to several key Halifax film and video artists and present their interpretations of making 'independent' film and video.[33]

Tales from Halifax

Both AFCOOP and CFAT have published their own histories in celebration of their achievements over the past three decades.[34] The AFCOOP catalogue devotes many pages to describing the prominent filmmakers and to documenting individual members' snapshot reflections on the nature of independent filmmaking. Several media artists wrote a CFAT history book to tell stories about their exploration of media art inside the organization. Based on the oral history interviews, this section discusses how people began to develop their occupational identites. The development of artist/filmmaker identity is an on-going process, intertwined with individuals' encounters with career challenges or opportunities, in the shifting political-economic contexts. The founding members of AFCOOP and CFAT had different backgrounds and diverse interests, and they chose to fight for their access of making independent film and video together. The pressure of financing independent production after the establishment of artist-run centres, however, never went away. These film and video makers needed capital and

labour that they generally could not afford. Eventually, they had to negotiate with different masters, including the NFB and the Canada Council.
Some founding members' final withdrawal from the artist-run centres raises
questions about what role these arts organizations have played in Halifax.

Going Down the Road

In the mid-1970s, journalist Connie Tadros wrote, in *Cinema Canada*, that
there were only a few functioning independent production companies in
the Atlantic region: ABS Productions in Dartmouth and Cal Film Productions in Halifax, which relied on commercial work and services charged
on post-production, and Fredericton's Fiddlehead Productions associated
with the New Brunswick government.[35] Then, in St. John's Newfoundland,
Memorial University's Extension Services housed a film crew that was at
one time involved with the *Challenge for Change* program (as discussed
in Jerry White's contribution to this book). The NFB and the CBC Halifax branch (CBHT) were the major producers of regional film and video.
NSCAD University also had film and video courses and basic production
facilities since 1969.[36] However, these resources were not accessible to the
people outside the institution, where video practices were confined to a
more specific artistic framework.

First encounters with film

Several founding members of AFCOOP revealed to me the production
conditions in early 1970s Halifax and their career and life interests. All
agreed that the local arts infrastructure was not helpful to those interested
in mastering the art of filmmaking. Chuck Lapp was one of the few people
who attended the first AFCOOP meeting:

> In 1972, I graduated from Dalhousie University. I worked in
> newspaper and Dalhousie student union photography depart-
> ment. I am interested in writing and photography. Film can re-
> ally combine both of them. My initial education as a journalist
> made me interested in social documentaries. Film was not an ac-
> cessible medium here [Halifax]. We could not find any cameras
> in the city and equipment in the province to make film. The only
> equipment available was in the NSCAD. They have a couple of

16mm cameras and super 8 cameras for students at that time. They were doing primarily art oriented production. I managed to get a student to book some equipment to make film. I decided that somewhere there must be an industry that I could tap into. I thought that Toronto and Montreal would have filmmaking industry that I could get some experience. I went to Toronto and decided to stay there.[37]

Chuck Lapp described himself as a self-motivated student who was eager to study filmmaking for social activism. The other two founding members, Chuck Clark and Bill MacGillivray, were more interested in the artistic and technological aspects of film. Chuck Clark admitted that he was fascinated by the technology:

> I was an art collage student in photography and printmaking. I became a tech-nerd. I worked in the audio and video department at NSCAD. In 1973, I took a film course taught by Robert Frank who is a famous film photographer. It got me interested in filmmaking. I was not ambitious enough to be interested in it in the beginning. But, I was interested in the technical side. I joined the film co-op.[38]

Bill MacGillivray, the first president of AFCOOP and now a renowned feature filmmaker, described his encounters with film as unexpected opportunities that came to him in his quest for a balance between life and art:

> I attended The Nova Scotia College of Art in 1964–5 (I think) and then went to study at what is now Concordia in Montreal for a few years where I made a short film on a borrowed Bolex. From there I went back to Halifax. Got a job teaching art in the school system – saved money and my wife at the time and I moved to London in 1970–1, where I attended the London International School of Film Technique.
> I am not a careerist – even though I had gone to film school (I didn't graduate, by the way – did just one of two years), I was never fully intent on becoming a career filmmaker, in fact

I didn't make my first 'real' film (*Aerial View*) until I was in my 30s and *Life Classes* wasn't made until I was 39–40.[39]

In contrast, for Chuck Lapp, participation in film is a form of grassroots social activism, advocating for a better representation of Atlantic Provinces and a fair allocation of public media production facilities in Canada:

> I thought that I would like to make film and a lot of other people wanted to make films. Let us create facilities here that allows people to express our culture by an art form that does not exist here. I grew up in PEI. I liked to stay in the region and the culture here, exploring the culture that is ignored. The Atlantic region is culturally ignored by the rest of the country. We want to get a medium that can reach the people beyond the region.[40]

With very different personalities and backgrounds in film, these individuals decided to form a film co-op together in Nova Scotia in the time of building "Canada's Hollywood."[41] The commercial film production was concentrated in Toronto and Montreal, where federal tax dollars, Canadian talent, and American capital were in a state of ferment. In contrast, Halifax filmmakers, who had been involved in filmmaking elsewhere, identified the instrumental value of film in projecting an Atlantic cultural identity and recognized the depressing economic situation in Halifax, where no institution had resources and an interest in creating production facilities for unknown filmmakers. When the Canada Council launched a sponsoring program, these "students" quickly made a decisive move to turn their frustration into concrete actions. In the fall of 1973, a group of young people held the first meeting to discuss the mandate and structure of AFCOOP in a lounge at the Dalhousie University Arts Centre.[42]

Atlantic flair

While criticizing an industrial mentality, these filmmakers repeatedly underscored that 'culture' was indispensable in the making of East Coast independent film. There are two different notions of culture emergent from these interviews. One is grounded in the local tradition and history, and is regarded as the source of creativity. The other was a working relation, slowly growing among the co-op members and providing them with emotional support as well as necessary technical and labour resources.

Bill MacGillivray stressed that staying within his community fuelled his creativity in filmmaking. He consciously stayed away from the industry practices:

> [Even] if I were to have been a full-time filmmaker, I would never have moved to Toronto. All my films are about the community I grew up in – near the ocean, in the Atlantic region. This is important to me – if I changed where I lived, not only would my greater community have changed, but so would have the people I worked with, and our particular, sympathetic/empathetic style of filmmaking.[43]

Lulu Keating joined AFCOOP in 1978 after she studied film at Ryerson University in Toronto. She saw her participation in the co-op as an escape from the competitive culture of the film industry as well as a reunion with her hometown folks:

> I found it [Ryerson] very competitive. What appealed to me about the co-op atmosphere was that you could get people to help you out. In Toronto, despite its good reputation, students were very cliquish and very competitive. For me, I always say my education really completed itself at the film co-op where I learned all the processes of filmmaking. I was there [the Toronto Filmmakers' Co-op][44] and saw some films coming from the co-op in Nova Scotia. Because I knew that I wanted to move back to Nova Scotia where I am originally from, I was thrilled to discover that there was a filmmaker's co-op. I watched their films and I was really impressed because they were about people in Nova Scotia. So, as soon as I returned to Halifax in the fall of 1978, I went right away to the film co-op and tried to join it.[45]

As I have discussed in the first section, the expression "independent film and video" often appeared in the policy statements made by the NFB and the Canada Council. What is striking about the interviewee narratives is that none described themselves as "independent filmmakers" in their early

Lulu Keating working on a flatbed edit table, courtesy Atlantic Filmmaker's Co-operative.

career stage. Instead, they always began with a story of a discontented "student," with deep roots in Atlantic Canada and desires of transferring his/her stories onto celluloid. They believed that their artistic lives could prosper by drawing on a *co-operative* energy in an artist-run organization; they did not make films in an isolated and independent manner. The narratives of these film artists can be contrasted with the ways in which the federal cultural institutions had envisioned the Canadian independent film and video.

First, the term "independent filmmakers" emerged as an appealing phrase appropriated by so-called "cultural bureaucrats" in the late 1960s, when the federal government was seriously planning a future life for the Canadian private film sector that mainly consisted of small production companies.[46] Michael Spencer, an executive producer of the Canadian Film Development Corporation (CFDC) during the 1960s, notes that he and his colleagues viewed "independent filmmakers" as cultural industrial talents/labourers, who would fuel a profitable feature film industry in Canada.[47] The second (and contrasting) argument for an independent media was put forwarded by the grassroots media organizations in the 1970s. Newly established artist-run centres in large cities, such as Toronto, Vancouver, and Montreal, often embraced an ideology of anti-American cultural imperialism, partially compatible with a Canadian nationalist objective inscribed in the post–World War II federal cultural policy.[48] From an artists' perspective, the idea of "independence" was used to define a distinguishing identity for Canadian media art and to support non-commercial art films and videos. As the first section shows, the NFB Halifax office and the Canada Council incorporated this art-oriented narrative of "media independence" in their policies that targeted a "vigorous" and "independent" film/video community in Halifax.

The founding members of AFCOOP and CFAT adopted the vocabulary of "independent Canadian media" to successfully obtain a start-up funding from the Canada Council. In addition to the nationalist rhetoric, their stories show a strong attachment to an east coast Maritime lifestyle, inspiring these young "students" to carve out a unique mandate for AFCOOP. Nevertheless, in the following years, through their interactions with different governmental agencies, these "students" had gradually grasped the State's meaning of "independent filmmaker," a meaning which had to be creatively negotiated with their own.

What Does It Mean to be an 'Independent Filmmaker'?

Could these filmmakers and artists create a 'utopian space' in the form of member-run centre? After having obtained a shared facility, the stress of financing non-commercial projects did not go away. The lack of a production fund put individual filmmakers in a vulnerable position, sandwiched between the market and the government. The Council did not give production money to organizations. Members had to find ways to support themselves and their projects, while the local employment opportunity in film at the time was highly controlled by a few cultural agencies, including the NFB and the CBHT. Film and video artists' perceptions of these governmental agencies reflect their relations with them.

For example, Bill MacGillivray characterized the NFB as reluctant to give away resources to local filmmakers:

> The National Film Board was beginning to set up a regional office here. We all thought that that was a good thing until we realized that they were bringing everyone down from Montreal to be the crew in that office and that none of us would get a job there. It was very unfortunate. And although they said that we would get to be the creative ones and they would 'help us' make our films, in reality most of the first films were made by their in-house staff. Subsequently they did help a lot – but there were growing pains.[49]

While dealing with the Canada Council fund, some filmmakers began to develop ambivalent feelings about their connections with the Council. Chuck Lapp recalled:

> In the spring, they [the Canada Council] approved the application and gave us $15,000. They wanted us to have a senior filmmaker to guide us. So they gave us $13,000. We paid [this filmmaker in Cape Breton] and made the Council feel better.[50]
>
> We continued to get money from the Canada Council. But they normally do not give money to organizations for production. They

have art grants for individuals, the money they gave is mainly for operation. They really want us to apply to them as individuals. They want to control. We did not want to be controlled. The Canada Council was in Ottawa and nobody knew anybody. Down here, we need to get the region and the community accesses to make any films.[51]

Despite the fact that they had basic production equipment, these filmmakers had to learn how to raise production funds by knocking on the doors of governmental agencies. They did so by tapping into a complex family of government funding programs. Lulu Keating made her film with the support of the NFB through a small program for co-op-based independent filmmakers – called PAFPS (Production Assistance for Filmmakers in the Private Sector), which did not provide any cash but did draw upon the resources of its now closed film laboratory and sound mixing facilities:

> I got thousands of dollars of services from the NFB to make *City Survival*. So I got the stock and they were processed in the NFB. It took a month to get my rushes. It was difficult when you tried to make a drama. You shoot and you have to go back to pick up rushes. It was impossible to wait for a month. The biggest heartbreak was when they were giving me my final mix. These independent films were always in low priority. We had a mix in October. All they had to do was to put it in a lab and make an answer print. I called everyday almost. They said, "Well, you have got bumped by somebody else." It took five months to process.[52]

Keating's encounter shows how the NFB's institutional structure and economic power may tend to limit the scope of grassroots filmmaking. From the institution's perspective, they were providing valuable assistance, and this contradiction goes to the heart of the struggles faced by regionally based filmmakers working in a very expensive medium.

The main instigator of CFAT is Brian MacNevin, who was a NSCAD student with an interest in community-based video art. When he worked in the NFB production unit, MacNevin first proposed a *Video Theatre* idea to his bosses:

Rex [Tasker] and others liked the idea (all for different reasons perhaps), but nonetheless, the support was there and we could have done it alone, done it within the NFB Halifax office that is.

I remember when the first discussion of *Tel-Ed*'s involvement happened, Rex asked me if we should involve them or not.... I remember thinking at the time, and telling Rex so, that if *Tel-Ed* became involved, because they were a non-profit society, outside the NFB, we could go after other government support, like the Canada Council, to raise funds for a *Video Theatre* and this seemed like a good idea at the time.

But once *Tel-Ed* became involved, I realized this was not where I wanted to put my energies. Independent video makers did use *Video Theatre*, but not "artists" so much, with the *Tel-Ed* and *Challenge for Change* influences, it seemed to "encourage" (as an institutional ideology that is, nothing stated of course) a certain kind of product. The place had the feel of a Government office (because it was housed in the NFB building). The independent video makers, who used *Video Theatre*, used video as a prerequisite to making their "film," or those who used video for social animation. At any rate, I was feeling a little frustrated regarding wanting to develop a community of artists interested in media arts, and realized that it would not happen at *Video Theatre*.[53]

MacNevin decided to break away from *Video Theatre*. In 1978, he started a new organization, the Society for Art Presentation, which would promote interdisciplinary art and artists. A video art gallery, the Centre for Art Tapes (CFAT), which focused on programming, emerged from this initiative. In the early 1980s, the Canada Council discovered that *Video Theatre* could not fulfill its dual mandate – social development and support for the arts community. Thus, the Council withdrew funding from *Video Theatre*; instead, it chose to negotiate with CFAT. Former board member Bruce Campbell recalls that the Council used CFAT's accumulated deficit as a bargaining chip to persuade the board of directors to turn CFAT into a video production organization.[54]

Interviewees highlighted the price they had to pay in order to be an 'independent' film or video maker. The desire to control the message as well as the whole process of production, post-production, and distribution were crippled by governmental interferences. Most individuals wanted to avoid

Clockwise from far left: Cathy Quinn, Amy Pfeiffer, Kathy Anderson, Carolyn Murray-Crick, Tim Bider, and others unidentified. The Allen Fox Workshop, Courtesy of Centre for Art Tapes (CFAT).

the market censorship; however, they discovered that they could in turn be absorbed into governmental cultural politics with its own corresponding limits.

Leaving 'Utopian Space'

With little capital in the way of production funds, artist-run centres could not insulate their members from contact with powerful agencies. The independent media producers were compelled to be dependent on the government. Although AFCOOP and CFAT were identified as production organizations, they strived to finance a very few small productions every year. The structure of artist-run centres became more problematic as the size of membership increased. Slowly, these organizations grew into education and equipment resource centres. Chuck Lapp decided to start his own film production company:

> I was one of the filmmakers who want to do social documentaries. We saw the co-op as a potential production house. We could do features. We actually got together, produced and financed social documentaries that nobody did. But the co-op only had the ability to do educational outreach to people who want to do film. I really felt that I could not continue to be in the co-op and make films that I want to do. I needed to go out and find my way.[55]

AFCOOP's financial problems had also created a dilemma for the senior members, when they saw an increasing number of newcomers demanding support from the co-op and who had different attitudes from those held by the founding members.

Bill MacGillivray described his biggest worry in the mid-1980s: "After *Stations* I realized that I could not make the larger films I wanted to make within a co-op – it was not fair to new members to ask for so much in the way of resources and there was the issue of changing attitudes within the co-op as it gradually became less and less vital (in my opinion) and gradually members began to look at the co-op as a training ground in preparation for the 'real industry.'"[56] Some AFCOOP members decided to join CFAT, which began its production services and programs in the early

1980s. Chuck Clark reduced his participation in AFCOOP because he saw the potential of video technology in art making as being less rigid than filmmaking: "I stayed with CFAT because the aspect of the technology. Film is magical. But it is expensive. And you need to learn how to get out there to communicate. It is a big debate. For many people, electronic stuff is more accessible, approachable, modern."[57] Funding constraints created huge obstacles for many who in fact began their first films and developed their skills in arts organizations. After several years, the 'grown-ups' could not find roles in what they saw as a 'nursery film school,' and they gradually left for resources and opportunities available in the market.

Epilogue

In the usual story of the artist-run media centre in Canada, the policy of "democratization and decentralization" allowed artist-run media centres to mushroom, creating space for a generation of Canadian film and video makers to mature without selling out to commercial interests. Yet, as my interviewees recalled, in practice these media producers did not often gain a much-desired freedom to produce films outside the dictates of industry or nationalistic protocols. Most members had to function within the constraints of small budgets and grant agency requirements.

Fast-forward to the present context: Halifax is now the fourth largest film and video production centre in Canada. Having gone through the early community development and the years of building facilities and skills, AFCOOP and CFAT have expanded their mandates to attract an ever-broader spectrum of Halifax citizens. One senior member, who has been working with both organizations for more than twenty years, described their pragmatic approach, which in his account responds to the new economic environment: "The mandate has to be broader. When it first started, there was more idealism. Now the mandate expresses the realism through a greater understanding of how people can be trained in the industry. We not only talk about artists but also professional development."[58]

In a frenzy of building up an Atlantic motion picture industry, the challenge for AFCOOP and CFAT has been understood as keeping up with the technology and allowing accessibility to all these new members. For example, the new membership structure of AFCOOP consists of four categories, Volunteer, Associate Member, Full Member, and Equipment Access

Member. Those who have full membership are required to participate in general meetings and volunteering work. Others only have to fill out an application and pay their fees. Now, AFCOOP and CFAT use a small business model to stress inclusiveness, moderate expansion, and flexibility. This entrepreneurial method does not break their financial and symbolic ties with the federal cultural institutions. Indeed, it provides ideological reinforcement of small organizations while also moving AFCOOP and CFAT closer to the film and video industry. Today, AFCOOP and CFAT identify themselves as the powerhouse of creativity. They do not want to be on the fringe of the Canadian state anymore. Instead, both organizations, to varying degrees, seek to fit themselves squarely into a nationwide system of media production and distribution.

Currently, a range of small and medium-sized media companies operate in Halifax. Nova Scotia Community Colleges offer technical courses in film and media production and NSCAD University now offers an undergraduate program in film production.[59] The Atlantic Film Festival attracts moderate crowds at its annual screenings. More and more government money and agencies, such as the Film Nova Scotia (formerly the Nova Scotia Film Development Corporation), have become involved in the film and video business. All of this activity raises the question of what is 'independent production' in the context of this new pragmatic model. I do not have the answer but want to conclude with MacGillivray's comments:

> It was very hard to raise the money to make one's own films in those days – but in many ways, now it is even harder. Especially if you are trying to invent your own cinema on any kind of scale – which is originally what a co-op was meant to do – give you a warm place to invent and grow. As budgets got bigger and Telefilm and the NFB got involved in projects people had to answer to too many masters.
>
> I feel there are fewer people trying to create a personal cinema now than there were in the earlier days – if that is progress – then so be it – but perhaps a new form of co-op should be created to answer this question: where do I go for emotional and technical support when I feel my voice is too small or too different to be heard within the industrial glamour that surrounds me?[60]

Acknowledgments

I thank Zoë Druick for providing me with useful materials on the National Film Board of Canada. Sylvia Roberts, liaison librarian from Simon Fraser University, helped me locate the literature on the Canadian grassroots media. I am grateful to the two anonymous reviewers and Darrell Varga, who patiently edited my manuscript and introduced me to the recent literature on Canadian film history. Tyler Pearce and Kevin Gould gave me useful comments on my final manuscript. None of these people has responsibility for anything I have written.

NOTES

1 For discussions on artist-run media centres in English Canada, see, for example: Jennifer Abbott, ed., *Making Video "In": the Contested Ground of Alternative Video on the West Coast* (Vancouver: Video In Studio, 2000); Keith Wallace, "A Particular History: Artist-run Centres in Vancouver," in *Vancouver Anthology: the Institutional Politics of Art*, ed. Stan Douglas (Vancouver: Talonbooks, 1991), 23–45; and AA Bronson, "The Humiliation of the Bureaucrat: Artist-run Centres as Museum by Artists," in *Museums by Artists*, ed. AA Bronson and Peggy Gale (Toronto: Art Metropole, 1983), 29–37.

2 In recent years, AFCOOP published a catalogue to commemorate its 30 years of activities: *30 Takes: Celebrating 30 Years at the Atlantic Filmmakers Co-operative* (Halifax: AFCOOP, 2004). CFAT members contributed to an essay collection, *Intersections: 25 Years of Connecting at the Centre of Art Tapes*, ed. James MacSwain (Halifax: Pottersfield Press, 2004).

3 Several conceptual artists from NSCAD University were singled out as the pioneering video art practitioners in Halifax. For an example of such an overview see Dot Tuer, "Mirroring Identities: Two Decades of Video Art in English-Canada," in *Mirror Machine: Video and Identity*, ed. Janine Marchessault (Toronto: YYZ Books, 1995). NSCAD University is the acronym for the Nova Scotia College of Art and Design. Because my interviewees used the full name, "the Nova Scotia College of Art and Design," when they answered my questions, I retain this use in the interview transcripts.

4 Although gender is not a variable in this study, I was inspired by feminist cultural policy critics, who emphasize the position of local knowledge and interests within the large political and economic context. See, for example, Annette Van Den Bosch and Alison Beale, "Introduction: Australian and Canadian Cultural Policies: A Feminist Perspective," in *Ghosts in the Machine: Women and Cultural Policy in Canada and Australia*, ed. Annette Van Den Bosch and Alison Beale (Toronto: Garamond Press, 1998), 1–3.

5 In this paper, the term "cultural policy" literally means government intervention in the cultural field, but also including business operations and civil society campaigns around the conditions and productions of cultural artefacts. Some use the term "cultural policy" to describe different technologies of citizenship: see Justin Lewis and Toby Miller, eds., *Critical Cultural Policy Studies: A Reader* (Oxford: Blackwell, 2003); and Jim McGuigan, *Rethinking Cultural Policy* (Berkshire: Open University Press, 1994).

6 Robert E. Babe, *Canadian Communication Thought: Ten Foundational Writers* (Toronto: University of Toronto Press, 2000), 59.

7 For academic reviews on Canada's postwar cultural policy, see, for example: Maria Tippett, *Making Culture: English-Canadian Institutions and the Arts before the Massey Commission* (Toronto: University of Toronto Press, 1990); Paul Litt, *The Muses, the Masses and the Massey Commission* (Toronto: University of Toronto Press, 1992); Dot Tuer, "The Art of Nation Building: Constructing a 'Cultural Identity' for Post-War Canada", *Parallelogramme* 17 (1992): 24–36.

8 Michael Volkering, "Deconstructing the Difference-engine: a Theory of Cultural Policy," *Cultural Policy* 2 (1996): 189–212.

9 Zoë Druick, *Projecting Canada: Government Policy and Documentary Film at the National Film Board* (Montreal & Kingston: McGill-Queen's University Press, 2007), 9.

10 Ibid., 127.

11 Ronald Dick, "Regionalization of a Federal Cultural Institution: the Experience of the National Film Board of Canada

1965-1979," in *Flashback: People and Institutions in Canadian Film History*, ed. Gene Walz (Montreal: Mediatext Publications Inc., 1986), 17–35.

12 Vancouver became the location of the first NFB regional production centre in 1972.

13 Rex Tasker, "NFB Atlantic Regional Office," *Cinema Canada* 30 (1976): 34.

14 For example, Nova Scotia Public Archives has published "A Brief History of Film in Nova Scotia," http://www.gov.ns.ca/nsarm/databases/easterneye/history.asp.

15 Janine Marchessault, "Amateur Video and the Challenge for Change," in *Mirror Machine: Video and Identity*, ed. Janine Marchessault (Toronto: YYZ Books, 1995), 13–26. Marchessault gives this important example, also discussed by White in his chapter of this collection: in 1966, the NFB produced a cinéma-vérité portrait of a poverty-stricken Montreal family called *The Things I Cannot Change*, where the film's 'truthful' footage was edited in a way that the representation of the family reinforced the subject's hopelessness and futility.

16 Peter K. Wiesner, "Media for the People: the Canadian Experiments with Film and Video in Community Development," *American Review of Canadian Studies* (Spring 1992): 65–99.

17 Marchessault, 13.

18 Druick, 126–58.

19 Gary Evans, *In the National Interest: A Chronicle of the National Film Board of Canada: The Politics of Wartime Propaganda* (Toronto: University of Toronto Press, 1984), 328–29.

20 Several essays describe the influence of NFB on the video access centres. For example, Scott MacKenzie, "The Challenge for Change in the Alternative Public Sphere," *Canadian Journal of Film Studies* 5 (1996): 67–83; Kevin Dowler, "Interstitial Aesthetics and the Politics of Video at the Canada Council," in *Mirror Machine: Video and Identity*, ed. Janine Marchessault (Toronto: YYZ

Books, 1995), 37. For an analysis of the development of the Canadian film industry, drawing upon Michel Foucault's concept of governmentality, see Michael Dorland, *So Close to the State/s: The Emergence of Canadian Feature Film Policy* (Toronto: University of Toronto Press, 1998).

21 This term is derived from a paper written by former Canada Council video officer Tom Sherman. It suggests how an economic dependency on funding agencies can affect artists' identities and their works. Sherman admits that his working experience in the Council helped him understand artists' dependent relationship with the funding agencies. Tom Sherman, "The Value of Privacy and the Effects of Cultural Engineering," in *Before and After the I-Bomb: An Artist in the Information Environment*, ed. Tom Sherman and Peggy Gale (Banff: Banff Centre Press, 2002), 84–99.

22 Dale McConathy, *The Canadian Cultural Revolution: An Appraisal of the Politics of Economics of Art* (Toronto: Society for Art Publications, 1976), 1–3.

23 Ibid., 3.

24 Dowler, 37. For a detailed history of the development of arts funding policy, see Clive Robertson, *Policy Matters: Administrations of Art and Culture* (Toronto: YYZ Books, 2006).

25 Druick, 144–50.

26 Nancy Shaw, "Cultural Democracy and Institutionalized Difference: Intermedia, Metro Media", in *Mirror Machine: Video and Identity*, ed. Janine Marchessault (Toronto: YYZ Books, 1995), 28.

27 Jan Peacock, "Body for Speaking: Body-Centred Video in Halifax 1972-1982," in *Video Re/view: the (Best) Source Book for Critical Writings on Canadian Artists' Video*, ed. Peggy Gale, Lisa Steele (Toronto: Art Metropole, 1996), 144–45.

28 McConathy, 2.

29 Tom Sherman, "The 'Media Arts' and the Canada Council: the Present Situation and a Glimpse of the Future," Canada

Council internal discussion document, 20 November 1982. Information provided by an anonymous source at the Canada Council.

30 Tom Sherman, author interview, 5 January 2006.

31 Ted Magder discussed the genesis and development of Canadian feature film policy from the late 1960s to the 1980s in his book *Canada's Hollywood: the Canadian State and Feature Films* (Toronto: University of Toronto Press, 1993), 129–66.

32 Jean M. Guiot has discussed how the Canada Council policy has affected the organizational culture of artistic production in "Arts Councils as Organized Anarchies and De Facto Regulatory Agencies: Some Comments on the Bureaucratization of Artistic Production," *World Futures* 28 (1990): 217–23.

33 This paper focuses on the NFB and the Canada Council. Also, other cultural agencies, such as CBC television, the Canadian Film Development Corporation (now Telefilm Canada), and the Canadian Radio-television and Telecommunications Commission, interact with the grassroots media communities in varied ways. At the provincial level, some researchers have shown that the government agencies actively designed different policies to create imaginaries of Nova Scotia. For example, Adrian Alexander Willsher examined cinematic representations of Nova Scotia by the provincial agency in his master's thesis *Where are the Roads?: the Tourist and Industrial Promotion Films of the Nova Scotian Film Bureau, 1945–1970* (Halifax: Dalhousie University, 1996).

34 See note 2.

35 Connie Tadros, "The Testing Ground," *Cinema Canada* 31 (1976): 32–34.

36 Peacock, 144.

37 Chuck Lapp, author interview, 3 October 2002.

38 Chuck Clark, author interview, 17 October 2002.

39 William D. MacGillivray, author interview, 28 March 2006.

40 Lapp, author interview.

41 Magder, 129–92.

42 Chuck Lapp wrote an essay, "In the Beginning there was an Idea, no, there was a Dream...," to review the process of getting the first grant from the Canada Council in *30 Takes: Celebrating 30 Years at the Atlantic Filmmakers Cooperative* (Halifax: AFCOOP, 2004), 6–7.

43 MacGillivray, author interview.

44 The Toronto Filmmakers' Co-op was established in the early 1970s. In 1977, Lulu got in touch with this film co-op, which eventually fell apart. Currently, the Liaison of Independent Filmmakers of Toronto (LIFT) plays a similar role in Toronto. Lulu recalled that she also worked on some projects at LIFT in the early 1990s.

45 Lulu Keating, author interview, 23 September 2002.

46 Michael Spencer with Suzan Ayscough, *Hollywood North: Creating the Canadian Motion Picture Industry* (Montreal: Cantos International Publishing, 2003), 61–73.

47 Ibid., 61–68.

48 Magder, 144–45. Magder presented an example of the Toronto Filmmakers' Co-op, which sent a brief to Gérard Pelletier, secretary of state, in 1972. The film co-op was very concerned with establishing a network of exhibition and distribution of Canadian films that stress artistic merit.

49 MacGillivray, author interview.

50 The filmmaker hired as mentor was Grant Crabtree, a career NFB staff filmmaker employed by the Board since the Grierson era and having retired in the Maritimes.

51 Lapp, author interview.

52 Keating, author interview.

53 Brian MacNevin, author interview, 1 March 2006.

54 Bruce Campbell, "In the Beginning," in *Intersections*, 11.

55 Lapp, author interview.

56 MacGillivray, author interview, 30 March 2006.

57 Clark, author interview.

58 Anonymous, author interview, 30 September 2002.

59 At the time of this writing there is also a proposal for a graduate-level MFA Program in film at NSCAD University, a far cry from the limited resources available at the time of the establishment of the co-ops, but also a move toward a greater institutionalization of this activity.

60 MacGillivray, author interview, 30 March 2006.

10

ARBITRARY PRODUCTIONS: THOM FITZGERALD'S *THE MOVIE OF THE WEEK*

BRUCE BARBER

> The very definition of the real becomes: that of which it is possible to give an equivalent reproduction. The real is not only what can be reproduced, but that which is always already reproduced. The hyper real. – *Jean Baudrillard*[1]

It is interesting to acknowledge that without music degree programs or classes in music history, theory or performance, art schools occasionally – arbitrarily – produce musicians and rock groups.[2] The same could also be said of filmmakers. A decade before NSCAD had instituted a film program, two fourth-year BFA Intermedia students, Thom Fitzgerald on exchange from the Cooper Union in New York City and Andrew Ellis, a student from Vancouver, produced a very ambitious film titled *The Movie of the Week*, the first feature-length film (75 minutes, 1990) to be produced at NSCAD in the century of its existence.[3] This is not to suggest that this film appeared in total isolation, for at least since the late 1960s several major independent filmmakers, dozens of video artists and a few critics and film theorists had presented their work and/or taught classes at NSCAD, among them Michael Snow, Robert Frank, Yvonne Rainer, Dan Graham, Lawrence Weiner, Martha Rosler, Betty Gordon, Darcy Lange, Sandy Flitterman, Lisa Steele, Judith Barry, Dara Birnbaum, Marion Barling, and Adrian Piper.[4] It should also be acknowledged in this context that 16mm film animation classes taught for many years by Henry (Ziggy) Orenstein and video classes taught by the

Andrew Ellis and Thom Fitzgerald at the Atlantic Filmmaker's Co-op in 1989–90 making *The Movie of the Week*, courtesy Emotion Pictures.

late David Askevold, as well as Jan Peacock, and David Clark, among others, including myself, have produced a number of accomplished film and video makers.[5] But it must be acknowledged that the Ellis and Fitzgerald film project marked a foundational moment in the beginning of a film culture at NSCAD.[6] With this historical background in view, this chapter explores the production and reception of *The Movie of the Week* with a special focus on how it represented both a departure from and an endorsement of NSCAD's conceptual heritage and specifically postmodern characteristics of the 1980s.[7] Arbitrary – yet not so arbitrary – *The Movie of the Week* raised the bar with respect to feature-length film production not only at NSCAD but also throughout Atlantic Canada.[8]

The Camera as Mirror

The Movie of the Week relates the story of Matthew (Thom Fitzgerald), a somewhat troubled young man who is so enraptured by his television set that he loses all sense of difference between what is real in his life and what is simulated. He comes to believe that the characters on TV represented in various scenarios – parodies of soap opera and melodrama vignettes – are his roommates, Eleanor and Jonathan, and that they speak through the tube directly to him. The narrative unfolds in what the script authors term a double language system, media representations which interrupt and augment an irregular dialogue between Matthew and his psychiatrist Dr. 'Brandy' McArthey. As the film's synopsis indicates, "[t]he goal of the film is to deconstruct mass media stereotypes and criticize the lack of realistic social or sexual roles on TV."[9] It should also be noted that this thematic interrogation of the mass media is a postmodern characteristic of Canadian cinema in the 1980s, most notably in the films of Atom Egoyan, but also in a different way in Bill MacGillivray's *Life Classes*, discussed by Darrell Varga elsewhere in this book.

Fitzgerald and Ellis structure the film around a narrative play between the camera lens, the mirror and the spectator, arguably the staple components of the cinematic apparatus.[10] Mirrors and mirroring (F. *mirour* L. *mirare* = to look at), appear throughout the film, either in the guise of a television set itself, frequently featuring Jordan Broadworth in a first-time role as the archly good-looking 'Television Man' – a games show host – mouthing "Money! Prizes! and the laconic gaze of the mostly untrained actors appearing innocently before the camera as if they were looking distractedly into a mirror.

This system of doubling engages split subjectivity – a post-Freudian consciousness that is marked by its multiple perspectives on reality. Matthew, the primary protagonist whose fractured psyche is configured in various guises throughout the film, represents a mirrored subject, alternately gazing at the camera or being reflected through a lens. Mirrors figure prominently in several sequences, including the first apartment sequence, a bedroom drama seduction, and the patient/psychiatrist scene, where Matthew performs a sado-masochistic bondage act with Brandy in an effort to prove his love can be as real as the only other 'true' love he has witnessed on television in his much beloved 'movies of the week.' The film is an elaborate conceit – a postmodern pastiche – in its play between obsessions, repressed homosexual desire, self-hate, and homophobia. The media represent the ideological 'matrix' that both obscures and provides the ground for a thoroughly postmodern split subject as this has been theorized in the post-Freudian writings of Jacques Lacan, Michel Foucault, Jean Baudrillard, J-L Baudry, Teresa De Lauretis, and Julia Kristeva.[11]

The film opens with *Espresso*, an exquisite short silent film that appears to be a found remnant from an earlier period of film history. The detached (anecdotal) narrative represented in this sequence shows a young man who is pursuing a beautiful and flirtatious waitress in a café. "As their eyes meet and their hearts swell, a mysterious elderly woman knocks the waitress and coffee into the young man's lap, ruining his chance to impress the woman of his dreams."[12] At the close of this short introductory film clip, we see the same young man, now identifiably Matthew, who is projecting *Espresso* onto the wall of his apartment.[13] He is then confronted by his own reflection in the bath water, the faucets, in windows, the mirrors in his apartment, and in the television screen that he feels compelled to switch on. On his television appears a trailer for 'a movie of the week' about desire and secret temptation revealing the doubling (schizoid) nature of the diegesis – from trailer to trailer; from film to video (television) to film, and from 'reality' to simulated – hyper – reality, thus providing the postmodern temporal and spatial coordinates of the film and also its dialectical play on the dynamics of representation and 'truth' within fiction. As the 'movie of the week' trailer ends, Matthew's psychiatrist, Dr. 'Brandy' McArthey, intrudes into the cinematic space with an accusatory, yet oddly conciliatory statement – another doubling conflation: "Call me what you like Matt, but I hope it won't be long before we start talking."

One register of the film's double narrative represents a 'coming-of-age' and another, a symbolic 'coming out' of Matthew, whose troubled subjectivity and sexual orientation issues are between a dream state of psychic alienation and desiring reverie signified in one bed scene where he is shown masturbating under the bedclothes. His existence is phenomenally inscribed in the media without which he would cease to exist, and the focus on mirrors and mirroring throughout the film traces his mediated consciousness, from desiring dream to abject reverie – "a man cut in half … by a window" – in the classic sense articulated by André Breton in the Surrealist manifestos. Through a series of interviews with Eleanor (the televised woman) and Jonathan, Matthew's former roommates and lovers, we learn details of his somewhat confused past, a back-story to his self-hate and cathected repression of homosexual desire. Intrusions of commercials represent the reality principle, and the double narrative secured in the opening sequences reveal that Matthew, having been the abused subject of the psychiatric profession – like the proverbial prisoner identifying with his jailer – now attempts to seduce 'Brandy' through a sado-masochistic entrapment fantasy.

Halifax film critic Ron Foley Macdonald wrote that the film had an "oddly realistic tone, which is sustained throughout the film. It is at once rigorously anti-romantic while maintaining an extremely subjective perspective. The main characters' inability to distinguish reality from media-mediated reality is reflected in the point-of-view which never clearly delineates what is real and what has been imagined."[14] On one important register the film articulates Guy Debord's thesis that the real is always distanced in the form of its representation; that reality is a consumable spectacle. The culture of desire manifested in *The Movie of the Week* is unable to be consummated or satisfied. In this sense desire is a negative value of the hyper-production/hyper-consumption (super ego) imperatives in contemporary capitalist society, where the truth – about satisfaction – is the Jaggerian: "I can't get no satisfaction …. no, no, no!" Desire becomes endlessly repeatable, at times onanistically satiable, but ultimately a super ego injunction that is patently irresolvable. Jean Baudrillard discusses this paradoxical situation in terms of the production of truth:

> Of course this is not a discourse on truth – not everything can be verified, there is no pretence about that. The same goes for the question of desire. To say that all desires are satisfied is nonsensical because desire as such cannot be satisfied, quite the

Thom Fitzgerald as Matthew in *The Movie of the Week*, courtesy Emotion Pictures.

opposite. But in this world of production, desire is at one and the same time productive and a means of satisfaction. Consequently we have lost touch with the whole concept of desire, desire as metaphor, and desire as promise, as something that cannot be satisfied or made a reality. I don't use the term 'desire' very often. The term had its day in the 1960s and 1970s. I suppose it's the same for me with the term "symbolic." Many of these paradigmatic terms were coined for other eras. "Desire" still clings to the world of the subject. Even Deleuze thinks of desire within a sphere of production, albeit a different and higher type of production. Molecular production was a big step for Deleuze, but even this proliferation and fractalization of the term 'desire' kept its original form and was never developed further.[15]

Mirrors and Mirroring

The Hanging Garden

Mirrors and mirroring as symptomatic of narcissistically inflected subjectivity and cathected desire also appear in several scenes of Thom Fitzgerald's first solo directed feature *The Hanging Garden* (1997),[16] a film that shares many of the same themes of *Movie of the Week*. After a decade away, Sweet William (Chris Leavins), the principal character, returns to the bosom of his Cape Breton family home to attend his sister's (Kerry Fox) wedding. The first mirroring scene occurs in the sequence when his grandmother (Joan Orenstein), who is suffering from dementia, is mirrored in the photograph of herself as a younger woman. Mirror scene #2 occurs at the conclusion of the homecoming sequence when William alights from his late model red convertible – a potent (sexually charged) symbol of his success – and he pauses to inspect and groom himself in the mirror attached to the car door, simultaneously referencing his narcissism and that "objects viewed through the rear view mirror are closer than they seem." In mirror scene #3, Sweet William detours around the wedding in progress, entering the house from a side door. A geriatric golden retriever is seen passing in the background of the frame and seemingly triggers an allergic asthmatic response in William that necessitates the use of an asthma puffer for relief. He looks in the mirror and laughs, perhaps an acknowledged memory of his earlier life and experiences in the family home.

The fourth mirroring scene occurs when Sweet William looks in the mirror as he tries on an oversized black sports coat – his own – from William's overweight teenage years, and as he does so, he sees the spectral image of his earlier rotund body reflected in the mirror. Similar to the first mirror sequence of his grandmother reflected in the photograph, this reflection occasions the spectators' knowledge of the imaging of youth; in grandmother's case the full bloom of youth without the ravages of age, and for Sweet William, the reflection signals his angst-ridden teenage years prior to his suicide. Mirror scene #5 in *The Hanging Garden* occurs when William takes Whiskey Jack, his drunken father, out of the bath where he had been placed to sober up and lays him on the bed. While this 'deposition' is in progress, he glances at himself in the mirror as if to mark his difference/distance from his father's alcoholism. This is one of two key scenes in which Sweet William assists members of his family, the other occurring when he is asked to hold up his sister's wedding train while she urinates in the lavatory. The sixth mirror scene reflects William's mother in the mirror as she delivers the Wildean line, "You've got to have a life to give it up Fletcher." The sister's wedding takes place in the garden where William previously had attempted to hang himself, and although his death is ultimately a major ambiguity in *The Hanging Garden*, the film's diegesis suggests that Sweet William was successful in his suicide (but the film, in magic realist style, posits two possible endings).[17] This 'fiction' is maintained through the regular appearance of the three figures of Sweet William: first as an innocent youth with the promise of successful rites of passage to adulthood; then as Willie the overweight teenager troubled by his parents' response to his emerging homosexual identity (his obesity and the size of his 'Willie'); and finally as William the successful young adult – returning 'from away' – whose spectral presence enables both a reconciliation with his past and a metaphysical 'settling of accounts' through a reiteration of the tragic narrative trajectory of his life. There are various other mirroring devices represented in this film as framed shots through doorways, windows, and reflections of human subjects in bottles, jars, and preserves on the kitchen and dining room shelves in the house.

As with *Movie of the Week*, the focus on mirrors and mirroring throughout *The Hanging Garden* traces the protagonist's split subjectivity, mediated consciousness, and cathected desire. It's ironic that the only flower that is not representing a character in the film is the petite paper white Narcissus,[18] the absence of which identifies the important *Ur*-theme of the narrative, the myth of Narcissus with all that this connotes with respect to onanistic self-love, prohibitions against incestuous desire, tragic death, transcendence, and regeneration.

The Mirroring of Desire

What is it about mirrors that have so fascinated filmmakers, visual artists, writers, and philosophers? Base narcissism? Or are they/we simply in the thrall of that divine mirror in which only perfect truth is reflected? Rudolphe Gasche argued that the reflection of the speculum was always potentially absolute,[19] and absolute reflection (speculation), as distinct from *mere* reflection, deliberately pursues a totalizing goal.[20] But Friedrich Nietzsche, another philosopher of the mirror, remarked: "When we try to examine the mirror in itself we discover in the end nothing but things upon it. If we want to grasp the things we finally get hold of nothing but the mirror – this in the most general terms is the history of knowledge."[21] Jean Baudrillard, the reluctant postmodern philosopher of the hyperreal, offers this advice on mirrors and mirroring: "Cowardice and courage are never without a measure of affectation. Nor is love. Feelings are never true. They play with their mirrors."

With dissertations on the mirror of this magnitude, it is not difficult to agree with Stephen Melville's assessment that Jacques Lacan has been somewhat "over-read as the theorist of the 'mirror stage.'" As Melville argues, the visual theory in Lacan's *Four Essays on Psychoanalysis* is less about the imaginary itself than an account of the symbolic underpinnings of the visual imaginary. Not what the mirror appears to reveal but "the seams that do not show, stains, or inscriptions that are the invisible condition of its apparently transparent reflexivity."[22] "Look that's you," the mother says to her infant as she holds him/her up to the mirror and the child (supposedly) recognizes its entry into a differentiated world in which s/he is both alone and not alone, different and yet the same. Is this the same Lacanian recognition/mis-recognition paradox that is provided by his celebrated sardine can anecdote? "Do you see that sardine can?" says the fisherman. "Well it doesn't see you!" When one sees oneself in the mirror, what does one see? You see yourself as another (you), not necessarily as others see you and often not how you think you look or should be seen, to be true! But does the mirror see you?

For centuries philosophers, writers, artists, and more recently, filmmakers have recognized how the mirror can both capture and betray truth; and how observation can eclipse reason. Early on in Jean Cocteau's *Orphée* (*Orpheus*), an iconic stage play and paradigmatically queered cinematic text, Heubertise, Orphée's guardian angel, tells him as they approach the mirror. "I am letting you into the secret of all secrets, mirrors are gates through which death comes and goes. Moreover if you see your whole life in a mirror you will see death at work as you see bees behind the glass in a hive."[23]

Mirroring and mirror imagery in Fitzgerald and Ellis's *Movie of the Week* and Fitzgerald's *The Hanging Garden* is not simply a cue to media hegemony and subject alienation. The appearance of the mirror in these films is part of a history of mirroring in painting and cinema that was initiated with the crisis of representation by the mid-nineteenth-century invention of the camera and the subsequent challenge to normative modes of representation. With their four years of art school education and as "out" gay men, Ellis and Fitzgerald probably had knowledge of paintings such as the famous painting *Self-portrait in a convex mirror* (c. 1523/4) by Francesco Mazzola, known as Parmigianino (1503–40), one of three famous paintings containing mirrors in the collection of the Kunsthistorische Museum in Vienna. This painting is a portrait of a young man, whose gender seems somewhat ambiguous, but which documentary sources inform us is the painter Mazzola, from the city of Parma, Parmigianino himself at the age of twenty-one. This *trompe l'oeil* image portrays this young prodigy "as lovely as an angel" as he was described, dressed in fur. "His hand that knew how to paint and draw so excellently" directs his *faux* innocent, imperious gaze toward the mirror, firmly announcing his arrival to his potential patrons in the Papal Court. This is a 'calling card' painting, much as Ellis and Fitzgerald's *Movie of the Week* is a 'calling card' film, produced in order to demonstrate the artist's obvious talent and thus win the favour and commissions of Pope Clement VII, and in the case of the filmmakers, the film financing agencies. Parmigianino has brilliantly painted his portrait on a convex piece of wood to enhance the illusion. Is this image a picture, or a mirror? In a crucial sense it is both, but it reflects none other than the painter himself, save in thought.

Another mirror painting in this extraordinary Viennese imperial collection is more conventional. *Young Woman at her Toilette* (1515), by Giovanni Bellini (c. 1433–1516), is one of hundreds of similar paintings that reinforce the objectifying proclivities of the male gaze through the agency of the mirror. As the young woman narcissistically inspects herself in the mirror, she becomes the object of desire of another, the (usually) male viewer. As feminist art historians have argued, this unbalanced visual axis of phallocentric power is played out in countless images in art, advertising, and film, perhaps no more provocatively than in the large painting *Susanna and her Elders* painted by Tintoretto (1518–1594). This painting represents an Old Testament story contained in the Book of Daniel 13. Susanna is portrayed after bathing in her bower (in nature), inspecting her body in front of a mirror placed symbolically before her in the middle ground of the painting, while she is surveyed (spied upon) by her elders, two wizened interlopers of the misogynist kind. When she spurns their lascivious intentions the men take revenge and accuse her of adultery to her husband. Only the judgment of the wise prophet Daniel releases Susanna from the death sentence regularly meted out to women accused of adultery at this time.

A Kaspar Hauser Look with the Nothing

The history of western art has many other important paintings with mirrors that would be of interest to filmmakers such as Fitzgerald and Ellis, not all of them emphasizing the phallocentric power axes of representation. Velasquez's painting *Las Meninas* (*Maids of Honour*), so brilliantly analyzed in necrophantic terms by Michel Foucault, and also Jan Van Eyck's magisterial portrait of *Giovanni Arnolfini and his Bride* (1434), function differently as philosophical vehicles for reflection. The ornate mirror reflects in miniature the interior of the bourgeois Flemish room in which these elegant subjects pose. The mirror in Van Eyck's painting reflects the backs of their bodies and the presence of two other figures in the room including the painter, and the fleeting chimerical play of light over its surface that threatens to erase this image forever. The elaborately carved and very expensive mirror frame containing ten scenes from the life and death of Christ, beginning with the Mount of Olives and ending with the Resurrection, reveals the high station of the subjects. The single lit candle in the candelabra, the little dog, the obviously pregnant wife, and the Christ Pantocrator position of Arnolfini's hand combine to signal the rich allegorical sigificance of this northern portrait of Joseph, the Holy Virgin Mary, Faith in the Lord, and redemption through his son Christ's incarnation, suffering, death and resurrection. In Van Eyck's painting the mirror becomes an incarnation of the all-seeing eye of an omniscient God, legitimating absolutely the sacramental rites of this solemn marriage ceremony.

The reader may perhaps recall the magnificent section from Foucault's *The Order of Things* in which the author discusses the large mirror in *Las Meninas*. The mirror offers the beholder "the enchantment of the double" which he argues is denied us as spectators: "Of all the representations represented in the painting" he insists, "this is the only one visible but no one is looking at it." Some of the individuals in the painting have their heads in profile but no one is looking directly at the mirror except the viewers outside the frame. "That tiny glowing rectangle which is nothing other than visibility, yet without any gaze able to grasp it, to render it actual and to enjoy the suddenly ripe fruit of the spectacle it offers."[24] Foucault notes that the mirror reflects nothing in the space of the room itself, or anything represented in the picture. It is not the visible that it reflects, like most Dutch and Flemish paintings of the period, excluding *The Arnolfini Wedding*, but the invisible. The mirror "cuts straight through the whole field of representation, ignoring all it might apprehend within that field, and restores visibility to that which resides outside all view."[25] But, as Foucault insists, this invisibility is not the invisibility of that which is hidden; rather, "it addresses itself to what is invisible both as a result of the painting's structure and its existence as a painting." Thus he offers a philosophical revelation on this phenomenon; another peak/pique of abitrariness – perhaps deconstruction – that has special relevance to the use of the mirror in the films of Ellis and Fitzgerald: "The Mirror provides a metathesis of visibility that affects both the space represented in the picture and its nature as representation; it allows us to see, in the centre of the canvas, what in the painting is of necessity doubly invisible."[26]

Mirrors, windows, and doors also figure as powerful philosophical tropes in sections of Walter Benjamin's magisterial unfinished *Arcades Project*.[27] His discussion identifies the paradoxical qualities of spectatorship and surveillance, the great philosophical motifs of doubling and reflection invoked by the evanescent qualities of the mirror and how these figure in the negotiation of space and place which has fascinated photographers and filmmakers since the invention of photographic representation. "The way mirrors bring the open expanse, the streets into the café – this too belongs to the interweaving of spaces, to the spectacle by which the flaneur is ineluctably drawn."[28] Further on in this passage Benjamin waxes poetically on the speculum in more philosophical terms which deserve to be quoted in full:

> Paris is the city of mirrors. The asphalt of its roadways smooth as glass, and at the entrance to all bistros, glass partitions. A profusion of window panes and mirrors in cafes, so as to make the inside brighter and to give all the tiny nooks and crannies, into which Parisian taverns separate, a pleasing amplitude. Women here look at themselves more than elsewhere, and from this comes the distinctive beauty of the Parisienne. Before any man catches sight of her, she already sees herself ten times reflected. But the man too, sees his own physiognomy flash by. He gains his own image more quickly here than elsewhere and also sees himself more quickly merged with this, his image. Even the eyes of passers-by are veiled mirrors, and over that wide bed of the Seine, over Paris, the sky is spread out like the crystal mirror hanging over the drab beds in brothels.

Benjamin poses two practical questions: "Where were these mirrors manufactured and when did the custom of furnishing bars with them arise?" and "when did the custom of replacing canvas with mirrors in the frames of old paintings begin?"[29] Benjamin leaves these questions unanswered, but they have been responded to somewhat since by a number of authors, including Benjamin Goldberg's study *The Mirror and Man* (1985).[30] Other mirror observations of Benjamin's are more interesting in this context. "Let two mirrors reflect each other; then Satan plays his favourite trick and opens here in his way (as his partner does in lovers' gazes) the perspective on infinity." Benjamin hails Stephane Mallarmé as the "genius of mirrors;" and Odilon Redon as the painter of subjects (*Silence*, 1911) "as if they appeared in a somewhat clouded mirror. But his mirror's world is flat, averse to perspective." In this section of his essay Benjamin turns his attention to discussing mirrors as lighting aids in the Paris arcades. He shifts from a rumination on egotism, narcisissm, to commerce, and place. "One may compare the pure magic of those walls of mirrors which we know from feudal times with the oppressive magic worked by the alluring mirror walls of the arcades, which invite us into seductive bazaars."[31] Benjamin cites

A.G. Meyer's *Eisenbauten* (*Iron buildings*, 1907), in which is introduced a discussion of how mirrors are destructive of architectural form. "The increasing transparency of glass in colourless glazing draws the outer world into the interior space, while covering the walls with mirrors projects the image of the interior space into the outer world. In either case the 'wall' as a container of space is deprived of its significance." In Versaille's Baroque Hall of Mirrors "this relation between surface and light was constituted in such a way that it is no longer the light that interrupts the surface area but the surface area that interrupts the light."[32]

We also must include cinema in this discussion. Even at his most practical and descriptive, Benjamin is never far away from philosophical speculation about the subject(s) at hand. In these aphoristic fragments he speculates on the double-edged nature of perception, mirroring. He proffers the fugitive, the furtive eye, and the *augenblick* – history moving at 1/24th of a second – the blink of an eye identified in his famous essay "The Work of Art in the Age of Mechanical Reproduction" and his "Theses on the Philosophy of History," as a powerful indicator of the arbitrary forces of modernity. What follows is an astonishing text that needs to be quoted in full to understand its fecundity as a font for both philosophical reflection and comprehension.

A look at the ambiguity of the arcades; their abundance of mirrors, which fabulously amplifies the spaces and makes orientation more difficult. For although the mirror world may have many aspects, indeed infinitely many, it remains ambiguously double edged. It blinks: it is always this one – and never nothing – out of which another immediately arises. The space that transforms itself does so in the bosom of nothingness. In its tarnished dirty mirrors, things exchange *a Kaspar-Hauser look with the nothing* (emphasis added). It is like an equivocal wink coming from Nirvana. And here we are brushed with icy breath by the dandiish name of Odilon Redon, who caught like no one else, this look of things in the mirror of nothingness, and who understood, like no one else, how to join with things in their collusion of non-being. The whispering of gazes fills the arcades. There is no thing here that does not, where one least expects it, open a fugitive eye, blinking it shut again; but if you look more closely, it is gone. To the whispering of these gazes, the space lends its echo. "Now what", it blinks, "can possibly have come over me?" We stop short in some surprise. "What indeed can possibly have come over you?" Thus we gently bounce the question back to it.[33]

This enigmatic "exchange of a Kaspar Hauser look with the nothing" and the "equivocal wink coming from Nirvana" requires some explanation here. Kaspar Hauser, you may remember, particularly if you have seen Werner Herzog's film *Jeder fur sich und Gott gegen alle: Der Geheimnis von Kaspar Hauser* (1974), translated as *The Enigma of Kaspar Hauser: Every Man for himself and God Against All*, is the nineteenth-century story of a foundling without the ability to communicate who arrives like a time traveller in a sleepy town square. After he is taught to speak he tells of being raised in a cellar and of never having seen another human being. The members of the town intelligentsia confront the enigma of his sudden presence in their town with the power of their learning and logic, but Kaspar reveals the severe limitations of such rationalism. He departs as mysteriously as he arrived; stabbed by an unknown assailant leaving behind a deathbed vision that is merely the beginning of his story. During his autopsy his doctors are left to ponder his enlarged liver and over-developed brain. Benjamin's allusion here is to the mirror's lure, or better *allure*, which he equates with nothing less than a philosophy of being, perhaps the displacement of space for place, which becomes a *locus standi* for presence, presentiment … existence itself. "And here we are brushed with icy breath by the dandyish name of Odilon Redon, who caught like no one else, this look of things in the mirror of nothingness, and who understood, like no one else, how to join with things in their collusion of non-being. The whispering of gazes fills the arcades." Benjamin subsequently quotes from his young friend Theodor Adorno's book on the philosopher Kierkegaard, specifically the agency of mirrored window as a function of the latter's agnostic existentialist philosophy that is images of interiors … as the great motif of (philosophical) reflection. "The function of the window mirror is to project the endless row of apartment buildings into the encapsulated bourgeois living room; by this means, the living room dominates the reflected row at the same time that it is delimited by it."[34]

I am reminded here of artist Robert Morris's untitled *Mirror Boxes* (1965), and later Dan Graham's canonical mirror and video works: *TV Camera performance* (1970) staged at NSCAD in 1970; *time delay rooms* and *opposing mirrors and video monitors on time delay* and the artist's *'Picture Window' piece*, all from 1974;[35] and Graham's later mirrored glass pavilions *Octagon for Muenster* (1987) and *Double Triangular Pavilion* (1989), each of which invoke the Merleau-Pontyian philosophy of perception associated with experiencing these in phenomenological terms that became an indispensible feature of the minimalist aesthetic. This, perhaps, is an enigma that becomes a paradox, a space that, arbitarily, becomes place. As students at NSCAD in the late 1980s, Fitzgerald and Ellis were exposed to the publications documenting Graham's work and, given their self-proclaimed status as film television and video art buffs, would have acknowledged the theoretical premises of this protoypical work with mirrors and mirroring, if not necessarily Merleau-Ponty's phenomenological theory that subscribes it.

> The enigma is that my body simultaneously sees and is seen. That which looks at things can also look at itself and recognise in what it sees, the 'other side' of its power of looking. It sees itself seeing, it touches itself touching; it is visible and sensitive to itelf. It is not a self through transparence, like thought, which only thinks its object by inherence of seeing in the sensed, a self therefore that is caught up in things, that has a assimilating it by transforming it into thought. It is a self through confusion, narcissism, through front, a back, a past and a future.... This initial paradox cannot but produce others. Visible and mobile, my body is a thing among things; it is caught in the fabric of the world, and its cohesion is that of a thing. But because it moves itself and sees, it holds things in a circle around itself.[36]

I am tempted here to invoke the name of Alfred Hitchcock, whose mirrors and mirroring paradoxes are legion among Hitchcock scholars, and one of a number of not so arbitrary signature features of his work. Hitchcock was also an important figure discussed in film theory history texts and in film studies classes during the time that Ellis and Fitzgerald were studying. Here we should mention key scenes from *Shadow of a Doubt*, *Rear Window* and *Vertigo* to illustrate how Hitchcock's use of mirrors and mirroring, windows and doors stimulate/simulate a philosophy of reflection and simultaneously an enunciation of place in space. French Hitchcock scholar Raymond Bellour has undertaken some brilliant analyses – readings – of

ARBITRARY PRODUCTIONS

Hitchcock's films. He argues that the mirrored construction "endlessly re-
fracted" of several of Hitchcock's films

> reveal the prerogative and purpose of a certain kind of cin-
> ema of representation: to privilege the imagistic nature of what
> is at stake here by stopping, as it were, its vertiginous movement
> by doubling it; the mechanism of the lure, cinema, becomes,
> through the work of enunciation in the film, the condition of
> pleasure by creating a mirror construction endlessly refracted,
> the irreducible gap of the scopic drive. Pleasure is the image that
> must be assimilated, retrieved; the impossible real, like murder,
> which is the sadistic reversal of pleasure. For the man-subject
> who is behind the camera, this image of fear or pleasure ascribed
> to woman as other is the bedrock of his fantasy. This is also for
> Hitchcock what it means to enunciate.[37]

But with Bellour's (and Hitchcock's) "irreducible gap of the scopic drive"
perhaps we end up in Freud – Matthew's Halifax Queen Street apartment
and Sweet William's parent's house – again (via Lacan); "the idea of another
locality, another space, another scene, between perception and consciousness."[38] For what are mirrors but uncanny doors that are both open and
closed simultaneously – an eclipsed space, yet an identifiable place – such as
Marcel Duchamp's apartment at Rue Larey where the door (1927) swings
one way, opening one domestic space, while closing the other. And if you
will excuse the pun, the door in Duchamp's place is always ajar.

NOTES

1   Jean Baudrillard, *Simulacres et Simulation* (Paris: Galilée (Editions), 1986), 146.

2   Arbitrary is used here in its widest connotations to corral the meanings associated with impulse or caprice, lightness, fancy, or improvisational manner, impulse, whim, or gay. Arbitrary Productions was also the name of the film company that Thom Fitzgerald and Andrew Ellis established to produce *The Movie of the Week* (1990).

3   Other feature length films had been made involving NSCAD before this, notably William McGillivray's *Life Classes* (1987), which uses the school as a key location, and his documentary about the place: *I Will Not Make Any More Boring Art* (1987). MacGillivray was an MA Student in Art Education in the mid-1970s who withdrew from the program before completing his thesis.

4   Rainer, Graham, and Snow have published work through the NSCAD Press, and many have their work and that of students in the non-print collection of the NSCAD Library.

5   Other notable instructors are: Dara Birnbaum, Joyann Saunders, Paula Levine, Gary Kibbins, Ed Slopek, Kathleen Tetlock, Fred McFadzen, and Chris Woods. Students include: Doug Waterman, Albert McNamara, Brian Macnevin, Dorit Cypis, Susan Britton, Wendy Geller, Linda-Joy Busby, Alex Busby, Mark Verabioff, Marc Adornato, Anne Verrall, Liz MacDougall, Stephen O'Keefe, Michael Greer, Katherine Stockhausen, and Dawn Windover, to name but a few. Invoking these names obviously suggests a much larger project, probably a separate monograph on NSCAD Film and Video. See appendix in Bruce Barber, *NSCAD Film and Video Then and Now* exhibition catalogue.

6   NSCAD University now offers a BFA major in Film and will soon institute a Master of Film degree program.

7   B. Barber, ed., *NSCAD: The 80s* (Anna Leonowens Gallery Exhibition catalogue, 2006), online http://www.nscad.ns.ca/pdf/NSCADThe80s.pdf.

8   The directors of *The Movie of the Week* were Andrew Ellis (listed in the credits as producer, director, editor, Director of Photography and in the role of 'Jonathan'); Thom Fitzgerald (playing the role of Matthew), whose credits list a one-act play *The Tongue of Man* produced at the Hewitt Hall, NYC in 1988 and bit parts in several films and videos; Angela Baker (editor and sound editor) with sound editing credits for William MacGillivray's *I Will Not Make Any More Boring Art* and *The Vacant Lot* and *Jackass Johnny*. Baker has produced two of her own films, *The Boland Twirlers* and *Where Duty Leads*; Stephen O'Keefe, a graduate from NSCAD Intermedia as Lighting director; Gary Swim (Brandy) production; and location manager Jordan Broadworth (The Televised Man) from Toronto.

9   Ellis and Fitzgerald, *The Movie of the Week* synopsis (promotional material in the author's personal collection).

10 Jean-Louis Baudry, "From the World in a Frame," in Mast, Cohen, and Baudry, eds., *Film Theory and Criticism*, 4th ed. (New York and Oxford: Oxford University Press, 1992).

11 As Baudry argues, the omniscient spectator/subject is positioned as both produced by, and *the effect* of, the cinematic text. Both Fitzgerald and Ellis were aware of contemporary developments in film theory through their classes at NSCAD and were enrolled in survey film history classes in which film history and theory texts were assigned. For example, Ellis writes in his studio summary for work that he would undertake in the semester he was engaged in editing MOTW. "After an intensive summer of reading film analysis/theory and critiques and devouring films that were produced between 1920 and 1950 (the 'golden age' of film that I feel has directed Western societies' values and moral

standards and continues to do so today), I realized that heterosexual society had had eighty-nine years of positive image reinforcement that by its very exclusive nature, has instilled an innate sense of self-loathing in not only Gay people but in EVERYONE (emphasis in original) who did not fit these images of who we (the public) supposedly are."

12   *The Movie of the Week* plot summary.

13   The apartment location in Queen Street, Halifax was rented by Jan Peacock, who acted as Thom Fitzgerald's studio advisor during the shooting of *The Movie of the Week*. Andrew Ellis's studio advisor was this author.

14   Ron Foley Macdonald, "Representation under Siege," Toronto *FUSE* (June–July 1990): 30.

15   Interview with Baudrillard by "Henri" posted on European Graduate School listserv, 25 April 2007.

16   *The Hanging Garden* was extraordinarily successful for a first feature, garnering major film festival awards at the Atlantic Film Festival, the Vancouver Film festival, and the Mar del Plata Festival in Argentina. It was voted most popular film at the Toronto International Film Festival and was awarded four Genie Awards. Fitzgerald also won the Claude Jutra award for best direction of a First Feature.

17   See Andrew Burke's discussion of this in his contribution to this book. See also Malek Khouri, "Other-ing the Worker in Canadian 'Gay Cinema': Thom Fitzgerald's *The Hanging Garden*," in Darrell Varga and Malek Khouri, eds., *Working on Screen: Representations of the Working Class in Canadian Cinema* (Toronto: University of Toronto Press, 2006), 134–47.

18   Paperwhites of the daffodil family (*Narcissus papyraceus*, from *papyrus* and *aceus*, meaning paper-like) are part of the Narcissus genus. The myth of Narcissus related in Ovid's *Metamorphoses* had an important influence on English Victorian homoerotic culture through the writings of Oscar Wilde, particularly the author's *The Picture of Dorian Gray* and also through the influence of Andre Gide's study of the myth, *Traite du Narcisse (The Treatise of the Narcissus)*, 1891. Narcissus was also a popular subject of the Pre-Raphaelite painters.

19   Rudolf Gasche, *The Tain of the Mirror: Derrida and the Philosophy of Reflection* (Cambridge, MA: Harvard University Press, 1986).

20   Ibid., 54.

21   Friedrich Nietszche, *Aphorism 243* of *Daybreak: Thoughts on the prejudices of morality.* quoted in Martin Jay, *Downcast Eyes: The Denigration of Vision in Twentieth-Century French Thought* (Berkeley: University of California Press, 1994), 31n.

22   Melville in Brennan and Jay, *Vision in Context: Historical and Contemporary Perspectives on Sight*, ed. Teresa Brennan and Martin Jay (New York: Routledge, 1996), 111.

23   Benjamin Goldberg, *The Mirror and the Man* (Charlottesville: University of Virginia Press, 1985), 243.

24   Michel Foucault, *The Order of Things: An Archeology of the Human Sciences* (New York: Vintage Books 1973), 7–8.

25   Ibid., 8.

26   Ibid.

27   Walter Benjamin, *The Arcades Project*, trans. Howard Eiland and Kevin McLaughlin (Cambridge, MA, and London: Belknap/Harvard Press, 1999).

28   Ibid., 537.

29   Ibid., 538.

30   Goldberg, 538.

31   Ibid., 541.

32   Ibid., 65–66.

33   Ibid. 66.

34   Theodor Adorno, *Critical Models: Interventions and Catchwords*, trans. H. Pickford (New York: Columbia University Press, 1998), 45; in Benjamin, 542.

35   Published in Dan Graham, *Video-Architecture-Television* (Halifax: NSCAD Press, 1979).

36 Maurice Merleau Ponty, *The Primacy of Perception: And Other Essays on Phenomenological Psychology, the Philosophy of Art, History and Politics*, ed. James M. Edie, trans. William Cobb (Evanston, IL: Northwestern University Press, 1964), 162–63.

37 Raymond Bellour, *The Analysis of Film* (Bloomington, Indiana University Press 2000), 237.

38 Jacques Lacan, *The Four Fundamental Concepts of Psychoanalysis* (New York: Norton, 1978).

11

SITE SPECIFIC: VISUALIZING THE VERNACULAR IN ANDREA DORFMAN'S *PARSLEY DAYS*

ANDREW BURKE

Bicycles play a significant role in Andrea Dorfman's debut feature, *Parsley Days* (2000). Not only is the protagonist, Kate, an expert in bicycle repair, but the film is also punctuated by a series of shots of Kate and others cycling through the streets of North End Halifax. The symbolic force of these images vastly outweighs whatever narrative function they may serve. These journeys by bike may get the characters from one scene to another, but, more importantly, they place them within a specific landscape and constitute a symbolic representation of their dreams, desires, and dilemmas. Moreover, the cyclist's eye view seems an appropriate figure for Dorfman's filmmaking practice itself. *Parsley Days* is a film immersed in, and committed to, the city and community it represents. In what follows I examine *Parsley Days* as a Maritime film that represents a compellingly contemporary Halifax and captures the texture of the everyday lives of its young characters as part of the fabric of the Haligonian cityscape.

Originally from Toronto, Dorfman's work to date binds her inextricably to the Maritimes and to Halifax in particular. Her two features, *Parsley Days* and *Love That Boy* (2003), are both set in Halifax: the setting for the former is the city's North End while the latter is set in the more suburban West End. Even though the city is never named as such in either film, the distinctive, vernacular architecture of the North End is immediately recognizable to viewers of *Parsley Days* familiar with the city. In addition to the architectural distinctiveness that grounds *Parsley Days* in a particular neighbourhood experience, Dorfman captures something of the surge in creative energy that characterized the city as a whole in the 1990s. Her characters circulate within a bohemian milieu fed by Halifax's art and music scenes and nurtured by the culture of its many universities. Her deft and empathetic representation of the lives of young artistic Haligonians is perhaps not surprising given that she studied at the Nova Scotia College of Art and Design (NSCAD). Graduating in 1994, Dorfman remained in Halifax and made several short experimental films under the auspices of the Atlantic Filmmaker's Co-op. As is so often the case with cultural production that emerges from the margins, *Parsley Days* seemed to some reviewers to have come out of nowhere. Yet the film, remarkably assured for a debut feature and distinguished by a well-established set of aesthetic preoccupations and a fully formed visual style, draws on both Dorfman's short work and a history of Atlantic Canadian filmmaking (particularly the work of William D. MacGillivray, Lulu Keating, and Thom Fitzgerald) in its form and substance.

Parsley Days tells the story of Kate who, in the midst of deciding how best to break to her boyfriend Ollie that she no longer wants to be in a relationship with him, discovers that she is pregnant. The film resists the temptation to shape the narrative around Kate's decision of whether or not to have the baby. She stands firm from the outset in her choice to have an abortion. The substance of the narrative rests in Kate gathering the courage to tell Ollie that she does not love him anymore. What makes this task particularly onerous is that she and Ollie are universally perceived to be the perfect couple. Indeed, they have become so inseparable in the eyes of their friends and families that they are known as "KateandOllie," a hybrid formation that has subsumed and liquidated their individual identities. *Parsley Days* is at heart the story of Kate's painful reclamation of an individual identity from within a relationship that on the surface does not seem in any way repressive or exploitative. Although it later emerges that Ollie isn't quite as perfect as he appears, Kate's decision is rendered all the more difficult by the general perception of Ollie as a caring, gentle partner.

Through Kate, Dorfman examines why, despite being enmeshed in a relationship and immersed within a community, it is nevertheless possible to feel alienated and alone. In a sequence during which Kate thinks back on the very beginnings of her relationship with Ollie, she comments in voice-over that "no matter who you are or who you are with, we are all ultimately alone." Dorfman presents Kate's predicament in striking visual

Megan Dunlop as Kate in *Parsley Days*, courtesy of Mongrel Media.

terms throughout the film. Ensnared in the final, numbing moments of a relationship that has effectively ended, Kate complains that she "can't feel anything anymore." Dorfman's camera captures a kind of catatonic blankness on Kate's face in these moments as she reaches inside for the feelings of guilt or sadness she should be having but is not. Later, when a friend prattles on rapturously about her latest love, Kate is shown in a parka and scarf and the sound of a blizzard drowns out the lover's nonsense that she can no longer bear.

Parsley Days is filled with these magical moments in which Kate's feelings are externalized and presented visually in a manner that breaks with strict realism. In this way, Dorfman's work can be connected to that of Thom Fitzgerald. In *The Hanging Garden* (1997), a film on which Dorfman served as a camera assistant, Fitzgerald crafts a story in which the past and the possible frequently irrupt into the present. Just as Fitzgerald has, for example, three embodiments of his protagonist onscreen simultaneously in order to show how the present bears within it the tensions and traumas of the past, so too do Dorfman's films frequently present the possibilities pregnant in the same moment. A common Dorfman strategy is to craft a fantasy sequence that shows how a scenario might unfold, or could tragically or would ideally unfold, only to cut back to show how things take place in reality. The climactic scene of *Parsley Days*, in which Kate cycles to a surprise party being thrown in her honour, operates in precisely this fashion. From the perspective of her bicycle saddle, she imagines a series of possible scenarios, both positive and negative, right up to the moment when she arrives and the real events play out. This counterfactual presentation of what could or should occur allows for the depiction of her characters' deepest desires and anxieties. Although two filmmakers do not necessarily constitute a full-blown school or movement, Fitzgerald and Dorfman both draw on the opportunities that magical realism provides in order to give concrete representation to internal dilemmas and psychic deadlocks, but also to represent something of the contradictions of contemporary Maritime life more generally.

As a mode, magical realism aims to overcome the limits of realism by introducing fantastical or supernatural elements, events, or occurrences that articulate the repressed truth of real conditions of existence. As such, the mode, from its origins in Latin American fiction, has long been understood as having progressive political potential, especially for subordinated and marginalized groups. Tom Waugh includes Fitzgerald's *The Hanging*

Garden in his Queer Canadian Canon and, although he does not address it directly, the film's use of magical realism can be understood as a representational strategy which, by challenging the restrictions of orthodox realism, also contests the hetero-normative assumptions that govern the reality that realism characteristically aims to represent and reproduce.[1] A similar queering of realism obtains in *Parsley Days*, since the film denaturalizes the hetero-normative force of its central relationship by giving voice to Kate's profound disillusion and disenchantment with the very idea of a romantic relationship. The film does not suggest that Kate is a lesbian, but rather has her question the social imperative to couple. When a friend observes that she is "the other half that makes up the whole" to Ollie, she feebly responds, "I am a whole person." She is able to assert this with greater and greater force as the narrative proceeds, but the hesitancy with which it is first said is an indication of why Dorfman finds visual figuration for Kate's predicament in an image of cold, windswept isolation. Kate is isolated within a community (and a wider world) that puts a premium on the idea of the romantic relationship. In her alienation from this social imperative, Kate is out of joint with her community and surroundings.

While *Parsley Days* and *The Hanging Garden* both draw on magical realism to destabilize society's governing hetero-normative assumptions, they also do so in order to represent something of the uncanny strangeness of Maritime life itself.[2] Indeed, each film treads a careful path in its representation of the Maritimes as a space and culture distinct from that of the rest of the country. The inherent danger in representing the particularity and peculiarity of a regional space is the sentimentalization of those elements that mark that place as different. In the case of Nova Scotia, the risk comes in the temptation to hypostasize provincial culture in a mythical past. As Ian McKay explains, this is precisely what happened to Nova Scotian culture over the course of the twentieth century:

> As tourism, folklore, and handicrafts all developed in the twentieth century, the people of the fishing villages came to be see as bearers of Nova Scotia's cultural essence: they became archetypal Nova Scotians living not on a barren patch of Atlantic shoreline, but on a mythified "Coast of Songs," which rang with their ballads and merriment. They came to be represented as stout-hearted, resourceful fisherfolk, who led a "simple life" by the sea, untroubled by urban stresses, nourished by the natural

beauty all around them.... These people and those like them became the Folk.[3]

Needless to say, any such vision of the rural picturesque is dramatically out of sync with the historical conditions of poverty from which the image ultimately derives as well as being incongruent with contemporary Nova Scotian life. Indeed, the performance of rural simplicity and general salt-of-the-earthiness for a touristic other is characteristically a modern phenomenon, an attempt to capitalize on the very conditions of poverty that the performance fetishistically embodies.

As such, magical realism does not represent an avenue of escape from the difficulties of real life, but rather constitutes an effort to depict the contradictions that structure it. In terms of the Maritimes, the lived experience of uneven development is one of mixed temporalities. The force of the mythified past is such that the present does not seem fully itself and the future, especially when it is spoken of in economic terms, seems condemned to being some perpetual recreation of the past in the form of an elaborate and profitable pastiche. This dilemma, perhaps not surprisingly, has had a profound influence on the province's film and television production. On the one hand, there is a long tradition of heritage productions, which, to varying degrees, draw on or diverge from dominant conceptions of the provincial past. Films such as *The Bay Boy* (1984, Daniel Petrie) or *Margaret's Museum* (1996, Mort Ransen), and television productions such as *Pit Pony* (1997–2002), on which Dorfman worked as an assistant cameraperson, serve as examples of productions that offer a limited critique of the mystifications of heritage cinema even as they parasitically draw energies from the form itself. On the other hand, there are works such as *The Trailer Park Boys* (television 1999–, film 2006, Mike Clattenberg) which, despite how they challenge the maintenance and manufacture of folk innocence that seems to plague even the most critical of heritage productions, end up producing other kinds of regional stereotypes that seem equally contradictory and problematic.

Parsley Days offers a way out of this dilemma not by effacing the differences between Maritime life and life elsewhere, but by immersing its characters in a deeply historical neighbourhood that is nevertheless very much part of the modern city. Dorfman conveys something general about the way in which community, wherever it may be and however it may take shape, influences the identities of those within it. To do so she draws upon the look and feel of a specific neighbourhood: Halifax's North End. The North End has historically been home to Halifax's working classes. As such, it suffered immensely during the long period of economic decline that followed on the heels of the city's modest postwar success. While the South End has long housed Halifax's professional classes and features many stately homes, the North End is characterized by a distinctive vernacular architecture. In recent years the neighbourhood has attracted a large number of young people, both students and those involved in the arts and small-scale cultural production. As a result, it has become home to a marginalized but fiercely independent community. The simple, colourful, boxy houses of the area are featured prominently throughout *Parsley Days* and, combined with the narrow, hilly streets, they serve as a metaphor for the closeness of community and the comforts of place. Indeed, as Jennifer Gauthier argues: "Dorfman uses a number of repeated images to emphasize her characters' sense of embeddedness in their local surroundings: Kate and Ollie biking through the neighborhood, Kate meeting her friends in the park or at the produce market, and Kate teaching her bike repair class in the community centre. These scenes ground the movie in Kate's everyday reality, despite the unusual circumstances in which she finds herself."[4] In addition to this, the specific topographical features of the North End also allow Dorfman to place her characters within a larger social frame. The streets on which *Parsley Days* are mostly shot stretch from the Halifax Commons down to the harbour. As a result, they provide a backdrop that is frequently askew, the foundations of the houses angled against the slope of the streets. This provides a visual metaphor for the characters. They are young people who are slightly out of sync, or off-level, with the world around them, existing in that liminal space between university and full-blown adulthood. Dorfman captures this moment of fleeting freedom and the sense of its precariousness very precisely, and she does it not simply through narrative, but through setting as well.

More problematic is the way in which *Parsley Days* focuses almost exclusively on this bohemian milieu at the cost of capturing the diversity of the neighbourhood and city in which they live. This is, on the one hand, perhaps not surprising given the virtual segregation that has historically split and separated communities (along lines of both class and race) in Halifax and, lamentably, continues to do so in the present day. The North End of Halifax was the site of Africville, an Afro-Canadian community that was forcibly displaced with the construction of the A. Murray MacKay Bridge and the expansion of the Port of Halifax in the mid-1960s.[5] The forced relocation of the residents of Africville has come to symbolize the deep racism that pervades Nova Scotian culture. Even though the destruction of Africville meant the scattering of the Black community to public housing closer to the city centre and to suburban sites such as Spryfield, a substantial Black community remains in the North End. In its representation of the neighbourhood, *Parsley Days* is constricted by the limitations of Kate's community, the tight circle of connections that give rise to the feelings of claustrophobia she experiences. Nevertheless, given the degree to which the film cinematically reproduces the organic street life of the North End, it is somewhat surprising that the signs of its traumatic past and the continued presence of its Black community do not find greater representation.[6] Yet, ironically, it is precisely in this elision and absence that the film is true to the historical divisions that structure Haligonian society. More recently, Dorfman has directed episodes of CBC's *North/South* (2006), a serialized television drama which focuses specifically on the racial and class divisions that geographically structure the Maritime city. *North/South* sticks to the conventions of soap opera, and while working within a genre places constraints on Dorfman's characteristic visual and narrative style, it also allows her to work on a broader canvas and with a greater range of characters than her modestly budgeted feature films have permitted. As such, in the interaction of four families of different classes and ethnicities, *North/South* presents a compelling picture of a contemporary city that bears the scars of historical antagonisms and traumas.

Whatever its limitations in terms of signalling both the presence and historical import of the North End's Black community, the film is in other ways engaged with the history of the city and the province. Once again, this is grounded in the film's representations of the North End and the streetscapes that define the area. In the past twenty years, the neighbourhood has been modernized, and to a certain extent the processes of gentrification have displaced the Black and working-class communities that have historically lived there, and even erased their contributions to the neighbourhood. *Parsley Days*, in contrast, dramatizes the sustainability of a neighbourhood, and even the desirability of traditional neighbourliness, in the way that it is grounded in a transformed, but not gentrified, neighbourhood.

There is an analogue to be made here with the work of Brian MacKay-Lyons, a Nova Scotia architect who has undertaken several projects in the

North End of Halifax in the past twenty years. Taking as his inspiration the vernacular buildings and maritime landscape of Nova Scotia, MacKay-Lyons has developed an architectural style that is regionalist without being sentimentalist. He draws on vernacular forms (barns, boat sheds, even boats themselves), yet eschews the ornamentation and romanticization that usually accompanies reworkings of the traditional. MacKay-Lyons's residential projects in particular exemplify the way in which the rigour of high modernism and its commitment to formal sparseness is in its own way matched by the vernacular plainness of traditional Nova Scotian buildings. His residential architecture stands at this intersection of tradition and modernity, and explores the conjunction, to echo the title of Malcolm Quantrill's book on MacKay-Lyons, of the plain and the modern.[7]

A tangible connection between MacKay-Lyons and *Parsley Days* is that his building at 2042 Maynard Street is featured in the film, and its exterior is used as Ollie's community contraceptive centre.[8] But beyond this direct connection, there is also a way in which MacKay-Lyons' architectural grammar and composition overlaps with Dorfman's cinematic vocabulary and phrasing. Indeed, both are concerned with community and its persistence, but they also share a commitment to simple construction and basic materials drawn from what is locally available. As such, both are committed to what might be termed a craft aesthetic. As MacKay-Lyons explains, "These projects employ a low-tech or 'folk-tech' approach to construction. They are, for the most part, within the vernacular material culture of the place that they sit."[9] The houses MacKay-Lyons has built in the North End of Halifax reference the area's traditional domestic architecture (the iconic box-framed, shingled, street-adjacent working-class house), but also integrate nautical and industrial elements that link them to the nearby Port of Halifax and the shipyards that have historically been central to the North End's economy. In terms of Dorfman's filmmaking practice, the commitment to a "vernacular material culture," to use MacKay-Lyons' phrase, translates into an indie aesthetic that thrives on location shooting and the particularity of place, mobilizes a repertoire of actors and non-actors as performers, forges connections between cinema and other artistic practices (including music, painting, photography, conceptual art, and literature), and, finally, imagines craft as art and art as craft.

Both Dorfman and Mackay-Lyons draw on the past in order to generate forms that speak to and inhabit the present. They visualize the vernacular in such a way that makes it part of the present rather than a residual

The Mackay-Lyons building on Maynard Street in North End Halifax, used as a location in *Parsley Days*. Photo by Darrell Varga.

or mythified element of the past. For Dorfman, this attentiveness to the relationship between past and present, art and craft continues and extends debates that have long been central to the Nova Scotia arts community. Indeed, the Nova Scotia College of Art and Design is central to these debates as they have played out both nationally and internationally. NSCAD's rise to prominence in international art circles in the late sixties and seventies had much to do with the growth and development of conceptualism within a local sphere that seemed much more hospitable to traditional forms of artistic practice. The success of NSCAD during that period did not rest on any wholesale repudiation of the local and vernacular, but rather understood it to be as compatible with and hospitable to avant-garde aesthetic practices as traditional ones.[10] Dorfman's time at NSCAD came after the years usually described as the College's golden ones, yet Halifax and NSCAD remained a crucial site of debate about the uses and abuses of the past in art well into the nineties, not least because of the rise in aesthetic standing of folk art. Indeed, as Cliff Eyland has argued, the "vernacular" is perhaps preferable to the idea of the "folk" because of its inherent elasticity. In his catalogue introduction to a 1994 exhibition of Nova Scotia art at the Dalhousie Art Gallery, Eyland explains that a greater variety of work can be assembled under the rubric of the vernacular than that of the folk since the latter seems to exclude those whose belonging to the place is mediated, or even contaminated, by formal training:

> Several of the art educated artists in this show are not simply making, as might be expected from their training, art historical references when they quote vernacular art. Their commitment to the content of their work runs much deeper than the word "reference" would suggest. Conversely, the "folk" artists in this exhibition make their work to a professional standard, sometimes through the direct influence of art world professionals. Very often the professional and the primitive meet half way.[11]

Eyland's argument is instructive in thinking about the practice of both Dorfman and Mackay-Lyons, as neither of them simply refer to the vernacular but rather integrate it into the very substance of their work. The latter routinely incorporates vernacular elements, particularly those relating to the shipbuilding and fishing industries, into his structures, while Dorfman, perhaps in a more oblique fashion, has her characters adopt a variety of traditional craft forms, most notably knitting. In each case, the vernacular generates a sense of location and tradition without being in thrall to either, and thereby bypasses the pitfalls of both antimodernism and folk nostalgia that Ian McKay so thoroughly documents in *The Quest of the Folk*.

The title of *Parsley Days* itself signals the film's interest in questions of the past and memory. When Kate learns that she cannot get an appointment at the abortion clinic for three weeks, she consults her herbalist friend Chloe (Marcia Connelly), who tells her that parsley is a natural emmenagogue capable of inducing abortion. Kate dutifully begins a parsley regime, eating copious amounts of the herb, bathing in it, and even, following Chloe's instructions to the letter, inserting it vaginally each night. As such, the film in a quite literal sense recounts Kate's parsley days. Dorfman's modification of the idiomatic expression "salad days" is significant. The phrase itself derives from Shakespeare's *Antony and Cleopatra* and is used by Cleopatra to describe the idealism and innocence of her youthful adventures. Reference to "salad days" has come to signify both the nostalgic reminiscence of a person's own vanished youth and a more general lament for lost innocence and the passing of a golden era. The term signifies the process of recollecting the perfection and purity of innocent days, yet it also points to how the errors of inexperience and youthful indiscretions form the intrinsic substance of melancholic reflection. While the concept of salad days conjures up a whole set of nostalgic fantasies most routinely associated with the grand spectacle of heritage cinema, the idea of parsley days invokes a sense of the past on a much smaller scale and far more intimate in its traumas and tensions. Even if Kate is in many ways representative of her milieu, precariously poised between a prolonged adolescence and the full traumas of adulthood, the film thankfully never raises her to the position of a generational emblem or waxes nostalgic about the innocence of youthful days. What the film accomplishes instead is an examination of how it is in and through its loss that the past is truly valuable. Kate worries throughout the film that leaving Ollie will result in her forgetting the happy times they had together, but in reality it is only when she severs herself from that past that the work of memory can begin. Before that moment she is in the grip of melancholic nostalgia, desperate for a future she cannot quite imagine and held back by the sheer weight of the past.[12]

Before Kate is able to confess to Ollie the news that she no longer loves him, Ollie has his own confession. He tells Kate that he deliberately punctured a condom so that she would become pregnant. This revelation has little emotional effect on Kate, but finally does give her the courage to tell Ollie how she truly feels. The entire scene takes place with the two of them sitting in a canoe in the backyard of Kate's North End home. An earlier montage sequence had established a summer at the lake as Kate and Ollie's happiest time together and the canoe as the symbol of the blissful early days of their relationship. By the end, however, their relationship has literally run aground. They spend the night lying entwined and reminiscing of what has passed, but the striking image of them in a canoe grounded on the grassy green of an urban backyard conveys the impossibility of returning to the past even as it communicates the difficulty in giving up the desire to do so.

Given the symbolic importance of Kate's bicycle, it is significant that bit by bit throughout the film parts of her bike are stolen. By the time she is almost completely worn down by her anxieties about telling Ollie the truth, her bicycle has been stripped bare and only the skeletal frame remains. This serves as a striking visual metaphor for how Kate fears that, without Ollie, she too might be reduced to nothingness. Yet there are two events that enable Kate to confront Ollie. First, her bicycle repair students give her a replacement bicycle, complete with a knitted bicycle sweater to protect it from the world. Second, the "slow student" from her class with whom she has shared a stolen kiss returns her original bicycle fully reconstructed, the parts having been stolen by his jealous girlfriend. The news of Kate's indiscretion shatters the public sense of the couple's perfection and paves the way for her to break with Ollie. But the gift from her class also facilitates Kate's decision in that it demonstrates that she has the love and support of her friends and community. As such, these two bicycles are the symbolic vehicles for Kate's future freedom as much as they have literally been the means by which she, over the course of the film, has navigated the streets of her North End Halifax community. *Parsley Days* is a film about being grounded in a history and a place, but in its breaks with strict realism, use of the vernacular, and recognition that the past can be acknowledged without being wholly determining, the film provides an example of contemporary Atlantic Canadian filmmaking that has its eye to the future.

NOTES

My thanks go to Holly Procktor, Stephanie Whitehouse, Candida Rifkind, and Andrea Dorfman for their assistance and advice in the preparation of this article.

1   See Thomas Waugh, "Cinemas, Nations, Masculinities (The Martin Walsh Memorial Lecture 1998)," *Canadian Journal of Film Studies/ Revue Canadienne D'Études Cinématographiques*, 8(1) (Spring 1999): 8–44; Waugh, *The Romance of Transgression in Canada: Queering Sexualities, Nations, Cinemas* (Montreal: McGill-Queen's University Press, 2006), 414. For a discussion of the importance of magical realism to postcolonial criticism see Stephen Slemon, "Magic Realism as Postcolonial Discourse," in *Magical Realism: Theory, History, Community*, ed. Lois Parkinson Zamora and Wendy B. Faris (Durham, NC: Duke University Press, 1995): 407–26. For a consideration of the role magical realism has played in contemporary Canadian fiction that pays special attention to its role in Nova Scotian literature, see Jennifer Andrews, "Rethinking the Relevance of Magic Realism for English-Canadian Literature: Reading Ann-Marie MacDonald's *Fall on Your Knees*," *Studies in Canadian Literature* 24(1) (1999): 1–19.

2   Malek Khouri argues that the queer politics of *The Hanging Garden* are compromised by a retrogressive representation of its working-class characters. Khouri is surely right to point to the ways in which Fitzgerald's film presents its character's liberation from the homophobia of his working-class roots to be thoroughly wrapped up in the acquisition of social and cultural capital, but in contending that *"The Hanging Garden* presents a much too abstract rendering of a concrete dilemma," he neglects to see precisely the way in which the concrete can be expressed through the abstract: Malek Khouri, "Other-ing the Worker in Canadian 'Gay Cinema': Thom Fitzgerald's *The Hanging Garden*," in *Working on Screen: Representations of the Working Class in Canadian Cinema*, ed. Malek Khouri and Darrell Varga (Toronto: University of Toronto Press, 2006), 141. For all the possible criticism of the content of the narrative, its chosen mode, whether it is put in terms of hyperrealism, surrealism (both positions Khouri identifies in criticism of the film), or magical realism, does not preclude a material and concrete analysis made via the metaphysical and abstract. For more on the avenues of political critique opened up by magical realism as well as the limitations of the mode, see Fredric Jameson, "On Magical Realism in Film," *Signatures of the Visible* (New York and London: Routledge, 1992), 128–52.

3   Ian McKay, *The Quest of the Folk: Antimodernism and Cultural Selection in Twentieth-Century Nova Scotia* (Kingston and Montreal: McGill-Queen's University Press, 1994), xv–xvi.

4   Jennifer Gauthier, "Where is Here?: Local Visions in Three Canadian Films," *Canadian Journal of Film Studies/Revue Canadienne D'études Cinématographiques* 14(2) (2005): 42.

5   For more on the history of Africville and its ongoing political and cultural significance, see Donald H. Clairmont and Dennis William Magill, *Africville: The Life and Death of a Canadian Black Community*, 3rd ed. (Toronto: Scholar's Press, 1999). There is also a National Film Board documentary, *Remember Africville* (1991), directed by Shelagh Mackenzie, that features footage of the razing of the community and interviews with many former residents. George Elliott Clarke's work, both critical and creative, comprises an ongoing engagement with the Black Nova Scotian, or Africadian, experience. See especially Clarke's review of Mackenzie's film: George Elliott Clarke, "The Death and Rebirth of Africadian Nationalism," in *Odysseys Home: Mapping African-Canadian*

Literature (Toronto: University of Toronto Press, 2002), 288–96.

6   *Life Classes* (1987, William D. MacGillivray) serves as an example of a Nova Scotia film that successfully integrates the history of the destruction of Africville into its contemporary narrative.

7   For a comprehensive overview of the work of MacKay-Lyons as well as an account of how the combination of regionalism and modernism in his work has garnered national and international acclaim, see Malcolm Quantrill, *Plain Modern: The Architecture of Brian MacKay-Lyons* (Princeton: Princeton Architectural Press, 2005).

8   The actual entrance is at 5658 Falkland St. About the project, MacKay-Lyons writes, "The blue clapboard row houses continue the residential grain of Falkland Street and extend it into a block where the original houses had burned down [...] The units are generic, side hall row houses built directly on the street line like their neighbors." ("2042 & 2086 Maynard Street," *Brian MacKay-Lyons: Projects 1986–97* (Halifax: TUNS Press, 1997), 79.)

9   Brian MacKay-Lyons, "Modest Means," *Brian MacKay-Lyons: Projects 1986–97* (Halifax: TUNS Press, 1997), 15.

10 William D. MacGillivray's 1988 documentary *I Will Not Make Any More Boring Art* provides an account of NSCAD's rise to international stature in the late sixties and seventies. In the film, MacGillivray observes how NSCAD to a certain degree bypassed the national as a frame of reference in its heyday, forging instead direct links between the local and the international.

11 Cliff Eyland, "Red Herrings, Clever Horses and the Benefits of Doubt," in *Uses of the Vernacular in Nova Scotian Art* (Halifax: Dalhousie Art Gallery, 1994), 9–24. Eyland's article remains the best discussion of the philosophical and political ramifications of the efflorescence of folk art in Nova Scotia from the seventies to the nineties. Eyland argues that the interest in folk art should not be understood to have developed subsequent to NSCAD's moment of high conceptualism, but rather was part and parcel of conceptualism's effort to displace traditional aesthetic forms. Eyland identifies Gerald Ferguson as an artist and curator who exemplifies the mutual compatibility between avant-garde and folk practices. Ferguson has been a professor at NSCAD since 1968 and curated what is usually identified as the first exhibition of Nova Scotia folk art at the Art Gallery of Nova Scotia in 1976. Eyland also lists Mackay-Lyons among those whose work fits with the remit of the exhibit but falls just outside it.

12 I draw here on Slavoj Žižek's revision of traditional understandings of melancholia. As conventionally conceived, melancholy signals the inability to give up the object even in the face of its disappearance or death. But, as Žižek argues, the condition belongs not to the period after the object has been lost, but to those moments before: "melancholy is not primarily directed at the paradisiacal past of organic balanced Wholeness which was lost due to some catastrophe, it is not a sadness caused by this loss; melancholy proper, rather, designates the attitude of those who *are* still in Paradise but are already longing to break out of it: of those who, although still in a closed universe, already possess a vague premonition of another dimension which is just out of their reach" (Slavoj Žižek, *The Fragile Absolute – or, Why is the Christian Legacy Worth Fighting For?* (London: Verso, 2000), 98). This is precisely Kate's predicament. She spends the majority of the film in the depths of melancholy, in the supposed paradise of a relationship with Ollie, haunted by the sense of its imminent end yet excited about what might come after.

12

THE SOCIAL PRODUCTION OF PLACE IN FOUR FILMS ABOUT ARTISTS

DARRELL VARGA

In this chapter I am interested in the dialectical relation between creative practice, the culture and politics of place and space, and how these terms are inflected under late capitalist conditions of media culture in this country. These conditions place the demand of international marketability onto independent cinema, posing a particular challenge to an art cinema practice that has an integral relation to the local and that has historically been sustained through state-funded cultural infrastructure. I examine the negotiation of these conditions through the figure of the artist in the following: *Life Classes* (Dir: William D. MacGillivray, 1987), *Candy Mountain* (Dir: Robert Frank and Rudy Wurlitzer, 1987), *New Waterford Girl* (Dir: Allan Moyle, 1999), and *Congratulations* (Dir: Mike Jones, 2000). These titles are by no means intended to represent the entirety of art film production in the Atlantic region; rather, they represent some of the possibilities and limits of the form as conditioned by their respective dates of production, from the zenith of the era of art cinema in the mid-1980s to the entrenchment of culture as industry at the end of the twentieth century.

Congratulations

Mike Jones is a key figure in the filmmaking scene in Newfoundland, working as the resident filmmaker for the comedy group Codco beginning in the 1970s as well as directing the feature films *The Adventure of Faustus*

Bidgood (1986), a wild political satire about a milquetoast bureaucrat who becomes president of the People's Republic of Newfoundland, and *Secret Nation* (1992), the comedy-conspiracy theory about Newfoundland joining Canadian Confederation. As in the stage and television work of Codco, these films situate regional difference within the framework of the rise of the modern technocratic nation-state and the chatter of a mass media culture. The target of satire is the peculiarities of language, social norms, gender and the mass media, political culture and the dominance of the Catholic church in Newfoundland life, as well as the marginalization of the region in the political and media discourse originating in central Canada. As Helen Peters describes the Toronto premiere of the first Codco theatre show *Cod on a Stick* in 1973: "The play was highly political, presenting Newfoundland culture to the mainland audience by turning the pain and embarrassment of being 'foreigners in a strange land' into side-splitting but pointed humour, a combination which left Ontario audiences not sure who was laughing at whom or why."[1]

There is a similarly uneasy relationship between the films of Mike Jones and the ethos of central Canada, an unease played out in *Congratulations* and throughout his work, beginning with his Codco collaborations. For instance, in *Sisters of the Silver Scalpel*, originally produced as part of the Codco stage play *Would You Like to Smell My ... Pocket Crumbs* (premiered in St. John's in 1975 and at Theatre Passe Mureille in Toronto in 1976), and completed as a film in 1981, the lead characters host a TV show called "Wilderness on Parade" and undertake a safari adventure to the Newfoundland hinterland in pursuit of a rare breed of nuns. They are anti-artist figures and serve as counterpoint to the discussion of *Congratulations* which follows. Upon arrival in "the socio-zoological wild country of Newfoundland," the TV-adventurers set up camp by expelling the residents of a rural dwelling, in a not too subtle reference to outport resettlement. In the televisual logic of the lead characters, which parodically mimics the logic of the church, a wild nun is "helped" by being captured and tied to the hood of their car as they drive through St. John's. Throughout the film, they speak with earnestly contented midwestern accents: "This little nun seems to have turned a blind eye to science. I guess she couldn't be expected to know, poor little thing, that what we were doing to her was for her own good. Would you just look at that, she just kept praying and praying the whole time." The voice of reason, paternally easing us into situations for our "own good," is set against the absurd logic of colonial relations.

THE SOCIAL PRODUCTION OF PLACE

Congratulations was commissioned as part of a series marking the twenty-fifth anniversary of the Toronto International Film Festival Group. The series included Jones and other directors from across the country (though most are based in central Canada), including Anne Wheeler, David Cronenberg, Atom Egoyan, Jean-Pierre Lefebvre, Guy Maddin (whose wild, Vertov-inspired film *Heart of the World* gained considerable acclaim in numerous international festival screenings), Don McKellar, Patricia Rozema, Jeremy Podeswa, and Michael Snow (the latter as the sole experimental filmmaker). Each director was given free rein to make a film on any subject but that would honour the festival by screening as a prelude to the regular programming during the event's anniversary year in 2000. In my experience attending the festival that year, audiences responded enthusiastically to Toronto icons Egoyan and McKellar, who each produced funny but inconsequential films based on the memories of their experiences with the festival prior to becoming "name" directors. These films, with references to the camaraderie of festival lineups and the idiosyncrasies of audiences, provided the satisfaction of an insider familiarity that is distinctly local but which implies the broader importance of the event to which that audience itself is invested. To my surprise, there was a less than generous response to Jones's *Congratulations*, which, on the one hand, is a straightforward commemoration of the festival but is also a sly parody of the antimodern construction of east coast life and of the dependent relation between the region and central Canada – where the film festival is one of a long history of cultural, social, and political institutions based in central Canada that exercise a measurable degree of power over regional activity insofar as the commercial market success of an independent Canadian film depends largely on receiving the imprimatur of quality signified by a festival screening.[2] In this respect, TIFF is the most important Canadian festival, presenting art cinema while also serving as a primary venue to the international cinema market where the latter is legitimized by the presence of the former.

Congratulations begins with the introduction of Jones, along with his brother Andy and sister Cathy, as "an ex-filmmaker of the cheap independent variety, a washed-up low-life television comedy actress, and a has-been stage actor dimly remembered now for his low-brow poo-poo humour." The setting is an old house by the ocean (shot in Bauline, Conception Bay) and the three, dressed in un-Toronto dirty work clothes, are hauling some firewood, digging in the garden, and carrying (in Mike's hands) a cod fish. The images emphasize not only regional underdevelopment but also the

Mike Jones, Cathy Jones, and Andy Jones in *Congratulations*, courtesy
Toronto International Film Festival Group.

displacement of gritty alternative cinema in the global marketing of independent film. *Congratulations* functions through a dialectic between the form of cinema and the fact of discord between region and centre. The film is also, in the words of Mike Jones, "autobiographical," insofar as he embodies the spirit of independent cinema in its gritty locality, a spirit displaced by the increasingly corporatized film industry.[3] The premise of the film is the honouring of the regional artist by employing him to honour and pledge allegiance to the central cultural institution, or ideological state apparatus in Althusser's terms, the festival itself. Indeed, the function of the centralized media industry is to suture together the nation in an imaginary coherence for the purpose of marketing symbolic exchange as culture industry for the global media marketplace. Consistent with industrial development in Canada, the region is a source of labour and provides a marketable and compliant folk image. While the short films do not in themselves have much exchange value, they serve to legitimize the institution, a major venue in the marketing of international cinema and for the launch of Hollywood product, as national centre of cultural value. What is being ironically congratulated, then, is the increased globalization of the culture industry and the diminishment of indie alternatives that evoke a specificity of place.

Regionalism has historically been a strong force of resistance to the centralization of power and the suturing together of Canada, and the articulation of regional distinctiveness has been an important component in the contemporary writing of Canadian history. In Atlantic Canada this task is carried out in the work of the *Acadiensis* scholars (as detailed in Colin Howell and Peter Twohig's contribution to this collection), against the grain of the "Laurentian Thesis" which situates Canadian political and economic activity in relation to the national centre.[4] Film Studies comes to this problem much later. As resistance to the coherence of the nationalist narrative began to take hold elsewhere, film scholars in Canada concentrated until recently on articulating a canon of national cinema that coherently articulates the nation.[5] Likewise in the context of critical theory, the concept of place and the local has been associated with the non-dialectical, while time has been formulated as the vehicle for history.[6] However, it is the specificity of place within a given text that undermines the hegemonic abstraction of the space of the nation; that is to say, the nation is not simply imagined but lived materially. These material conditions include conditions of labour, social organization and exchange, and access to resources, but also systems of symbolic exchange – cultural interaction, education, and the mass media.

Atlantic Canada as a concept is produced through specific material conditions and relations of exchange, but also through the production of an antimodernist narrative of innocence, particularly, as Ian Mckay has demonstrated, in the creation of a market for folk art and in the development of the tourism industry.[7] This marketing of place through a pre-industrial ideal erases the real conflicts through which place is formed, as Mckay suggests: "The emergence of the Folk was perfectly suited to the perspective of those who were seeking new ways of imagining their communities, yet who also had every reason to hope that these new ways would entail the restoration of a comforting conservative ideal."[8] Antimodernism is a frequent subject of parody in film and television production from the region; yet films and videos, as a consequence of the integration with the financial, juridical, and distribution apparatus, are necessarily modern forms of representation created through highly sophisticated uses of technology and the organization of labour, and integrated with the economic and institutional forces of the global media marketplace.

The tension between the new and the folk is played out in the skies over Newfoundland. Following the introduction of the Jones family a helicopter appears on the horizon, emblazoned with the logo of the Newfoundland Independent Film Cooperative (NIFCO) to lift this trio away from the outport and onto their mission in the imperial centre. The helicopter, this high-tech tool of military aggression, commodity image-making, and police surveillance, serves to affirm the central Canada stereotype of the wealth of subsidies available to regional cultural industries. It is a device that is the antithesis of alternative cinema – film co-operatives, especially in the earlier era of art cinema, are generally more likely to be equipped with a rusty wheelchair to facilitate moving camera shots, though I should point out that NIFCO is exceptionally proficient at raising funds and is presently outfitted with an impressive technological infrastructure. In any case, the helicopter is standard equipment in the very kind of film prominent in the global media marketplace and screened at the Toronto Film Festival. It also demonstrates the ease with which the isolated regional worker-artist can be re-inserted into the marketplace when the image of the folk has some useful exchange value. Jones splatters the cod onto the floor of the helicopter, they climb aboard and, as they fly over the rugged coastal landscape and startlingly beautiful icebergs they fall asleep, dreaming themselves into the

THE SOCIAL PRODUCTION OF PLACE

present through memories of their collective cinematic past. Their dreams consist of excerpts from Mike Jones's earlier feature films *Secret Nation* (1992) and *The Adventure of Faustus Bidgood* (1986), including a scene from the former where we see Mary Walsh scream at Cathy Jones, recalling for insiders at least the volatile tensions existing between members of Codco. The excerpts also reveal a rich and complex body of work rooted in the local and unbeholden to the conventions of documentary-style realism important to the canon of Canadian cinema. For that Toronto festival audience, they may simply be baffling images, as these films are no longer in circulation and the ephemeral nature of cinema culture diminishes historical memory. They are also images quite unlike those associated with the Toronto New Wave, decidedly gritty and fantastical rather than slick and existential.

The helicopter lands on the concrete outside of a glass and steel structure with NIFCO signage, again, corporate spatial logic at odds with the grassroots and urban space typically used by arts organizations. (The building is in fact the Department of Fisheries and Oceans in the White Hills overlooking Quidi Vidi Lake and the east end of St. John's.) The real NIFCO is located in the old downtown of St. John's in an unassuming house sans identifying signage. Inside, the outporters are met by a team of hairdressers, make-up artists and wardrobe personnel who groom and dress the roughworn trio into a more marketable media image – wool socks and work boots exchanged for more a fashionable base beneath evening gown and tuxedo. In the studio, they perform for the camera congratulatory praise for the festival. But is even this minor integration into the apparatus only a dream? The film concludes with the three in the kitchen of their saltbox house, pausing wistfully as the radio voice of the late Lister Sinclair, former CBC radio standard bearer for a public culture that is not beholden to the marketplace, announces the upcoming twenty-fifth Toronto International Film Festival. The men quietly continue their card game at the kitchen table while Cathy Jones begins to gut the cod, over top of the St. John's *Telegram* newspaper with the headline: "NIFCO Celebrates 25 years of Service," an anniversary that is extremely important to the fostering of local alternative cinema culture, but that passes unremarked upon in central Canada. As the film's prescient introductory narration has stated: "They are old now, and not much use to anyone."

Life Classes

> When a film undertakes the representation of "art" as a theme
> or engages an artwork as motif, it is, whatever else it is doing,
> also more or less openly and more or less knowingly enter-
> ing into a contemplation of its own nature and at some level
> positing its own unwritten theory of cinema as art. – *Susan*
> *Felleman, Art in the Cinematic Imagination*[9]

Life Classes tells the story of Mary Cameron (Jacinta Cormier) who has
grown up in a small town on Cape Breton Island, works in her father's
drugstore and passes the time with a paint-by-numbers hobby.[10] Upon
becoming pregnant by her sometime boyfriend Earl (Leon Dubinsky), the
local bootlegger turned satellite TV pirate-entrepreneur, she moves to the
big city of Halifax to raise her child. To earn extra income she becomes a
drawing-class model at the local college (the Nova Scotia College of Art
and Design, now known as NSCAD University) and is drawn into a world
of new ideas, eventually becoming an artist herself. The film, then, is about
Mary's process of self-discovery and transformation from consumer to producer, a process that follows matriarchal lineage. Important to the film is
Mary's relationship with her grandmother, her memory fragments of her
own mother, and the birth of her daughter. Along the way the film engages
with the question of the relationship between region and centre, concepts of
culture and value, technology and place, and the body as subject and object
in the work of art.

Mary has a job in a department store and, like her art-student co-
worker Gloria, is bored by the mundane day-to-day routine, which she expresses at a lunch break where she also laments the absence of tinned milk
(evaporated milk packaged in tin cans and popular in Cape Breton). It is
this mundane detail of the everyday followed upon by Gloria's invitation for
Mary to come to her dreadfully dull art history class that prompts Mary's
transformative entry into the world of art. While Gloria discreetly assuages
her boredom during her art history class by wearing headphones to listen
to music, Mary gazes intently at the slide show presentation of modernist
canonical paintings. While the professor flatly proclaims their importance,
it is up to Mary to sort through questions of value, a question grounded in
the body. In a post-class discussion with Gloria, she expresses unease with

abstraction in figural representation, saying: "I don't really understand the fuss you people make over pictures you can't even understand. I mean those paintings of women we saw tonight, they were, like, evil or something." Gloria then slyly suggests that Mary can use her body to earn some extra money – by becoming a drawing-class model. Mary then enters the art studio as a worker seeking much-needed income, and to engage directly the question of the body as object and subject of art.

The drawing-class scenes on the one hand evoke the critique of objectification suggested by Susan Felleman in a discussion of the French New Wave: "Art film's readiness to bare its own devices comes to seem predicated on its insistence on baring the female body, too, and preserving, indeed naturalizing, a sexist ideology of culture for which the nude is emblematic."[11] This may indeed be Mary's initial experience, for her expression, as she listens to the drawing instructor for the first time, suggests both unease and a stubborn resolve to do the job. The instructor's comments to the students refer to her body as a mass: "Try to see her skeleton with X-ray eyes. It's not supposed to look like anything.... Continue working into what you have so you start off with a scribble and start working into the drawing so what you'll probably end up with is a dark mass of something that looks like nothing." The students stare intently at Mary's body as they work. Through this collective experience, Mary, along with the class, is learning to see with great precision the form of the body through which they may come to understand its place in the world.[12] Later, when Earl comes to visit Mary's Halifax apartment where various drawings are on display, he is only able to see them as nudes. Mary, however, is gradually transformed from object to active agent, no longer interested in paint-by-numbers, now beginning to create, and create herself anew. This creative identity is mirrored by her generative experience in becoming a mother. The making of art is not romanticized or posited as a mysterious process; instead, it is connected with labour, the grounding of identity in place, and the complexities of material experience.

The new is intertwined with the past. As Mary becomes an artist she is compelled to return to Cape Breton and witness the death of her maternal grandmother. Grandmother is the film's connection with the past, with Gaelic heritage, and with a premodern concept of place and culture. However poignant her death, it is not a moment of nostalgia and lament but part of Mary's process of engaging more fully with the present. Of Mary's small-town home, Robin Wood writes: "The small town/country community

Jacinta Cormier and Jill Chatt in *Life Classes*, courtesy of Picture Plant.

THE SOCIAL PRODUCTION OF PLACE

is never sentimentalized, either past or present. The film's view is that, if there ever was once a form of 'organic culture' there of any character or distinction, it is now irretrievably lost, and nostalgic laments for its passing would be a waste of time; if it ever existed, its traces have been thoroughly obliterated by the irresistible flood of consumer capitalism, technology, and the media."[13] Mary's life in the present is not a simple rejection of the past but is also not beholden to it. When she returns to Halifax and is back at work as a drawing class model there is a distinct shift in her self-consciousness. In the first classroom scene the camera is in close as it arcs around the body, now the camera is more distant as it travels around the room revealing the many varied drawings in progress. Here, Mary is represented in a multiplicity of ways, as a subject in the process of becoming, and the instructor's voice, again commenting on the student work but projected onto Mary, is more generous: "There's a real softness to it."

There are many important aspects to Mary's development as an artist, culminating in her "One-Man" show of nude drawings of Earl and subsequent return to Cape Breton to reclaim her grandmother's house, but I want to concentrate on her position as both artist and worker whereby the concept of art is grounded in material circumstances and the specificity of place. A New York artist visits the college to stage a video "happening" in which Mary and various students participate for a fee of two hundred *American* dollars. They each stand naked in a translucent condom-like tube and create a speech or chant based on a significant childhood memory while a musician improvises alongside. This performance evokes the nature of video art in the 1980s (and is, according to MacGillivray, specifically influenced by American artist Les Levine, whose work concentrates on the idea of time rather than art as a fixed object) as well as the character of the film's location, NSCAD University, which was during the 1970s a major centre of conceptual art – attracting many important visiting artists and functioning in relation to other international art locales rather than to central Canada. Indeed, the fact of border-crossing is central to the scene insofar as the performance is intended to be viewed, via satellite, in New York, but culture can neither be contained by borders of the nation-state nor by the technological apparatus and is picked up by Earl's pirate satellite dish and distributed to Mary's home community – forcing her to reconcile her self-image with her public face in her home town.

What we see in this electronic transmission is not the cultural homogenization of globalization, where culture is an object of capital, but an expression of the specificity of place and identity. Mary's performance becomes the dominant element of the video happening, and her contribution, while drawing on personal history, is not at all about nostalgia. The idea of place is not the antimodern tourist image of the region; rather, it is about holding onto fragments of the past as one lives in the present – fragments which, in Walter Benjamin's words, flare up briefly and just as quickly vanish. She sings in both Gaelic and English, the folk-like lament: "My child is my mother returning. Her mother, my daughter the same. She carried us all in her yearning, our sorrow, our joy, our pain." The lyrics speak of matriarchal lineage and evoke a sense of place that is poetic and sensual rather than instrumental. Mary's trajectory throughout the film is toward that sense of place, moving through an abstract and instrumentally ordered space. In the live moment of the video performance broadcast across space, from margin to imperial centre and incidentally to Cape Breton Island, Mary casts back to her own mother's story, and back to her Gaelic heritage in order to tell a story about her own daughter.

She tells a story of origins that knows its history, but is about finding a way to see oneself in the present. While she fled her home community upon becoming pregnant with an "illegitimate" child, the song and her performance is a literal declaration of legitimacy. When the folks back home in Cape Breton see the performance (on an "illegitimate" receiver) it is embarrassing to Mary, but this allows her to make a home that is unconstrained by the dominant vision of place, signalling that she no longer accepts the terms of illegitimacy cast upon her while also refusing to disavow her relationship with place and history. Her movement here is made possible by the intersection of technologies of globalization and media culture with her own particular experience grounded in the social. It is significant that this possibility occurs while she is situated as a worker, a paid performer in someone else's project, one where authorship is both diffuse and strictly held. This process makes it possible for Mary to return to, and begin the rehabitation of, her grandmother's house, a place which becomes a distinct mixture of past and present, of traditional culture and Mary's experience in the urban artworld. The film concludes as she refuses Earl's awkward marriage proposal and clears a view to the ocean; that is, to an image of mobility and to the source of life.

Candy Mountain

The conclusion of Robert Frank and Rudy Wurlitzer's *Candy Mountain* has the central artist-character, a renowned guitar maker named Elmore Silk, set his creations ablaze on the shore of Cape Breton Island rather than have them fall into the hands of profit-minded investors and record company executives. This moment of destruction also signifies both the spark of creativity and the filmmaker's own antagonism toward the business of art. It is interesting that while this film is set at the margins of the music industry and at the margin of the nation (and is punctuated by a great indie soundtrack), the main artist is not a musician but a maker of things to be used in the creative practice of others. As an international co-production (Canada, France, Switzerland), the film narrates the borderland of film, art, and finance in relation to the concept of regional and national culture. It is not a film that sets out to explicitly comment upon regional conditions; instead it encounters the region as a consequence of the transnational forces of art and culture. Likewise, film is simultaneously an object of exchange in the arena of international finance and an embodiment of the local where the local is not simplified as "authentic" alternative to the placelessness of cultural homogenization, but formed out of the dialectic of border crossing.

This idea of border crossing is important to an understanding of the artist Robert Frank (Swiss-born, American-professionalized, global wanderer, Canadian recluse), for whom *Candy Mountain* is thinly disguised autobiography. The film unfolds through a journey, on the part of a young would-be guitarist named Julius from New York City, through the American rust belt and eventually into Nova Scotia. Julius is employed by record company executives (one is played by the influential political documentary filmmaker and New York artworld figure Emile De Antonio) to find Elmore Silk, who, like the reclusive Robert Frank, is in hiding in Cape Breton and who maintains a high degree of distrust toward the business of art.[14] *Candy Mountain*'s concluding fire anticipates Frank's own performative gesture of disgust: "In 1989 he became so fed up with the commercialization of the photography market that he nailed a stack of his rare vintage photographs to a board, tied it up with bailing wire, and called that his art work."[15]

While Frank's gesture is fuelled by a certain contempt, it is co-extensive with the relation between creation and destruction in his artwork and with the processes of development and underdevelopment through which a given place comes into being. The film's road trip covers some of the terrain of Frank's seminal photography book *The Americans*, which was originally published in Paris in 1958 and subsequently became a kind of map of the beat era.[16] The book, made on the road through America, raises the question of who belongs and who has power. This theme can be read in this film and Frank's earlier work such as his *Cocksucker Blues* (1972), about the Rolling Stones during the *Exile on Main Street* American tour, a film that is utterly unimpressed by the gloss of celebrity. The everyday grime and desperation found on the road in *Candy Mountain* is the antithesis of the tourist image of Nova Scotia which has been constructed as a pastoral antimodern ideal; here it is revealed as the product not of nature but of the forces of capital. Frank's gaze posits landscape as carceral space, where we are both fixed within and uncomfortably looking in from outside, as one critic of his photography describes: "In Frank's transforming vision of America, a car is a casket, a trolley a prison, a flag a shroud. As for us, we stand in odd groups and stare at some impossibly sad event beyond the frame of Frank's camera, while he captures us and the event itself is forgotten."[17] *The Americans* is influenced by the New Deal–era images of Walker Evans and Dorothea Lange which, while stark, are informed by a social-missionary optimism of the New Deal. However, there is no nostalgia or local pride in this book or in Frank's films, which must not be read as metaphor but as metonymic engagement with place.[18] The relationship between this film and the body of photographic work is not simple coincidence, for in his more contemporary work, Frank often rephotographs earlier images, not with lament or nostalgia but to critically recontextualize the past.

Candy Mountain is set not in the counterculture era taken up by Frank's oeuvre, but in the mean-spirited 1980s, where the border-crossing of international finance is facilitated by the implementation of investor rights agreements, while the optimism of the New Deal is drained away by high unemployment and cutbacks in social programs. These social-political conditions form the landscape for the film, a bleakness mitigated by the spark of creativity maintained by the characters. A *Cinema Canada* review from the time of release pointed out that "there is a real attempt to reconcile the idealism of the past with the realities of the present."[19] It is a reality shaped by labour exploitation, as the wanna-be rock star Julius hopes to exchange his labour for a chance at music industry fame and fortune, and it is indeed a journey through 1980s celebrity iconography. He is paid a small amount of expense money which he quickly loses to various contacts, including half of his money to Tom Waits, who plays a sleazy celebrity and brother of Elmore. Waits sells him a car and a contact address, and then recommends that as a young person he should take up golf. The contact leads to a brother–in-law of Elmore as played by Dr. John, who swindles him out of his car. Julius, world-weary but ever determined, sets out again only to be placed under arrest and imprisoned in a makeshift home jail by a Nova Scotia justice of the peace played by Leon Redbone. The remainder of Julius's cash is a bribe for his release. These images of exploitation consist of standard Canadian stereotypes of American culture, but here the ruthless machinations of finance are unconstrained by borders and, indeed, the border-crossing experience of the filmmaker tempers any nationalist idealization of place.

The landscape is harsh and unfriendly, but not in the cliché of wilderness constructed in Canadian cultural criticism; rather, the harsh reality of economic exploitation stands in for the processes of development and underdevelopment through which space and place are formed. On the open road, few favours come without a cost. Julius does, however, share a few moments of warmth with some of the people he meets along the way. These moments are never neutral or innocent, but there is a notably increased sense of freedom, however temporary, as Julius gives up (or loses) material comforts. He gets a lift from a native woman (played in low-key brilliance by Tantoo Cardinal) driving the four-wheeled emblem of British colonialism, a Land Rover, who first wants to shoot a deer. The image of city slicker Julius stumbling through the bush on the one hand is predicated on stereotypes of Canadian life consisting of roughing it in the bush. However, the land is not romanticized. It could care less whether the subjects survive. When the two take shelter in a shuttered cottage, the woman explains, as she smashes in the door with the butt of her rifle, that it is owned by "summer people from The States," suggesting a relation between capital, nation-state, and privilege. Here, explanation no longer matters; it is cold and they are inside. When asked about living near the ocean in comparison with his life in New York City, Robert Frank simply says: "You don't have that much time to contemplate nature in that way. You have to keep the house warm, you have to split the wood, you have to make sure the water is right and that the wind doesn't get through the cracks."[20]

The lesson throughout this journey is for Julius to grab hold of the moment rather than cling to the fantasy of success and glamour manufactured by the music industry. He finally meets Elmore and this encounter motivates the selling of his guitars – but not to Julius, whose appearance instead provides motivation to recover anonymity on the open road once again. Elmore sells his guitars to a Japanese collector, both for money and because, as the film implies, there is some respect on the part of the purchaser for the aesthetic value rather than simple market returns. This deal involves the exchange of twelve guitars, an agreement not to manufacture any more of this kind, and an agreement to destroy all others (thus the scene of burning guitars described earlier). It is a deal with the devil, but it does provide financial security and facilitates the artist's ability to move on to other projects rather than remain rooted in past successes. In this way it precisely mirrors Frank's own career decisions, particularly his decision in the 1960s to stop making personal photography and instead turn to moving pictures.[21]

In its desire to identify a place less determined by financial exchange, the film exploits the exoticization of the Asian other, a beautiful woman representing unnamed Japanese investors, who is both representative of economic domination and a mysterious figure of tradition and power evoking the importance of art as "lineage" rather than simple commodity. The Asian presence is not simple stereotype but also autobiographic, for the first retrospective book of Frank's photographs, *The Lines of My Hand*, was published by Japanese publisher Kazuhiko Motomura in 1972, and it was a highly personal collection. Value requires destruction rather than the generation of art, but in the context of the culture industry this becomes a viable alternative to the production of the commodity fetish offered by the music industry. Julius obviously does not win fame and fortune. Like most workers, he remains stuck in the same exploitive position in which he entered the cycle of production. But he does share a few moments of genuine pleasure with Elmore, jamming on a guitar (an especially garish, circa-1980s neon model) as it is being set ablaze. It is an image that encapsulates what Greil Marcus describes as the essence of Frank's images, that "the whole of life can be found almost anywhere."[22] But at the same time, the end of the road in this film also marks an end to the era of art cinema and a shift toward production that is better defined within the terms of genre, as is the case with *New Waterford Girl*.

New Waterford Girl

The opening image of *New Waterford Girl* is of laundry hanging to dry on an outdoor line. It is precisely the same image as that used in a contemporaneous Web and television advertising campaign for Newfoundland and Labrador tourism. In both cases, the image plays off of the idea of regional disconnection from the centre of culture, and both evoke this disconnection as a virtue. Likewise, the main character and narrator Moonie Pottie is characterized by a yearning to be located within culture rather than at the margins, in turn raising the question of the concept of culture – as associated with depth and tradition or whether it can be found in the quotidian everyday. We first see her standing by the side of the road, hitchhiking and holding a cardboard sign that says "Mexico." We later learn that this is a frequent pose, even though she only ever gets a ride as far as the nearby town of Sydney, Nova Scotia. Her narration similarly punctuates the stark Cape Breton landscape with poetic references to signifiers of "real" culture: "Ask me anything. I know that fine Italian espresso has unbroken cream on the top. I know the street map of Paris by heart."

This narration occurs over the scene of her brother's wedding, occasioned by pregnancy and held jointly with a funeral to save costs – emphasizing the film's obvious relation between adulthood and death in the isolated region. In turn, Moonie's character, as artist, is cast separately from her environment. We see her walking through town reading as a way of creating an imaginative barrier against the brutal environment, while we see kids beating each other up and an adult yells to her: "You're going to be killed doing that." When the new neighbours arrive, the gleeful awe at the landscape is undermined by Moonie's sarcastic guided tour: "My house. Your house. There's the shore. The mine. The main drag. Hospital. Tavern. Church. Tavern. Church. Church. School. Train station. Road to Sydney." The town landscape is marked by Catholic iconography, deployed in the narrative to mark the characters as hidebound to suspicion rather than to engage a critical understanding of the relation between culture and institutions of power.

Moonie is coming-of-age as teenage outsider in the rough-worn town of New Waterford, on Cape Breton Island. Her plan of escape is to get accepted into a New York art school, but when her parents refuse this goal she performs an elaborate charade of sexual promiscuity in order to convince her parents that she is pregnant and must be sent away. In this way, the film draws upon the stereotype of small-town sexual backwardness in order to position the artist-character as having purchase on the concept of place and authenticity. While the film inverts the teen coming-of-age genre's typical privileging of male sexuality – here, much of the comedy comes at the expense of the town boys, through Moonie's acts of faux conquest – it restores gender and genre conventions by maintaining her virginity. The concept of sex is performative rather than embodied pleasure. It is through this process that Moonie comes to see the beauty of the place from which she yearns to escape. This yearning for authenticity is punctuated by a 1970s rock music soundtrack which likewise signifies the film's Canadian identity while deploying that identity as part of the kitsch cultural landscape – 8-track tapes, plaid, gas-guzzling cars and beer-swilling boys, hockey, street fighting, white bread, and whisky. Moonie's fast friend Lou, the new neighbour who is from New York but staying in New Waterford for the summer, marks her outsider status by playing soul music at a party. While the scene is played for laughs, it functions to contribute to the depoliticized image of nostalgic representation of place, which in turn legitimizes the role of popular culture in producing place, an ideological sleight-of-hand predicated upon underdevelopment.

This is a popular genre film that takes for granted the ideological context; yet within the context of mainstream Hollywood film – where Hollywood is not simply a place or a national cinema but is understood instead as an apparatus of commercial activity – it is an independent production. Canada's function in what Toby Miller and others have described as the New International Division of Cultural Labour, describing Hollywood's location not geographically but in the division of labour, is as a part of the U.S. domestic market.[23] From the perspective of the development of a feature film industry in Atlantic Canada, this market function signifies success insofar as place is no longer articulated in relation to concepts of identity and cultural meaning, but functions instead as a free-floating signifier of authenticity for the global media marketplace, detached from the literal ground.

I do not make this point in order to reiterate the over-simplified division between industrial production in contrast with art film activity characteristic of earlier considerations of Canadian cinema. While the film's director Allan Moyle proclaims his affinity with American cinema culture, he also has claim to Canadian art cinema legitimacy as actor, writer, and/or director of the marginalized 1970s films *Montreal Main* (1974) and *Rubber Gun*

(1977).[24] A critical understanding of regional film activity must avoid the essentialization of authorship in relation to the concept of authenticity. This limited understanding occurs, for instance, in Ottawa-based film critic Tom McSorley's claim that this film merely makes use of the region as colourful backdrop for a story that is not authentic to this place.[25] It is worth mentioning, in contrast, that the film's screenwriter Tricia Fish has described the film in autobiographical terms.[26] While I agree with the general thrust of McSorley's criticism, the point of my analysis is not to reiterate questions of authorship but first of all to note the importance of genre conventions as symptom of the industrialization of filmmaking throughout Canada, an outcome of policy and finance rather than individual authorial predilection. Analysis then begins with the question of the degree to which a film critically engages with, rather than merely reproduces, these narrative conventions, through which arises a critical examination of social context, and of the very forces through which this place comes into being.

Moonie's agency and her eventual escape from New Waterford are facilitated by her American friend Lou, the girl-next-door boxer who asserts the sexual autonomy of the town's women by throwing a knock-out punch at the boys who have cheated on them. Lou's aggressive tactics are her means of belonging, against the declaration of her outsider status by a group of local girls: "What are you, on vacation? Try living here when it's hailing … ice pellets spiking you in the eye." The concepts of belonging and authenticity are linked to the environment, which is romanticized as both brutal experience and place of timeless beauty untouched by the forces of production. In an especially nostalgic moment that plays at odds with the marking of Moonie and Lou as outsiders, the idea of belonging is evoked through a scene of teens singing a folk song around a campfire.

Later, Lou's description of New York situates this dream destination as rather less enchanting than the Cape Breton landscape: "The Hudson River is filled with piss, cola and sludge. There's hardly any water in it." Viewers in Atlantic Canada would, like movie-goers everywhere, know the iconic value of an on-screen reference to a New York location, but would also be aware of the close proximity of the present Cape Breton cinematic location to the Sydney Tar Ponds, the most polluted location in Canada (a notorious toxic open-pit reservoir left over from a century of industrial waste and covering an area of three city blocks). This reference would be irrelevant to the broad global media audience whose constituents probably have their own toxic sludge to worry about.[27] The scene instead plays as lament for the ideal of community and an image of landscape untouched by modernity. The film concludes with Moonie's tearful train trip away from New Waterford to New York, where she repeats her "Ask me anything" refrain, but this time it is in celebratory description of her home-town.

In this way, the idea of the artist as outsider character facilitates the film's turn away from the forces of production through which society, place, and landscape are constructed for the sake of antimodern nostalgia that reifies place in service of genre. In more conceptually challenging films, the image of the artist is to engage inquiry into the nature of representation, whether through veiled autobiography as in *Candy Mountain*, as means of narrating the experience of work, place, and parenthood as in *Life Classes*, or as sly commentary on the relation between region and centre, as in *Congratulations*. In the genre conventions deployed in *New Waterford Girl*, the artist is outsider through which we see the region not in new and productive ways, but as stereotype.

Together, these films tell us that the concept of the region is neither uniform across its various locales, nor inherently a product of nature. Rather it is constructed through social processes, not the least of which is the process of representation. This creative process occurs neither in a vacuum nor as pure artistic insight free of social context; rather, it is a product of local conditions as well as cultural policies and financial constraints as much as it is an outcome of the history of film activity in this country. If there is a single point of reference linking all of these films it is the political, economic, and social relationship between region and centre. Here region is both idea and geography while centre is both physical and about the forces of culture and capital. The transformation I have described, from self-conscious art cinema toward a more commercial approach to movie-making, is likewise not an inevitable outcome but is a consequence of specific policy decisions. The various provincial film development offices in this country are established foremost as agents of economic development, and this activity privileges the attraction of off-shore production, primarily American television production, in addition to fostering local filmmaking. In this context, the latter is influenced by the former.

The funding policies of Telefilm Canada have systematically shifted away from auteur-driven cinema toward supposedly more marketable genre productions. The iconic value of select auteurs, notably Arcand, Cronenberg, and Egoyan, are put forward while at the same time the conditions through which the best of this kind of work has been nurtured are diminished precisely because the work is idiosyncratic to place and sensibility rather than to a market formula which is always determined by past box office success (instead of less tangible insights into the present). This shift began, arguably, with the transformation of the Canadian Film Development Corporation into Telefilm in 1984, signalling the context of broadcasting in the making of films in this country. Telefilm did originate with a cultural mandate and out of disappointment with the tax shelter years (the Capital Cost Allowance Act, providing 100 per cent tax write-offs for investment in Canadian film, 1974–82) as well as with the systemic problems of distributing theatrical films.[28] Jim Leach summarizes the dilemma of state investment: "On the one hand, the Corporation [CFDC] was responsible for investing public money and expected to generate a profit. On the other, as a public institution, it was under pressure to ensure that the films that it supported were culturally respectable and/or distinctively Canadian. It was open to attack when it invested in films with strong commercial potential but no apparent cultural pretensions ... but it was also criticized for poor business practices when the films it supported did not make money."[29] This conflict also points to the vexed place of the artist in this country, and as these films demonstrate, the artist character is often deployed as an outsider through which the nature of place can be illuminated, whether explicitly or symptomatically.

In any case, Telefilm's turn to broadcasting as a more viable means of providing Canadians with access to the country's films certainly made the form of mainstream television the dominant model for narrative. However, I do not wish to idealize a fixed notion of cultural production cast apart from commercial considerations; there are always a range of forces influencing the form and content of a given film, including funding imperatives and market conditions, but also creative preferences, as well as formal and genre trends and influences that can come from anywhere in the world. While the agency established the Feature Film Fund in 1986 to foster theatrical filmmaking, it is guided by the rhetoric of capital, by "market discipline," in the words of then agency head Richard Stursberg.[30] The current mandate of the FFF is now explicitly stated as: "encourag[ing] the making and marketing of Canadian feature films that have high box office potential."[31] This emphasis is reproduced in the Canadian Television Fund, established in 1996 in part through a levy on cable carriers. Richard Stursberg has since become the vice-president of CBC-TV and has brought to the national broadcaster the same simple-minded market formula, this time inflected by a particularly

Canadian populism. As he states in an interview: "CBC Television needs to be more like Tim Hortons and less like Starbucks ... It is not a service that is built for elites."[32] Putting aside long-standing institutional and economic obstacles to the popular distribution of Canadian cinema, the comment reflects the marginal place of art in this country's network of social relations. This marginalization is not a function of the preferences of individual citizens (whether for movies or donuts); rather, it is produced through specific cultural policies, policies reflected in the narrative turn of these films. Of the four films under consideration, only *Life Classes* is explicitly and fully about art and its fundamental integration with everyday life. *Candy Mountain* turns its back on the kind of industrial appropriation of art that drives the production of *New Waterford Girl*. Finally, *Congratulations* reveals a double marginalization: of art and region at the hands of the twin forces of culture and capital.

NOTES

1   Helen Peters, ed., *The Plays of Codco* (New York: Peter Lang, 1992), xii. The 1974 performance of *Cod on A Stick* at Memorial University in St. John's was filmed by Mike Jones. A copy is deposited in *The Papers of Codco*, Memorial University Archives 13.12.008 and 13.12.009. See the introduction of the Peters collection for an overview of the history of this amazing performance group.

2   My view of audience response is based on personal observation. *Congratulations* was played in high rotation as a prelude and this may have contributed to the audience fatigue; however, the Toronto audience response does resonate with the themes of the film.

3   Personal interview with the author, 15 October 2007, St. John's. *Congratulations* is included on the DVD of *The Adventure of Faustus Bidgood*. The author is the producer of this DVD re-release (funded by the Audio-Visual Heritage Trust of Canada in 2008). For information on availablility, see: www.nifco.org. A brief excerpt of *Congratulations* is also available at: www.popeproductions. com.

4   In literary criticism, the starting point for understanding Atlantic-based writing against the grain of canonical assumptions is Janice Kulyk Keefer, *Under Eastern Eyes: A Critical Reading of Maritime Fiction* (Toronto: University of Toronto Press, 1987). Kulyk Keefer acknowledges Patrick O'Flaherty's book *The Rock Observed: Studies in the Literature of Newfoundland* (Toronto: University of Toronto Press, 1979) as serving a similar function for writing in that province.

5   The primary critique of canonization is Peter Morris, "In Our Own Eyes: The Canonizing of Canadian Film," *Canadian Journal of Film Studies* 3(1) (Spring 1994): 27–44. The limits of the concept of national cinema are neatly summarized by Andrew Higson, "The Concept of National Cinema," *Screen* 30(4) (Autumn 1989): 36–46.

6   Contemporary Marxist Geography, in the work of Doreen Massey, David Harvey, and others, turns this idea on its head by concentrating on the social forces through which space and place are constructed.

7   Ian Mckay, *The Quest of the Folk: Antimodernism and Cultural Selection in Twentieth-Century Nova Scotia* (Montreal and Kingston: McGill-Queen's University Press, 1994). Related Arguments can be found in James Overton, *Making a World of Difference: Essays on Tourism, Culture and Development in Newfoundland* (St. John's, NL: ISER–Memorial University, 1996).

8   Mckay, 36.

9   Susan Felleman, *Art in the Cinematic Imagination* (Austin: University of Texas Press, 2006), 2.

10 *Life Classes* received considerable critical acclaim at the time of its release, and was the official Canadian selection for the Berlin International Film Festival. Like many Canadian films, however, it never received adequate theatrical distribution. I am pleased to be producer of the film's DVD re-release, funded by the Audio-Visual Heritage Trust of Canada and available from the filmmaker's website: www.pictureplant.com.

11 Felleman, 4.

12 MacGillivray has expressed to me in conversation the importance of this experience as fundamentally transforming a student-artist's way of seeing the world.

13 Robin Wood, *Sexual Politics and Narrative Cinema: Hollywood and Beyond* (New York: Columbia University Press, 1998), 305.

14 The journey is reversed in a documentary film made about this iconoclastic filmmaker. In *After Frank* (Dir: Walter Forsyth, 2005) the filmmaker journeys from Halifax in search of Frank's

isolated ocean-front house in Mabou, Cape Breton and then to New York City. In the end, Frank, off-camera, refuses to be represented but conveys the necessary lesson that art must move forward rather than return to the past. We can extend this lesson to the concept of place, not as something to be viewed nostalgically, but as a process formed in dialectical confluence of history, geography, and culture. On this documentary, see my article: "Reading, Regarding, and Waiting: Three New Documentaries from Nova Scotia," *CineAction* 69 (May 2006): 60–63.

15 Brian Wallis, "Robert Frank: American Visions," *Art in America* (March 1996): 75.

16 The English text is introduced by Jack Kerouac, who says: "Anybody doesn't like these pitchers don't like potry, see." Republished as: Robert Frank, *The Americans* (New York and Washington: Scalo–National Gallery of Art, 2000).

17 Tod Papageorge, *Walker Evans and Robert Frank: An Essay on Influence* (New Haven, CT: Yale University Art Gallery, 1981), 8.

18 This is the key insight of Jno Cook, "Robert Frank's America," *Afterimage* (March 1982): 9–14. The argument is made against the claims of John Brumfield, "'The Americans' and The Americans," *Afterimage* (Summer 1980): 8–15. My thanks to Alvin Comiter for sharing his Robert Frank file with me.

19 Greg Clarke, "Candy Mountain, *Cinema Canada* (December 1987): 30.

20 Wallis, *Art in America*, 76.

21 Anne W. Tucker, "It's The Misinformation That's Important," in *Robert Frank: New York to Nova Scotia*, ed. Anne Wilkes Tucker (Houston and New York: Houston Museum of Fine Arts–New York Graphic Society Books, 1986), 96.

22 Greil Marcus, "Robert Frank: Driving and Crying," *Artforum International* 33(3) (1994): 56.

23 Toby Miller et al., *Global Hollywood* (London: BFI, 2001), 3.

24 Cynthia Amsden, "The Rules According to Moyle," *Take One* 27 (Spring 2000): 32–35.

25 Tom McSorley, "The Centre Cannot Hold: The Cinema of Atlantic Canada," *Self Portraits* (Ottawa: Canadian Film Institute, 2006), 272. *New Waterford Girl* is cited in a listing of the inauthentic in footnote 2, p. 296.

26 Tom Lyons, "Bringing it All Back Home: Writer Tricia Fish and the Real New Waterford Girl," *Eye Weekly* (Toronto, 1 June 2000): 30.

27 For a history of the Tar Ponds, see Maude Barlow and Elizabeth May, *Frederick Street: Life and Death on Canada's Love Canal* (Toronto: Harper-Collins, 2000).

28 For a solid examination of this era of Canadian film read against the grain of the dominant cultural argument, see Peter Urquhart, "You Should Know Something – Anything – About This Movie. You Paid For It." *Canadian Journal of Film Studies* 12(2) (Fall 2003): 64–80.

29 Jim Leach, *Film in Canada* (Toronto: Oxford University Press, 2006), 3.

30 Etan Vlessing, "Telefilm Canada Draws Fire Over Commercial Bent," *Hollywood Reporter* (March 2–8, 2004): 90.

31 According to the guidelines published on the agency website at the time of this writing: http://www.telefilm.gc.ca/03/311. asp?lang=en&fond_id=1.

32 Kate Taylor, "CBC's No. 2 Stursberg Sees a Kindred Spirit in the New Boss," *Globe and Mail*, 7 November 2007, R1.

13

SEARCHING FOR PORTIA WHITE

SYLVIA D. HAMILTON

This chapter is part of my ongoing engagement with the story of African Nova Scotian born contralto, Portia May White, who in 1997 was designated as a person of national historical significance by the Historic Sites and Monuments Board of Canada. Canada Post's Millennium special postage series honoured her along with Glenn Gould, Guy Lombardo, and Félix Leclerc, and the Government of Nova Scotia has created the Portia White Prize, a major arts award valued at $25,000, in recognition and memory of her achievements. Portia White was an accomplished concert artist who forged an international career during the turbulent 1940s and 1950s. Known as 'Canada's Singing Sensation,' she was applauded by critics and audiences alike in Canada and abroad. Government and civic leaders of the day created the Portia White Trust, an unusual state action at the time, to help finance her budding career. Now called the Nova Scotia Talent Trust, it provides grants to an array of Nova Scotian artists. She died in 1968 at the age of fifty-seven. Contemporary Canadian female singers making their mark on the international scene may not know they have a trail-blazing foremother in Portia White. In spite of her fame and the indelible mark she made on her many admirers and her former voice students, no print or film biography about her existed. I grew up knowing her name but little else about this singular artist. In 1990, I embarked on what became a decade-long journey to document her life and career. Marked by the release of my documentary film *Portia White: Think on Me* in 2000, it appears to have no end.

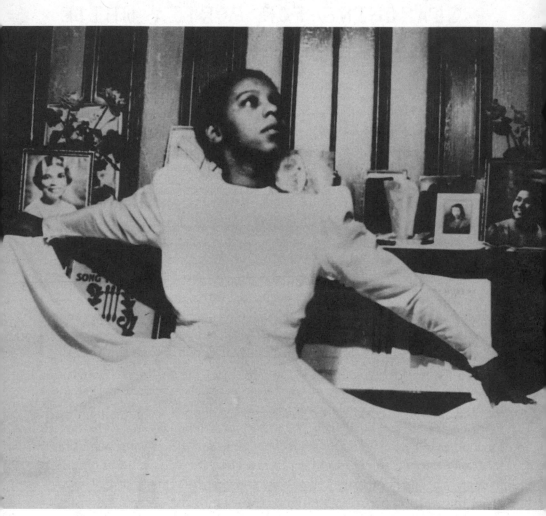

Portia White in her home on Belle Aire Terrace, Halifax, possibly prior to her debut concert at the Eaton Auditorium on November 7, 1941. Courtesy Maroon Films.

Beginnings

An examination of representations of women of African descent in Canada yields at least two well-established categories: the invisible and the stereotypical. The third, 'a credit to her race,' while less common, is nonetheless still present. African-Canadian women were either not there in the collective Canadian consciousness, as framed by publications and reflecting Canadian institutions, or they were represented by derogatory stereotypes, the residue of slavery, that were etched into the public's unconscious by Hollywood movies and American television shows of the 1950s. Consequently, coupled with the pervasive sexist stereotypes of women in general, African-descended women in Canada were saddled with offensive stifling and soul-destroying representations. There is the image of Aunt Jemima from the pancake box, recently updated, and the girl-child Topsy; both names were used against Black women and girls as racist slurs and put-downs by white children and adults alike. It is not uncommon to hear the phrase "grew like Topsy," uttered by speakers who may not know the origin of these words, nor its affront to women of African descent.[1] They were maids, housecleaners, or whores. Such images did not square with my experiences of Black women who surrounded and nurtured me and the other children in my village. The 'credit to her race' category is a case of damning with faint praise. The accomplishment is recognized, but the individuals are set apart from their background and roots, as somehow being not *like the others* of their kind. Somehow *different*.

Within her constituency, however, Portia White may be celebrated as an example of what *we* can do, and claimed as our own. I knew I had to make a large space for Portia White, in the same way that St. Claire Bourne had done for poet Langston Hughes, actor and vocal performer Paul Robeson and photographer/filmmaker Gordon Parks, and that Michelle Parkerson had done for blues great Betty Carter and a capella sensation Sweet Honey in the Rock, in the documentaries they produced. Reflecting on his career during which he had produced over thirty films, Bourne asserts that: "Everyone should have the right and opportunity to see themselves reflected in the cultural expressions of the land in which they live. Hollywood has proven that, up to now at least, it is incapable or unwilling to do that so it is up to us, the independents, to fill that vacuum."[2] Those independents include women such as documentarian Michelle Parkerson, who says emphatically that "Being a Black Woman filmmaker requires your best womanish and womanist (i.e. courageous, wilful) behaviour. To keep producing is a constant test of your artistic and political commitment."[3]

Race, and how it defines the lives of individuals, remains an area that is prickly for people to face directly, without excuse or defence. In interpersonal relationships it can become explosive when individuals from dominant white society are asked to take personal responsibility for changing their own attitudes toward race and encouraging those who look like them to do likewise. The common perception many Canadians have of their nation is that it is more tolerant, less racist (or at least less overtly so) than the United States, where race operates as a signifier sharply etched into American society. The United States is Canada's race measuring stick for the status of race relations. That 'we' are not like 'them' perception seems to persist in the face of the daily experiences of many African Canadians, and other people of colour, and Aboriginal people, that underline racism as a brutal fact of Canadian life. It is our whale in the room; we see a blow every now and again above water, say it is an 'isolated' incident, point to how bad it is south of the border, and carry on. Whether documentary or fiction, films' engagement with race within their narrative may be viewed as meditations (intentional or unintentional), as third party interventions within the discourse. They throw the images and the themes they carry into large relief, and depending on the public viewing context within which they are shown, have the potential to break open the discussion about how the complexity of race permeates the everyday lives of people of all classes and backgrounds. Conversations about what is seen and represented on film can become a way, albeit a rather safe one, into an examination of this tenacious issue without it necessarily becoming directly personal. The participatory question and answer session, often an integral element of the public screening experience, may offer such direct engagement. Audience members can continue the discussion on an informal basis once the film screening is over, in the lobby, on the street and behind closed doors at home.

The experience of a question and answer session during a class at Mount Saint Vincent University is offered by way of example. As guest lecturer in a sociology class, I presented my documentary *Speak It! From the Heart of Black Nova Scotia* (1992). The film is set in a predominantly white Halifax high school and follows a group of African-Canadian students as they try to find reflections of themselves in their school; it charts their journey as they cope with issues of race, identity, and belonging. Following the screening, I encouraged students to identify and to discuss any themes they found in the film. The class was mixed racially but the majority of students were of European background. One difficult scene in the film shows a school bathroom wall scrawled with violent racist graffiti using the word 'nigger.' While some students were shocked by this scene, a few students entered the discussion by saying 'they,' meaning Black people, "are allowed to call it to themselves, but we are not allowed to use it. It's a double standard."

The debate created a way for me to talk to them about the derivation, and the historical and contemporary use of this word as a weapon against African-descended people, about the power and meaning of language, and the individual's responsibility in how language is used. I called to their attention the daily experience of those African-Canadian students who would have had to try to avoid that stall when they entered the bathroom. There was also the question of what other students felt when they saw the graffiti.[4] While I allowed that many hip hop artists use 'nigga,' a derivation of the 'nigger,' as a way to declaw the original, to remove its power, others argue that it is a word that simply cannot be reclaimed. The late Richard Pryor's story is telling. After a trip to the continent of Africa, he stopped using it. Perhaps Michael Richards, affectionately known as Kramer (the character he portrayed on the television show *Seinfeld*), whose racist rant caused a storm of controversy, might view video of Pryor's later standup act in which he tells his conversion story, as part of his self-re-education.[5]

At other screenings of *Speak It!*, with students in various locations across Canada and elsewhere, the scene that touches on the issue of interracial relationships provoked lively debate; it was the focus of many questions and comments that broadened the discussion beyond Black and white, to encompass other racial/cultural groups and intergenerational conflicts over values and customs and the how and why of social change. I screened Karen Cho's documentary *In the Shadow of Gold Mountain* (2004) during a Canadian History on Film class I was teaching at Acadia University, and some students seemed puzzled as to what it had to do with them, *now*. I used the film to open a discussion about the history of racial superiority in Canada and how it was manifested in regulations such as the Chinese Exclusion and Head Tax Act (1885–1947), and the internment of Japanese Canadians. At the core of these events was unvarnished racism, fear of the other, and an assumption of white superiority. The *now* part of the discussion raised the Japanese-Canadian Redress Movement and the subsequent Canadian government apology to Japanese-Canadians and the establishment of the Canadian Race Relations Foundation. Within the wired classroom context,

I brought in various Web sites to extend the conversation. My approach was to encourage students to think more broadly and historically when they read about or encountered debates about racism in Canada today. Part of that conversation hinged upon questions about the erasure of events, organizations, communities, and people such as Portia White from narratives about Canadian history and society. My documentary *Portia White: Think On me* can serve as counter-memory standing in opposition to erasure.

Home Is Where Her Heart Was

> Portia kept in touch with every member of the family. And I could phone her on Friday and she would tell me about everyone in Halifax and how Mildred was in Cleveland and she made a point of keeping in touch with everyone.[6]

Portia was born in 1911, in Truro, Nova Scotia, the third of Izie Dora and William Andrew White's thirteen children. William, a graduate of Acadia University's Divinity School, was pastor at the Zion African Baptist Church in Truro. Izie, a pianist and contralto, instilled a love of music in her children. When Portia was still young, Rev. White moved his family to Halifax, where he assumed ministerial duties at Cornwallis Street African Baptist Church. When she was three years old, World War I was declared. In Nova Scotia, Black men joined the lines of citizens volunteering for the war effort. Unlike the majority of citizens, however, they were routinely turned away because of their colour, told it was a 'white man's war.' After protests from Black leaders and their white supporters from across Canada, and a debate in the House of Commons, a compromise solution was reached: a separate, segregated Black Construction Battalion would be commissioned. Portia's father, William White, became its chaplain. She was six years old when he left his young family to go overseas to France in 1917. Portia, along with her siblings, joined the church choir that in later years she directed. As one of the oldest children, Portia had many family responsibilities; she saw her family through hard economic times, the death of siblings and of her beloved father. Once she graduated from high school, because of her race, school teaching was the only professional job available to her. Even then, she had to teach in Black segregated schools in Africville and in Black communities in Halifax County. She spread her meagre salary of less than thirty-five dollars a month a long way – helping at home and paying for music lessons.

Race was an exclusionary factor in Canadian society that had a legacy of slavery, segregated schools, racial restrictions in employment, housing and in the provision of all manner of services. Distinguised legal scholar Constance Backhouse states emphatically:

> It is essential to recognize that racism is located in the systems and structures that girded the legal systems of Canada's past. Racism is not primarily manifest in isolated, idiosyncratic, and haphazard acts by individual actors who from time to time, consciously intended to assert racial hierarchy over others.... Racism resonates through institutions, intellectual theory, popular cultures, and spiritual beliefs. Education, employment, residence, and the freedom of social interaction were sharply curtailed for all but those who claimed and were accorded the racial designation 'white.'[7]

How is it then that a young Black girl dreams of performing on the concert stage? And how is it that she succeeds? The creative drive is a powerful life force, perhaps paralleled only by the support, guidance, encouragement, and blessing of a family. Portia White had both: an remarkable creative drive and a family that supported and encouraged her to reach for and touch her dream. Most important, however, is that she possessed one of the finest vocal instruments Canada had ever seen. My search began with fragments of her story.

Journal Entry: Letter to Portia

Dear Portia:
I am writing a letter to you, though it's a letter you will never read, at least as far as I know. But there are unknowables. Then again, just because I don't know a thing, does not mean that that thing does not exist. Herewith my letter to you. It is an uncertain journey I have started, searching for you. My growing list of questions is matched only by my increasing uncertainty about what answers I will find. There are so many things I want to

know about you, your family, your life, your friends, your career – and you above all. I don't know if I will find answers to all of my questions, but I am drawn to you. You left me little to work with. No diaries, no bundles of letters, no script of your life story. There is much to piece together, much to understand.

A Musical Convergence

I think that the rhythm of the Negro spirituals is the rhythm of the North American continent, really. I think that is the music that is native to this continent. – *Portia White*

To understand Portia White's historical significance, I had to consider the cultural and political context and social climate of the times during which she lived. Her life spanned two world wars, the Great Depression, and the civil rights movement. She died in February 1968, just two months before Martin Luther King Jr. was assassinated. What was the world like during Portia's early years? In Paris, Josephine Baker was turning heads as she appeared dressed in feathers at the Theatre des Champs Élysées in 1925. When Billie Holliday recorded the arresting, uncompromising song "Strange Fruit" in 1939, Portia was a twenty-four-year-old teacher who lived a double life: teaching children by day, rushing off to voice lessons after school, and performing in concerts and festivals whenever she could. In this same year, the Daughters of the American Revolution prevented contralto Marian Anderson, who would later figure in Portia's life, from performing a concert at Constitution Hall in Washington, DC.

Like Portia's father, Anderson's and Bessie Smith's fathers were also key figures in Black Baptist Churches. The years 1921 to 1931 are considered the peak years of the Harlem Renaissance, that period of flourishing artistic and cultural development within the African-American community, when writers such as Langston Hughes, whom Portia would later meet in Detroit, Zora Neale Hurston, and Claude McKay produced some of their finest literary work. Musicians, including composers and performers, were central to this creative movement, with the 'Negro' spiritual becoming a significant point of convergence between African and European traditions. What Portia could not know when she learned to sing these spirituals at her father's Cornwallis Street African Baptist Church in Halifax was that she would eventually meet Harry T. Burleigh, a Black composer who arranged these songs which became a constant and much-loved part of her repertoire and that of other Black classical performers. The creative and pioneering contributions of people of African descent in the field of Euro-classical music is a deeply buried story, so much so that it is commonly believed that Black people have no history, or at best a very slim one, in this arena. While she may not have known it when she began, Portia had companion travellers, female and male on this path: Martina Arrayo, Grace Bumbry, Shirley Verrett, Carol Brice, Leontyne Price, Dorothy Maynor, Paul Robeson, Todd Duncan, Roland Hayes and Marian Anderson, to whom she would be often be compared. When Portia eventually signed with Columbia Concert Management in New York, she joined Paul Robeson and Dorothy Maynor, who were also represented by this agency, the largest in North America at the time.[8]

When violinist Rosalyn M. Story began a book on Black divas in 1986, she was questioned about her choice of subject. From her point of view, "The project seemed a natural course for the black violinist whose only role models in classical music were the women who sang so-called 'serious' literature. Marian Anderson and Leontyne Price were icons who presented me with a universe of possibilities."[9] Story's *And So I Sing: African American Divas of Opera and Concert* surveys early performers such as Sissieretta Jones, who was born in 1869 in Portsmouth, Virginia, and Elizabeth Taylor-Greenfield, who "had a voice the likes of which the American public had seldom heard from any singer, white or black."[10] Story concludes with a glimpse into the contemporary careers of Barbara Hendricks, Jessye Norman, and Kathleen Battle. The lives and career achievements of these early artists that Story unearthed during her research reclaimed their space:

> The notion of knowing and defending one's rightful place loomed large over the pages of newspapers and scrapbooks I found that detailed the lives and careers of black women in this overwhelmingly white profession. In opera there have been many Rosa Parkses, strong black women who stood their ground and firmly, knowing that their place was wherever they chose to be.[11]

Collective Sites of Memory

Who is responsible for remembering when those who kept the memory, the memory keepers, are gone? Consider the way a particular song is sung by people who can't read or write music, yet know the melody and lyrics in their bones, They kept the 'song' to sing it for others to learn, to pass on. When this 'keeping' skips a generation, and unless recorded in some way, it will be lost to future generations. People in African Nova Scotian communities knew the name Portia White, though many never saw her perform and knew little about her career. They *knew* she was very important. Collectively, they held her in their memory. Individuals interviewed for *Portia White: Think On Me* each held highly personal memories, which combined to offer a composite portrait of the sister, artist, teacher, colleague, and friend that was Portia.

French historian Pierra Nora provides a context within which to view my search. He writes of his concept of *lieux de mémoire*, which exists "where memory crystallizes and secretes itself at a particular historical moment, a turning point where consciousness of a break with the past is bound up with the sense that memory has been torn – but torn in such a way as to pose the problem of the embodiment of memory in certain sites where a sense of historical continuity persists."[12] In *History and Memory in African-American Culture*, scholars Geneviève Fabre and Robert O'Meally bring together an engaging and vibrant collection of essays that use Nora's theoretical concept to tackle the theme of history and memory in African-American culture. They explain that:

> For us African Americanists perhaps the most significant aspect of the idea of *lieux de mémoire* was its capacity to suggest new categories of sources for the historian: new sets of sometimes very difficult readings. We considered, for example, how to read certain dances, paintings, buildings, journals, and oral forms of expression. More than ever, we saw novels, poems, slave narratives, autobiographies, and oral testimonies as crucial parts of the historical record. These varied repositories of individual memories, taken together, create a collective communal memory.[13]

Although there were no essays on film, either fiction or non-fiction, and its role in this endeavour that is so central to diasporic Africans, there were obvious markers that offered direction in my own rescue mission of Portia White. Nora explains that we create these *lieux de mémoire* by deliberately creating archives, maintaining anniversaries, organizing celebrations etc. *Lieux de mémoire* may be historical or legendary, events or figures. They become sites of personal and collective memory. Not only did I want to know more about Portia, but from the little I did know, I did not want her erasure from the Canadian historical artistic landscape to continue. To my knowledge, Portia White had no parallel, regardless of race, in Canadian history. Portia White would become my *lieux de mémoire*.

Portia the Artist

> Nobody ever told me to sing, I was born singing. I think that if nobody had ever talked to me, I wouldn't be able to communicate in any other way but by singing. I was always bowing in my dreams and singing before people and parading across the stage as a very little girl. – *Portia White*

Between 1941, when she had her Toronto debut at Eaton Auditorium, and 1944, when she astonished and satisfied New York audiences and critics in her first Town Hall performance, Portia White captured the full attention of arts critics and music lovers throughout Canada. Interviewed in 1964, when she returned to Halifax to perform in a special concert to raise funds for the Nova Scotia Talent Trust, she explained, "But I was sort of naïve, approaching every concert as though it was just a dress rehearsal. This sort of dulls the real shock, you see."[14] Her success took her by surprise; the truth was, nervousness took over before her concerts. "Often before a concert, I am too nervous to sleep. I lie awake and go over the whole program complete with encores," she admitted to interviewer Thelma Le Cocq. Once she stepped on to the stage, her calm appeared: "I have a faculty for dividing myself in two. Putting one half of me in the wings while the other half sings on stage. I have a great time in the wings mocking at the onstage me. I say, 'Do people really think she's a wonderful artist? Why, there's so much she has to do yet.'"[15] Reviewer Augustus Bridle believed she was. In his words, her stage presence was "the acme of studied elegance in deportment."[16] She was a superb concert performer who sang in Italian, Spanish, French, and German. After hearing her sing, *Globe and Mail* critic Hector Charlesworth raved that "Her tonal volume is remarkable, and she makes beautiful use of it."[17] Portia's teacher, Ernesto Vinci, had a lot to do with the production of her vocal performance. He came to Nova Scotia in 1939 from Europe, via New York, taking her on as his prized student; he trained Portia in the *bel canto* technique, an Italian vocal style that means 'beautiful singing.' Vinci diligently schooled her and through rigorous training shifted her voice into the contralto range. Portia's earliest performances included selections by composers such as Mozart, Bizet, Handel, Schubert, Purcell, Verdi and Rachmaninoff and Negro spirituals, many arranged by H.T. Burleigh.

Ruth Barrie, a contralto and voice teacher based in Ottawa, who combines teaching with a singing career, understands the special relationship a singer has with her audience. "You really feel you have to draw the audience toward you and to develop a rapport with them. And when that happens, it's magic, it really is." Many felt Portia's magic. Barrie never learned about Portia when she went to music school, nor did she see her in concert, but after hearing a performance recording said:

> That it was a glorious instrument. A beautifully warm, rich and velvety tone. A lot of depth and a lot of colour to it. Impeccable German which I found very interesting when you consider someone growing up in Nova Scotia, it's not a language you would think they would be exposed to a great deal. Very good English diction as well.... I think it's important to say that for me, I definitely had a sense of the person behind the voice, which I think is something that is difficult to do.[18]

Winnipeg-born soprano Mary Morrison, who trained at Toronto's Royal Conservatory of Music and, coincidentally, also studied for a time with Ernesto Vinici, had the pleasure of seeing Portia perform. She remembers that:

> Portia had a wide range and a beautiful voice, so liquid, [it] poured out of her. She did programmes that had something for everybody in them. I like the top of her voice very much and I think maybe as she went along, she discovered more of the top of the voice. The lower register was very full of course. It was quite

even throughout, the voice doesn't stand still. And as she went along, she probably discovered notes that maybe she didn't even know she had. We don't hear many contraltos today and it's very fascinating. And the repertoire she chose, some of it is definitely mezzo, not so much contralto. She had a good high range.... Portia was probably the first Black person I'd heard and I think what struck me probably was not only the beautiful voice, but the sincerity she brought to the music and to the text.[19]

By the time she died in 1968, at the age of fifty-seven, Portia White had given a command performance before Queen Elizabeth II, had been featured in national and international magazines and had performed in nearly one hundred concerts across Canada, South America, the Caribbean and the United States. After her career was sidelined by ill health and poor management, she established herself as a consummate music and voice teacher in Toronto. She was the vocal teacher and coach of choice for Canadian theatre and radio performers including Lorne Greene, Don Franks, Ann Marie Moss, Dinah Christie, and Judith Lander. But even as she was being praised in the media and performing in concert halls throughout Canada, her race was rarely forgotten. Historian Hilary Russell points out that:

> Partly because she contradicted generalized negative images often applied to her race, members and consumers of the mainstream media were fascinated. They loved her looks, her regal bearing, and her Horatio Alger-like story; they were wowed by her well-spoken and cultivated intelligence; and they relished the opportunity that she provided for Canada, Nova Scotia, Halifax and even Toronto to take credit for her extraordinary success. Best of all, perhaps, her mere presence on the concert stage and in the media seemed to speak volumes about the absence of racial barriers in this country, especially by comparison with the United States.[20]

Portia did encounter discrimination, and in the manner of people of her generation, as interviewer Thelma Le Cocq discovered, had developed her own coping strategies:

The story is told that on one occasion she registered at a luxury hotel in a large Canadian city, was accepted and shown to her room, and then told she would be expected not to appear in the main dining room. She pointed out to the manager that it was very strange that someone sponsored by a government of Canada should not be acceptable. The manager went away very upset, returned to say she would be welcome in the dining room. "Thank you very much," she replied, "but I always prefer to eat in my own room."[21]

Although Portia is remembered vividly by former students such as performers Dinah Christie and Judith Lander, and her devoted accompanist Gordon Kushner – all of whom appear in the film – and anyone who saw her perform, her life and her work remained largely unknown to most Canadians.

Written Out of Music History

Portia White, young Canadian contralto who made her New York debut in Town Hall in March of last year [in 1944] and gave another recital in the same hall last fall, appeared here for a third time last night before a large audience that was warm in its response. The recital was under the auspices of the government of her native Nova Scotia.[22]

In outlining the two purposes of the book *Music in Canada*, by Ernest MacMillan, published in 1955, then Governor General Vincent Massey explains in his introduction that it will give readers a "true and comprehensive account of music in this country from its beginnings ... in this story of music in Canada, we can find a vivid reflection of a broader theme – the growth of Canadian nationality."[23] I could find no mention of Portia White in the overall text, and most surprising is her absence from the chapter on Solo Artists by Ettore Mazzoleni. He writes about Lois Marshall, who received her musical training in Toronto and "was on the way to becoming known to the whole country when she won the Naumburg Prize in New York. This gave her a Town Hall debut, which led at once to a contract with Columbia Artists Management, one of the dominating agencies in the concert field."[24]

When this book appeared, Portia White had already distinguished herself as a leading international soloist, having had her New York debut in 1944, after which she was signed by Columbia. She occupied a pre-eminent place in the Canadian arts during the 1940s and 1950s; her concerts were widely reviewed in the popular media. She was known as 'Canada's Singing Sensation' and 'The New Star of the Concert Stage,' and 'Canada's Marian Anderson,' among other monikers. Ernest MacMillan, also a performing artist, was represented in 1942 by Oxford University Press, which at the time, had set up a concert management division to represent artists including Portia, Ernesto Vinci, and violinist Kathleen Parlow, among others.[25] The music scene in Toronto and Canada was small; clearly, Portia was known to him, but given her excision from his book, she was 'invisible.'

Moreover, Portia White was known to strongly voice her opinions about the importance of Canadian artists receiving training in Canada. That she received her foundational training in Nova Scotia was her special badge of honour. When interviewed by journalists she freely offered her beliefs about Canadian artists, the importance of state funding for artists and the excellence of Canadian teachers. Her encounter with novelist Ernest Buckler, also a Nova Scotian, on assignment for *Saturday Night* in 1948, illustrates her passionate views. They were discussing concerts in small towns. Buckler wondered why anyone in a small town would go to a concert. Portia told him people in the Maritimes were "eager and hungry" for good music.

> *Buckler*: And here an almost evangelical fervour staccatos her usual calm.
> *Portia*: "Why should we grovel in the dust (!) to American talent, when right here in Canada we have bigger and better voices, because we're farther north? I told them everywhere we went, there is plenty of Canadian talent which could give you just as good a show as we've done. But there's no outlet for Canadian artists, they can't live. Why can't their talent be organized and heard?"
> *Buckler*: "She's got something there."[26]

Granted, Portia White had experienced career setbacks by the mid-1950s that led to her withdrawal from the concert stage and consequently, from the broad public visibility she had enjoyed. However, between 1941 and

1960, she dominated the Canadian concert scene and was regularly featured in Canadian magazines and newspapers and performed on radio broadcasts. She was anything but an unknown; however, she is absent from a primary text written during her lifetime and in the city where she had performed, lived, and worked. How could someone so widely known be expunged from the cultural record, despite being so carefully and lovingly preserved in the memories of her family, those who worked and studied with her, and significantly, those who saw her perform? To make the documentary, I needed to unearth the taproot of these memories in my search for answers to these nagging questions. Since she died in 1968, I would have to comb the personal recollections of those who knew her, or saw her perform – family, colleagues, friends, concert goers, and former students. Together, they would offer a collective memory that I would juxtapose against material memory – archival documents, photos, recordings, film footage, and physical spaces.

Journal Entry: Remembering Portia

I remember my mother always saying that Portia White had taught in our one-room segregated school in Beechville just before she had. She remembered that music played a big role in Portia's classroom teaching. This was before I was born. My uncle, who is eighty-six, says that when he was about sixteen, he had a crush on Portia, though she never knew it. Portia boarded with my great aunt Emma, whose home was a regular stop for anyone coming into the community. Aunt Emma saw a lot of my eager uncle, because he wanted to see Portia.

> She [Portia] was an extraordinary worker.... We did chat, but only at the end of what she wanted to accomplish each lesson. I never came away from there without having learned at least three important things. And I never ruined my voice again.
> – *Former Voice Student Dinah Christie, 1990*

How do I remember someone I have never met? And how is it that one can spend so much time thinking in detail about this 'someone' they never knew? Thinking about how her day was organized, what she ate for breakfast. What made her laugh. What excited her. What her presence felt like if you were in a room with her. What it was like for her to step onto the

Portia White, likely taken in Toronto in the early 1960s, courtesy of Maroon Films.

stage at New York's Town Hall at a time when so few others like her had done so. How it felt to be refused a room at a hotel in your hometown, then to experience the wonder and excitement of a three-month concert tour to South America and the Caribbean where you are feted and applauded everywhere you sing. Maybe the memories of others go deep inside to become your own.

Brazeal Dennard, Choir Director, Detroit, Friday March 6, 1998, notes from telephone conversation:

He remembers attending the Negro Music Festival where Portia White performed. It was at the Briggs Stadium, now called Tiger Stadium. It is still in Detroit. Holds about 70,000 to 80,000 people and he remembers it was full. He was in a choir organized by Robert Noland and was about fourteen or fifteen at the time. The year was 1944. He said, recall that this was just after the time when Marian Anderson was refused entry to Constitution Hall. Everyone knew of Marian Anderson, and Portia White was billed as 'Canada's Marian Anderson.' He remembers being mesmerized, enthralled by her: "quite a magnificent singer. Remember I was a young impressionable teen. She was statuesque, very beautifully gowned.... I recall her as a lovely woman. Making a lovely sound. She had a lovely sound, not better than Marian Anderson, different from her." He says in those days there was a natural association because of the race. It was not a real comparison. There was Dorothy Maynor, Paul Robeson, Marian Anderson and Roland Hayes and that was it. Not like today. He tells me there was a huge turnout. People were looking for something. She was a draw, this woman coming in from Canada, for this Festival. He is eager to participate in the film. If I can get to Detroit, he will be an amazing interview.

The Making of *Portia White:*
Think On Me - Tracing a Life

I chafe under the term *Atlantic Region* because it collapses four unique provinces as if they were one specific geographic place. (It is akin to Africa being spoken of as if it were a country, rather than a continent.) I use Atlantic Region advisedly, for the purpose of offering some general observations regarding the challenges faced by creators living in Canada's easternmost region. Artists working in the Atlantic provinces are often a tough-minded and good-humoured lot. Filmmakers who have chosen to make films here arguably might have to be the toughest of the lot.[27] The majority of the funding available for film production is tied to broadcasters. To access funds from provincial funding agencies, such as Film Nova Scotia (formerly the Nova Scotia Film Development Corporation), and from the Canadian Television Fund (CTF), a producer needs to have a broadcaster attached to the project by way of a licence agreement. Keeping up with the ever-changing guidelines of the various agencies is a job in and of itself. Many independent producers both direct and produce their work; such juggling can have a significant negative impact on the creative process, which by definition is already a complex, stress-inducing affair. A scan of the credits of most Canadian documentaries reveals a patchwork of sources independent producers use to piece together budgets to produce their work. The challenge when the filmmaker is both producing and directing is how to hold firm and true to the integrity of the "director's vision" at the same time as pragmatically figuring out, as a producer, how to stretch the limited dollars to most effectively translate it to the screen, not to mention making time to respond to the ongoing demands and requirements of the agencies and broadcasters. As producer of *Portia White: Think On Me*, I dealt with over twenty individuals in eight agencies during the various stages of development and production.

"Independent" filmmaking takes on a particularly contested meaning in a Canadian industry where the financial resources come predominately from state sources by way of tax credits and equity investment. Filmmaker-producers sign off on lengthy contracts that accord specific rights, in relation to the film, to the investing broadcasters and agencies. Such rights include script and rough cut approvals etc. Not all rights are exercised all of the time; the salient point is that such rights are entrenched and are legally binding. Filmmakers who fund their projects solely with grants from arts councils and private investment will not run such gauntlets. However, with more creators entering the field, competition and demands expand, thereby making it difficult to raise enough funds from such sources.[28]

It is precisely because there is a significant level of public investment in the film and television industry that filmmakers and producers of colour and First Nations filmmaker-producers have over many years initiated a concerted lobby of state funding agencies/departments and public media institutions such as the National Film Board of Canada, the Canadian Broadcasting Corporation, and Telefilm Canada to advocate for more access to, and the equitable distribution of, public funds. Lobbying worked in some measure and agencies and broadcasters began to take steps to address the barriers. This advocacy and the growing public discussion and emphasis on 'cultural diversity' in Canada had an ironic result: media production from so-called 'mainstream' producers, already well into the queue for funds, began to include, often superficially, the notion of diversity as a theme, or story line.[29]

Consequently, producers of colour and First Nations filmmakers, after their advocacy, often found themselves not only in competition with each other ('only a few at a time' approach and always limited funds) but with 'mainstream' filmmakers who, in the search for 'fundable' projects, pitched stories with 'diverse, or ethnic' story lines. During the late 1980s and '90s there were many heated debates regarding who has the right to tell what stories both in the literary and media worlds. During the development of my Portia White film, I received a call from an individual who informed me that 'someone had already pitched my story on Portia White and it was well underway ... '; the clear message was that I should move on to some other story because this story was already being done. At one point, when pitching my current film, *The Little Black School House*, I was told that there were already films in the running that had 'Black' themes of some type.[30]

For a period in the 1990s VisionTV played a significant role for many documentary filmmakers across Canada and especially in the Atlantic Region. Fil Fraser, then head of VisionTV, was an early supporter of my Portia White film project, was keen to see the film made, and signed on without question.[31] VisionTV provided letters of intent and development licences to filmmakers that enabled them to get a foot in the door of the various provincial film agencies, or other funding bodies which would only consider applications for equity investment, at either the development or production stage, from producers whose projects have a broadcaster attached. Even though the VisionTV licence fees were small, they enabled filmmakers to launch projects on a wide range of subject areas, and VisionTV was a national broadcaster. However, by 2001–2002, it shifted its program mandate, and subsequently the type of documentaries supported at the development level. Many projects, including *The Little Black School House*, slid completely off the table, leaving filmmakers scrambling to find new broadcasters and funds to advance their films.[32] With the necessary patchwork of funds, the Portia White documentary project, which became *Portia White: Think On Me*, got underway. The research was exhaustive. I created a multi-layered research map to chart the information: clues, fragments, people, places, and any references to archival audio and visual material. These would be the ingredients for the construction of a composite filmic view of Portia's life and career. When one sets out to tell a version of a person's life, one needs some idea of where the journey might lead; the landscape, the geography, the contours, the switchbacks, all become part of the adventure.

Many years had passed since Portia White's concerts in the 1940s. With the passage of time, tracings become faint, making the research complex, daunting, and often, overwhelmingly discouraging. My map was in constant flux, as routes and by-ways were created when new information came into view. I added a birth to death chronology, noting the dates of the various known events in her life. I kept 'to do' and 'to find' lists, coloured file cards of notes, several notebooks, computer files, many filing boxes of material (including newspaper clippings, photographs, letters, sheet music, and concert programs) and early recordings of other singers such as Marian Anderson, Renata Tebaldi, and Ghena Dimitrova.

I began with Portia's family in Halifax, Toronto, and Montreal and was guided by their stories, suggestions, and memorabilia. Their co-operation was generous, always supportive, and most encouraging. Later I added the names of Portia's friends, professional associates, and colleagues to my 'to find' list. Anyone I succeeded in finding gave leads, more fragments, more clues. In the process, individuals who had seen her perform, or who had been her voice students, were uncovered. I followed even the most remote leads, some of which were dead ends, others that pointed to someone, or something else. I sought out experts in the field who could provide context and understanding of the life and career of a concert performer at that time. Historian Hilary Russell, who had completed research on Portia White for the Historic Sites and Monuments Board of Canada, which subsequently designated Portia as a person of national significance, was an invaluable colleague who shared her research, and serendipitously, her family. While researching, she discovered that her mother, Jean McFarlane, had seen Portia perform in Kingston, Jamaica, during Portia's three-month tour of Central and South America and the Caribbean in 1946. Both agreed to be interviewed.

I took advantage of any public opportunities to promote the research and placed an ad in the *Globe and Mail*'s personals column with the hope of turning up people or material. Elated, I received responses to the ad that led directly to two significant interviews. I searched public and private archives, libraries, and historical societies in Canada and the United States. Any details that emerged or that were gleaned from conversations were accorded a place on the map or in the chronology.

I shadowed Portia. I walked where she walked in Halifax, to Cornwallis Street Baptist Church. I rode the train to Moncton, New Brunswick, and walked the streets of the Toronto neighbourhood where she lived and taught in her studio. I stood in the expansive field at Detroit's Briggs (formerly Tiger) Stadium where she performed, spent nights at Winnipeg's Fort Garry Hotel where she met her faithful accompanist, and later my very generous interview subject, Gordon Kushner, and sat in the balcony of Ottawa's First Baptist Church, the venue for her last public performance.

During the research process I spoke with more than fifty people about Portia White, her life and career. From this initial grouping, I selected twenty-two people for on-camera interviews, which were filmed in and around Halifax, Nova Scotia, Toronto, Ottawa, and Detroit. We filmed archival material at the Nova Scotia Archives, the Ontario Black History Society in Toronto, York University Archives, Toronto Reference Library, National Archives and Library in Ottawa and the Detroit Public Library. I collected additional archival and still material from personal and public sources and filmed it in Halifax. Moving image and sound material came from sources such as the National Film Board of Canada and the Canadian Broadcasting Corporation Television Archives.

Portia's Voice:
The Spine of the Narrative

> 1948 ... It's almost 50 years. And it's like yesterday. When I
> hear that voice, I say, oh, yeah, that's her. And I hope she will be
> remembered. – *Gordon Kushner, Accompanist*[33]

Finding the right structure for a documentary is like panning for gold, a
lot of sifting and shaking, always some movement until the glint presents
itself. Once a structure is found, a lot of the anxiety that characterizes the
editing process subsides. Logically, the film rested on the spine of Portia's
voice – her singing voice and her speaking voice. We posted file cards with
a variety of possible narrative structures on our corkboard and used the
piles of research notes and the interview transcriptions as key elements in
structuring the narrative, which fell into three acts. The first ended with her
debut at Eaton Auditorium, the second with her illness and the move back
to Toronto from New York, and the third began with her career as a vocal
teacher and a life out of the limelight.

Surprisingly detailed and poignant memories characterized both the
research and on-camera interviews. It seemed as though those interviewed
had been waiting, in some cases for fifty years, to speak about Portia
White. Memories, and often tears, flowed quickly and easily. Her imprint
was strong and palpable. We pored over every available image of Portia,
either archival stills or footage, and began to structure the through line
of her life using the chronology the patchwork of materials and her voice.
Since the limited amount of moving image footage of Portia had to be used
sparingly, we (editor Angela Baker and myself) were challenged to create a
visual approach that would keep her image at the centre of the film. Cin-
ematographer Kent Nason's lighting and fluid shooting style gave the many
still photographs a quality not unlike actuality footage, and, further aided
by sound designer John Rosborough's work on the archival voice and sound
material, we evoked Portia's presence throughout the piece. Another fundamental structural element was the decision that I should be the on-camera
narrative guide for the film. It was not the choice I had initially intended,
but in prepping for the shoot, we decided it was wise to shoot some footage
with me in the different locations, as a 'just in case' option. I had embarked
on this story-journey, and after so many years was completely inside it by

this point. Could I even write it for someone else to tell? The 'just in case' became the case.

The Launch

> As a fellow Nova Scotian I was not aware of who Portia White was until I watched your show. I am amazed and disappointed that there is no park, street or building named in her honour in Halifax, as one of the most famous Nova Scotians. I think it is well overdue, for it is truly deserving. I would like to thank Sylvia Hamilton for her informative biography on an extraordinary talented woman. – *Cynthia K., Toronto, March 08, 2002, e-mail transmission*

> Many thanks for your program tonight. Listening to the black entertainers of the 50s and 60s was easy and enjoyable listening, but I was most interested in your last hour on Portia White. You introduced me to a famous Canadian that I was unaware of. I was impressed with her life and her voice. – *Barry Fisher, Calgary AB, March 7, 2002, e-mail transmission*

> I was a resident of Branksome Hall.... I was frequently one of the few girls in the house over the weekend and Miss White often took her turn at weekend duty. On one occasion she and the school nurse took me Christmas shopping – it all came back to me during the references to Christmas in the program." – *Shelley Tidy, March 8, 2002, e-mail transmission*

Portia White: Think On Me was screened at festivals and on several television networks.[34] In many ways the story told in the fifty-minute film was not completely contained therein, and not simply because of the limitation imposed by the form. The film is an entity, or as Paula Rabinowitz says, "film is itself a document, each with its own history."[35] It exists in the world and is subject to the responses that come precisely because it exists. But it can't tell its own history, part of which is the way people respond to it, part of which is how it came to be – a birth story, what material remains that was not included, what decisions were made and why, and what struggles ensued about where 'truth' was found. Rabinowitz reminds that:

> Documentary films theorize themselves as truth tellers and do so with reference to their historicity – their inclusion in a film history and their representation of another time or place. As film viewers we too bring our histories to bear on the images; documentary film can describe historical reality, demonstrate its effects, and evoke its experience for its viewers simultaneously. But it is this very immediacy which demands refusal so that we understand our own historicity in order to begin to see what we bring to the viewing process, and more importantly, what we get from it.[36]

Viewers who saw *Portia White: Think on Me*, either during the public screenings or on the television broadcasts, brought their histories: they came forward with memories and information about Portia White triggered by what they saw. With the swiftness of e-mail transmissions, I received messages not long after the film was televised. Viewers went online, found the broadcasters' Web sites, and sent messages that were in turn forwarded to me. Their notes included memories of meeting her or seeing her in concert. Some wrote to say how pleased they were to see the film because they had not heard of her, and that she is someone Canadians should know about. Traditionally, after a public film screening, the filmmaker may engage with the audience in a question-answer session in the theatre; lively conversations spill into the lobby after the formal session has ended. Ten years ago, after a television broadcast, only those who could make time and who were able to track down an address would write a letter to the filmmaker. Many viewers may have wanted to, but it was not an effortless matter. The internet gives instant access. I responded to the messages and in a few cases exchanged several correspondences with some of those who wrote.

What Remains

Portia White: Think On Me represented my *take* on Portia White's life at a particular moment on the continuum of my journey. It was a story I could present within the frame and finite time of the form, and available financial resources. What I knew about Portia White shifted and expanded as

I conducted my research. At times, a fragment of information that seemed insignificant a few years into the process became more important and made sense as I accumulated more pieces of her story. At times, I grappled, and still do, with conflicting elements of her story resulting in more questions to answer, more puzzles to solve. My fascination with this unique artist has not diminished. I look ahead but can't see the next marker; my search continues.

NOTES

1 Topsy is the name of a small Black girl character in Harriet Beecher Stowe's *Uncle Tom's Cabin* (1852). Although Stowe's book was considered an anti-slavery publication, the Black characters are presented as caricatures, rather than people with humanity.

2 "Bright Moments," by St. Claire Bourne, *Z Magazine* (March 1989): 40–41.

3 Michelle Parkerson, "No More Mammy Stories: An Overview of Black Women Filmmakers," *Gallerie Women's Art Annual* (1989): 13–15.

4 *Speak It! From the Heart of Black Nova Scotia*, producer, Mike Mahoney, director, Sylvia D. Hamilton, 28 min. 50 sec., National Film Board of Canada, 1994, 16mm. The explicit graffiti: "Niggers should be locked up in chains...." At one point in the film, Krista Brodie said, "If we could reach into the minds of a lot of white people you'd be surprised about what they think of Black people." Shingai Nyajeka, another lead student, said, "Teachers think this a racism free zone but it is not."

5 In November 2006 Michael Richards set off a blitz of his own when he verbally assaulted and insulted several audience members who were attending his show at the Laugh Factory in West Hollywood on 17 November. He let out a triad using the word 'nigger.' YouTube and other websites carried footage of his vicious rant. For a discussion of the derivation of and the contemporary debate about the use of the term 'nigger,' see Randall Kennedy, *Nigger: The Strange Career of a Troublesome Word* (New York: Pantheon, 2002).

6 Jack White, Interview by Sylvia D. Hamilton, The Portia White Project, Maroon Films Inc., Toronto 1998.

7 Constance Backhouse, *Colour-Coded: A Legal History of Racism in Canada, 1900–1950* (University of Toronto Press, 1999), 15. Another equally informative text examining racism in Canada from a historical and legal perspective is James W. St. G. Walker, *"Race," Rights and the Law in the Supreme Court of Canada* (Waterloo, ON: Wilfrid Laurier Press, 1997).

8 Columbia Concerts Inc., Community Concerts Promotional Brochure, 1946–1947. Other artists in the roster include baritone Todd Duncan, soprano Camilla Williams, singer and guitarist Josh White, all three African Americans, and violinists Jascha Heifetz and Yehudi Menuhin, pianist Serge Prokofieff, tenor Jussi Bjoerling and soprano Helen Traubel.

9 Rosalyn M. Story, preface to *And So I Sing: African-American Divas of Opera and Concert* (New York: Amistad Press Inc., 1990), xiii–xvii.

10 Ibid., 1–19

11 Ibid., xiii–xvii.

12 Pierre Nora, "Between Memory and History: Les Lieux de Mémoire, in *History and Memory in African-American Culture*," ed. Geneviève Fabre and Robert O'Meally, trans. Marc Roudebush (New York: Oxford University Press, 1994), 284–300.

13 Geneviève Fabre and Robert O'Meally, eds., introduction to *History and Memory in African-American Culture* (New York: Oxford University Press, 1994), 3–17.

14 Portia White, Interview by unidentified host of AM Chronicle, CBC Radio, Halifax, October 1964.

15 Thelma Le Cocq, "A Voice From Nova Scotia: Portia White," *Chatelaine* (December 1945): 26.

16 Augustus Bridle, *Mail Star*, 6 May 1943, 6.

17 Hector Charlesworth, "Portia White's Rare Promise," *Saturday Night*, 15 September 1941.

18 Ruth Barrie, Interview by Sylvia D. Hamilton, The Portia White Project, Maroon Films Inc., Ottawa, 19 October 1999.

19 Mary Morrison, Interview by Sylvia D. Hamilton, The Portia White Project,

Maroon Films Inc., Toronto, 21 October 1999.

20   Hilary Russell, "Portia White 1911–1968." Historical Services Branch, Canadian Parks Services, 1995, unpublished.

21   Thelma Le Cocq, "A Voice from Nova Scotia.".

22   *New York Times*, 6 December 1945, 31.

23   Vincent Massey, foreword to *Music In Canada*, ed. Ernest MacMillan (Toronto: University of Toronto Press, 1955), v. All of the 18 contributors to the book were male, one of whom, Leslie Bell, a lecturer, newspaper columnist, and broadcaster, knew Portia White because he conducted an interview with her for CBC Radio in Toronto.

24   MacMillan, 106–13.

25   Promotional advertisement for Oxford University Press, Canadian Branch, for its artists on its management roster, appears in *Canadian Review of Music*, October 1942, 21.

26   Ernest Buckler, "Maritimes Letter: Island has a Legislating Flurry; Halifax's Million Dollar Voice," *Saturday Night*, 17 April 1948, 26–27.

27   Documentary filmmakers such as Chuck Lapp and Teresa MacInnes, in Nova Scotia, and Gerry Rogers and Barbara Doran in Newfoundland, for example, who both produce and direct films, are standard bearers in this regard.

28   Canada Council, for example, as a condition of its funding, requires that the filmmakers retain creative control over their projects. Raising funds from arts councils for projects having budgets of $200,000 or more is a tall order. Canada Council offers support at the various stages of development of a project, so a filmmaker could receive research, production, and post-production funds from the Council, but not all within the same fiscal year. Peer juries review the projects so there is no guarantee of approval.

29   Discussion of the advocacy efforts and their results is beyond the scope of this essay. In light of the current state of the film and television industry, it is a topic ripe for further research and analysis. National cultural institutions such as the Canada Council for the Arts, the National Film Board of Canada, and the CBC, began equity programs in the 1980s as a result of the advocacy and pressure from artists and cultural workers. More recently, media organizations such as CHUMTV (now part of CTVglobemedia), Telefilm Canada, and Global have begun various programs.

30   *The Little Black School House* is a one-hour documentary shot in Nova Scotia and Ontario in 2006 about the little-known history and experience of Canada's segregated schools. It premiered at the 2007 Atlantic Film Festival in Halifax.

31   Along with Fil Fraser at VisionTV, his colleague Peter Flemington was eager to see the film go into production and fully endorsed it. CBC Halifax's Penny Longley, then Head of Independent Production, was a major supporter and brought CBC firmly on board. Other funding agencies that financed the film were the Nova Scotia Film Development Corporation, Telefilm Canada, the Canadian Independent Film and Video Fund, and Rogers' Telefund. The film was completed in the spring of 2000 and had its first screening in the fall at the Atlantic Film Festival, where it won an award for Sound Design. It is distributed by Moving Images, a Vancouver-based distributor.

32   In 2007 a group of documentary makers from the Maritimes lodged a formal complaint with the Canadian Radio-television and Telecommunications Commission (CRTC) alleging that VisionTV breached the regional conditions of its licence. See "Documentary makers criticize Vision TV," Gayle MacDonald, *Globe and Mail*, 24 October 2007.

33   Gordon Kushner, Interview by Sylvia D. Hamilton, The Portia White Project, Maroon Films Inc., Toronto, 22 October 1999.

34　Available from Moving Images Distribution, www.movingimages.ca. There have
been national telecasts on CBC's Opening Night, Bravo!, VisionTV and regional
telecasts on CBC Maritimes, and British
Columbia's The Knowledge Network.

35　Paula Rabinowitz, "Wreckage Upon
Wreckage: History, Documentary and
the Ruins of Memory," *History and
Theory* 32(2) (1993): 119–37.

36　Ibid.

Select Bibliography

Acland, Charles. *Screen Traffic: Movies, Multiplexes, and Global Culture*. Durham, NC: Duke University Press, 2003.

Althusser, Louis. *For Marx*. New York: Verso, 1990.

Anderson, Benedict, *Imagined Communities: Reflections on the Origin and Spread of Nationalism*. New York: Verso, 1996.

Apparudai, Arjun, ed. *Globalization*. Durham, NC: Duke University Press, 2001.

Armatage, Kay et al. *Gendering the Nation: Canadian Women's Cinema*. Toronto: University of Toronto Press, 1999.

Aronowitz, Stanley, and Jonathan Cutler, eds. *Post-Work: The Wages of Cybernation*. New York: Routledge, 1998.

———, Barbara Martinsons, and Michael Menser, eds., with Jennifer Rich. *Technoscience and Cyberculture*. New York: Routledge, 1996.

Atlantic Filmmaker's Co-operative. *30 Takes: Celebrating 30 Years at the Atlantic Filmmaker's Cooperative*. Halifax: AFCOOP, 2004.

Backhouse, Constance. *Colour-Coded: A Legal History of Racism in Canada, 1900–1950*. Toronto: University of Toronto Press, 1999.

Barber, Bruce, ed. *Conceptual Art: The NSCAD Connection 1967–1973*. Halifax: Anna Leonowens Gallery/NSCAD University, 2001.

Barthes, Roland. *Mythologies*, translated by Annette Lavers. New York: Harper Collins, 1972.

Beard, William, and Jerry White, eds. *North of Everything: English Canadian Cinema Since 1980*. Edmonton: University of Alberta Press, 2002.

Beaty, Bart, and Rebecca Sullivan. *Canadian Television Today*. Calgary: University of Calgary Press, 2006.

Berland, Jody. "Space at the Margins." *Topia* 1 (Spring 1997): 55–82.

Bhabha, Homi. *The Location of Culture*. London and New York: Routledge, 1994.

Cavell, Richard. *McLuhan in Space: A Cultural Geography*. Toronto: University of Toronto Press, 2002.

———. "Theorizing Canadian Space: Postcolonial Articulations." In *Canada: Theoretical Discourse*, edited by Terry Goldie et al., 75–104. Association for Canadian Studies, 1994.

Charland, M. "Technological Nationalism." *Canadian Journal of Social Theory* 10(1–2) (1986): 196–220.

Charney, Leo, and Vanessa R. Schwartz, eds. *Cinema and the Invention of Modern Life*. Berkeley: University of California Press, 1995.

Clairmont, Donald H., and Dennis William Magill. *Africville: The Life and Death of a Canadian Black Community*, 3rd ed. Toronto: Scholar's Press, 1999.

Clandfield, David. *Pierre Perrault and the Poetic Documentary*. Toronto Film Festival/Indiana University Press, 2004.

Clarke, George Elliott. "Honouring African-Canadian Geography." *Borderlines* 45 (1997): 35–39.

———. *Odysseys Home: Mapping African-Canadian Literature*. Toronto: University of Toronto Press, 2002.

Conrad, Margaret R., and James Hiller. *Atlantic Canada: A Region in the Making*. Toronto: Oxford University Press, 2001.

Cox, Kevin, ed. *Spaces of Globalization: Reasserting the Power of the Local*. New York: Guilford Press, 1997.

Dick, Ernest J. *Remembering Singalong Jubilee*. Halifax: Formac, 2004.

Dorland, Michael. *So Close to the State/s: The Emergence of Canadian Feature Film Policy*. Toronto: University of Toronto Press, 1998.

Drache, Daniel. "Canada in American Empire." *Canadian Journal of Social and Political Theory* 12(1–2) (1988): 212–29.

Eco, Umberto. *A Theory of Semiotics*. Bloomington: Indiana University Press, 1976.

Elder, R. Bruce. *Image and Identity: Reflections on Canadian Film and Culture*. Waterloo: Wilfrid Laurier University Press, 1989.

Elmer, Greg, and Mike Gasher, eds. *Contracting Out Hollywood: Runaway Productions and Foreign Location Shooting*. Lanham, MD: Rowman & Littlefield, 2005.

Evans, Gary. *In the National Interest: A Chronicle of the National Film Board of Canada from 1949 to 1989*. Toronto: University of Toronto Press, 1991.

Eyland, Cliff, and Susan Gibson Garvey. *Uses of the Vernacular in Nova Scotian Art*. Halifax: Dalhousie Art Gallery, 1994.

Fabre, Geneviève, and Robert O'Meally, eds. *History and Memory in African-American Culture*, translated by Marc Roudebush. New York: Oxford University Press, 1994.

Feldman, Seth, ed. *Take Two: A Tribute to Film in Canada*. Toronto: Irwin, 1984.

Feldman, Seth, and Joyce Nelson, eds. *Canadian Film Reader*. Toronto: Peter Martin, 1977.

Forbes, Ernest. *Challenging the Regional Stereotype*. Fredericton, NB: Acadiensis Press, 1989.

Forbes, Ernest, and Del Muise. *The Atlantic Provinces in Confederation*. Toronto: University of Toronto Press and Acadiensis Press, 1993.

Francis, Daniel. *National Dreams: Myth, Memory, and Canadian History*. Vancouver: Arsenal Pulp Press, 1997.

Frank, David. "One Hundred Years After: Film and History in Atlantic Canada." *Acadiensis* 26 (Spring 1997): 112–26.

Fuller, Kathryn H. *At the Picture Show: Small-Town Audiences and the Creation of Movie Fan Culture*. Charlottesville, VA: University Press of Virginia, 1996.

Gasher, Mike. *Hollywood North: The Feature Film Industry in British Columbia*. Vancouver: UBC Press, 2002.

Gauthier, Jennifer. "Where is Here?: Local Visions in Three Canadian Films." *Canadian Journal of Film Studies* 14.2 (2005): 38–53.

Gittings, Christopher E. *Canadian National Cinema*. London: Routledge, 2002.

Gunning, Tom. "The Cinema of Attractions: Early Film, Its Spectator and the Avant-Garde." In *Early Cinema: Space, Frame, Narrative*, ed. Thomas Elsaesser with Adam Barker, 56–62. London: BFI, 1990.

Harcourt, Peter. *Movies and Mythologies: Towards a National Cinema*. CBC, 1977.

Hardt, Michael, and Antonio Negri. *Empire*. Cambridge, MA: Harvard University Press, 2000.

Harper, Bill. *A Picture by Christmas: Early CBC Television in Nova Scotia*. Halifax: Nimbus Publishing, 2002.

Harper, Marjory, and Michael E. Vance. *Myth, Migration and the Making of Memory: Scotia and Nova Scotia 1700–1990*. Halifax: Gorsebrook Research Institute for Atlantic Canada Studies, 1999.

Harvey, David. *The Condition of Postmodernity*. Cambridge, MA: Blackwell, 1990.

Held, David, and Anthony McGrew. *The Global Transformations Reader*. Cambridge, UK: Polity, 2000.

Higson, Andrew. "The Concept of National Cinema." *Screen* 30:4 (Autumn 1989): 36–46.

Hiller, James K., "Is Atlantic Canadian History Possible?" *Acadiensis* 30(1) (Autumn 2000): 16–22.

Hjort, Mette, and Scott Mackenzie, eds. *Cinema and Nation*. London and New York: Routledge, 2000.

Howell, Colin. "Film and History in Atlantic Canada." *Acadiensis* 11(2) (Spring 1982): 24–145.

———. "Development, Deconstruction and Region: A Personal Memoir," *Acadiensis* 30(1) (Autumn 2000): 23–30.

Innis, Harold A. *The Bias of Communication*. University of Toronto, 1951.

Jameson, Fredric. *Postmodernism or, The Cultural Logic of Late Capitalism*. Durham, NC: Duke University Press, 1991.

———. *The Political Unconscious: Narrative as a Socially Symbolic Act*. Ithaca, NY: Cornell University Press, 1981.

———. *The Geopolitical Aesthetic: Cinema and Space in the World System*. Bloomington: Indiana University Press, 1992.

———. *Postmodernism, or, The Cultural Logic of Late Capitalism*. Durham, NC: Duke University Press, 1991.

Jancovich, Mark, Lucy Faire, and Sarah Stubbings. *The Place of the Audience: Cultural Geographies of Film Consumption*. London: BFI, 2003.

Jones, D.B. *Movies and Memoranda: An Interpretive History of the National Film Board of Canada*. Ottawa: Deneau-Canadian Film Institute, 1981.

Kellner, Douglas. *Media Culture: Cultural Studies, Identity and Politics Between the Modern and the Postmodern*. London and New York: Routledge, 1995.

Keohane, Kieran. "Symptoms of Canada: National Identity and the Theft of National Enjoyment." *CineAction* 28 (1992): 20–33.

Khouri, Malek. *Filming Politics: Communism and the Portrayal of the Working Class at the National Film Board of Canada, 1939–46*. Calgary: University of Calgary Press, 2007. .

Kroker, Arthur. *Technology and the Canadian Mind: Innis/McLuhan/Grant*. Montreal: New World Perspectives, 1984.

Leach, Jim. *Film in Canada*. Toronto: Oxford University Press, 2006.

Lefebvre, Henri. *The Production of Space*. Blackwell, 1991.

Loiselle, André. "Novel, Play, Film: The Three Endings of Gordon Pinsent's *John and the Missus*," *Canadian Journal of Film Studies* 3(1) (1994): 67.

Loiselle, André, and Tom McSorley. *Self Portraits*. Ottawa: Canadian Film Institute, 2006.

MacGregor, Gaile. *The Wacousta Syndrome: Explorations in the Canadian Langscape*. Toronto: University of Toronto Press, 1985.

MacSwain, James, ed. *Intersections: 25 Years of Connecting at the Centre of Art Tapes*. Halifax: Pottersfield Press, 2004.

Mckay, Ian. *Quest of the Folk: Antimodernism and Cultural Selection in Twentieth Century Nova Scotia*. Montreal and Kingston: McGill-Queen's University Press, 1994.

McTavish, Lianne. "Beyond the Margins: Re-Framing Canadian Art History," *Acadiensis* 30(1) (Autumn 2000): 104–117.

Magder, Ted. *Canada's Hollywood: The Canadian State and Feature Films*. Toronto: University of Toronto Press, 1993.

Marchak, Patricia. "Nationalism and Regionalism in Canada." *Canadian Review of Studies in Nationalism* 7(1) (Spring 1980): 15–30.

Marchessault, Janine, ed. *Mirror Machine: Video and Identity*. Toronto and Montreal: YYZ-CRCCI, 1995.

Massey, Doreen. *Space, Place, and Gender*. Cambridge, UK: Polity, 1994.

———. *For Space*. Thousand Oaks, CA: Sage, 2005.

———, et al. *Rethinking the Region*. New York: Routledge, 1998.

Melnyk, George. *One Hundred Years of Canadian Cinema*. Toronto: University of Toronto Press, 2004.

———. *Radical Regionalism*. Edmonton: NeWest, 1981.

Miller, Toby, Nitin Govil, John McMurrua, and Richard Maxwell. *Global Hollywood*. London: BFI, 2001.

Mitchell, W.J.T., ed. *Landscape and Power*. Chicago and London: University of Chicago, 1984.

Morley, D., and Robins, K. *Spaces of Identity: Global Media, Electronic Landscapes, and Cultural Boundaries*. London: Routledge, 1995.

Morris, Peter. *Embattled Shadows: A History of Canadian Cinema, 1895–1939*. Montreal: McGill-Queen's University Press, 1978.

———. "Backwards to the Future: John Grierson's Film Policy for Canada." *Flashback: People and Institutions in Canadian Film History,* edited by Gene Walz, 17–35 Montreal: Mediatexte, 1986.

———. "In Our Own Eyes: The Canonizing of Canadian Film." *Canadian Journal of Film Studies* 3(1) (Spring 1994): 27–44.

———. "The Uncertain Trumpet: Defining a [Canadian] Art Cinema in the Sixties." *CineAction* 16 (May 1989): 6–13.

Musser, Charles. *The Emergence of Cinema: The American Screen to 1907.* New York: Charles Scribner, 1990.

Naficy, Hamid, ed. *Home, Exile, Homeland: Film, Media, and Politics of Place.* New York: Routledge, 1999.

New, William. *Borderlands. How we Speak About Canada.* Vancouver: UBC Press, 1998.

Nichols, Bill. *Ideology and The Image: Social Representation in the Cinema and Other Media.* Bloomington: Indiana University Press, 1981.

Overton, James. *Making a World of Difference: Essays on Tourism, Culture and Development in Newfoundland.* St. John's: ISER-Memorial University of Newfoundland, 1996.

Palmer, Bryan D. *Cultures of Darkness: Night Travels in the Histories of Transgression.* New York: Monthly Review Press, 2000.

Peacock, Jan. "Body for Speaking: Body-Centred Video in Halifax 1972–1982." In *Video Re/view: the (Best) Source Book for Critical Writings on Canadian Artists' Video,* edited by Peggy Gale and Lisa Steele, 144–45. Toronto: Art Metropole, 1996.

Pendakur, Manjunath. *Canadian Dreams and American Control: The Political Economy of the Canadian Film Industry.* Toronto and Detroit: Garamond – Wayne State University Press, 1990.

Pike, David L. "Canadian Cinema in the Age of Globalization." *CineAction* 57 (March 2002): 2–10.

Quantrill, Malcolm. *Plain Modern: The Architecture of Brian MacKay-Lyons.* Princeton: Princeton Architectural Press, 2005.

Rabinowitz, Paula. "Wreckage Upon Wreckage: History and Documentary and the Ruins of Memory." History and Theory 32(2) (1993): 119–37.

Ramsey, Christine. "Canadian Narrative Cinema from the Margins: 'The Nation' and Masculinity in Goin' Down the Road." *Canadian Journal of Film Studies* 2(2–3) (1993): 27–49.

Ranger, Terrence, and Eric Hobsbawm, eds. *The Invention of Tradition.* New York: Cambridge University Press, 1983.

Reid, John, and Stephen Hornsby, eds. *New England and the Maritime Provinces: Connections and Comparisons.* Montreal: McGill-Queen's University Press, 2005.

Riegel, Christian Erich. *A Sense of Place: Re-Evaluating Regionalism in Canadian and American Writing.* Edmonton: University of Alberta Press, 1997.

Robertson, Clive. *Policy Matters: Administrations of Art and Culture.* Toronto: YYZ-Books, 2006.

Rompkey, Ronald. *Grenfell of Labrador: A Biography.* Toronto: University of Toronto Press, 1991.

Rutherford, Paul. *When Television Was Young: Primetime Canada 1952–1967.* Toronto: University of Toronto Press, 1990.

Sherbert, Garry, Anne Gérin, Sheila Petty, eds. *Canadian Cultural Poesis: Essays on Canadian Culture.* Waterloo, ON: Wilfrid Laurier University Press, 2006.

Shields, Rob. *Places at the Margins: Alternative Geographies of Modernity.* London: Routledge, 1991.

Smith, Neil. *Uneven Development: Nature, Capital and the Production of Space.* Blackwell, 1990.

Sussman, Gerald, and John A. Lent, eds. *Global Productions: Labor in the Making of the 'Information Society.'* Cresskill, NJ: Hampton Press, 1998.

Taras, David, Frits Pannekoek, and Maria Bakardjieva, eds. *How Canadians Communicate.* Calgary: University of Calgary Press, 2003.

Thompson, Marie. "The Myth of the Vanishing Cape Breton Fiddler: The Role of a CBC Film in the Cape Breton Fiddle Revival." *Acadiensis* 35(2) (Spring 2006): 5–26.

Tinic, Serra. *On Location: Canada's Television Industry in a Global Market.* Toronto: University of Toronto Press, 2005.

Tippett, Maria. *Making Culture: English-Canadian Institutions and the Arts before the Massey Commission.* Toronto: University of Toronto Press, 1990.

Tomlinson, John. *Globalization and Culture.* Chicago: University of Chicago Press, 1999.

Trew, Johanne Devlin. "Conflicting Visions: Don Messer, Liberal Nationalism and the Canadian Unity Debate," *International Journal of Canadian Studies* 26 (Fall 2002).

Underhill, Frank. *The Image of Confederation.* Toronto: CBC, 1964.

Urquhart, Peter. "You Should Know Something – Anything – About this Movie. You Paid For It." *Canadian Journal of Film Studies* 12(2) (Fall 2003): 64–80.

Varga, Darrell, and Malek Khouri, eds. *Working on Screen: Representations of the Working Class in Canadian Cinema.* Toronto: University of Toronto Press, 2006.

———. "Reading, Regarding, and Waiting: Three New Documentaries from Nova Scotia." *Cineaction* 69 (Spring 2006): 60–63.

Walker, W. St. G. *"Race," Rights and the Law in the Supreme Court of Canada.* Waterloo, ON: Wilfrid Laurier Press, 1997.

Walz, Eugene, ed. *Flashback: People and Institutions in Canadian Film History.* Montreal: Mediatexte, 1986.

Wasko, Janet. *Hollywood in the Information Age.* Cambridge: Polity Press, 1994.

Waugh, Thomas. "Cinemas, Nations, Masculinities (The Martin Walsh Memorial Lecture 1998)." *Canadian Journal of Film Studies/ Revue Canadienne d'Études Cinématographiques* 8(1) (Spring 1999): 8–44.

————. *The Romance of Transgression in Canada: Queering Sexualities, Nations, Cinemas.* Montreal: McGill-Queen's University Press, 2006.

White, Jerry, ed. *The Cinema of Canada.* London: Wallflower, 2006.

Williams, Alan, ed. *Film and Nationalism.* New Brunswick, NJ: Rutgers University Press, 2002.

Williams, Raymond. *Culture.* London: Fontana, 1981.

————. *Television: Technology and Cultural Form.* London: Wesleyan University Press, 1974.

Wilson, Robert, and Dissanayake, Wimal. *Global/Local: Cultural Production and the Transnational Imaginary.* Durham, NC: Duke University Press, 1996.

CONTRIBUTORS

BRUCE BARBER is a professor of Media Arts and director of the MFA program at NSCAD University. Since 1972 he has exhibited his artwork internationally, including these venues: Paris Biennale 1977; Sydney Biennale 1979; *The Art of Memory, The Loss of History* (New Museum, NYC 1985); *Resistance Anti-Baudrillard* (White Columns, NYC); *A Different War: Vietnam in Art,* curated by Lucy Lippard, travelling 1989–1992); *Memory Works: Post-Modern Impulses in Canadian Art,* curated by Mark Cheetham; *Streaming: A Laboratory,* Walter Phillips Gallery, Banff Centre,1999; *Interactions* Festival, Poland 2000; *Post-Object and Performance Art in New Zealand 1970 and Beyond,* Robert McDougall Gallery Christchurch, N.Z. 2000. He has also published many essays and reviews and is author of the forthcoming *Popular Modernisms: Art, Cartoons, Comics and Cultural In/Subordination.*

ANDREW BURKE is an assistant professor in the Department of English at the University of Winnipeg. He works on nineteenth-century British literature and culture, critical theory, and contemporary film. His current project is on representations of modernization and modernity in postwar British cinema. Recent articles have appeared in *English Studies in Canada* and *Historical Materialism.*

GREGORY CANNING has taught film history and theory at both Cape Breton University and Mount Saint Vincent University. He has a Masters of Arts in history from Saint Mary's University, with a thesis on American cinema during the Great Depression and the role of censorship through the Hays Office during this period. His research interests continue in early film exhibition and in the American cinema, looking at censorship as well as in the exhibition of American films, and he is currently a PhD candidate in the Interdisciplinary program at Dalhousie University.

NOREEN GOLFMAN is Professor of English and Dean of Graduate Studies at Memorial University of Newfoundland, where she teaches film studies, critical theory, and Canadian literature. She has been a regular film columnist (*Canadian Forum*) and presently writes an arts column ("Standing Room Only") for *The Independent* newspaper published in St. John's. She is also Vice Chair of the Newfoundland and Labrador Film Development Corporation and, among other subjects, has written about the development of regional film.

SYLVIA D. HAMILTON is a Nova Scotian filmmaker and writer. Her first film, *Black Mother Black Daughter*, has been seen in over forty film festivals throughout North America and Europe, and her films have gone on to win awards and be screened in festivals in Canada, the United States, Europe, and the Caribbean. *Speak It! From the Heart of Black Nova Scotia* received both the 1994 Maeda Prize awarded by the NHK-Japan Broadcasting Corporation, and a 1994 Gemini Award. *Portia White: Think On Me*, is a documentary about the extraordinary Canadian contralto who was known as Canada's Marian Anderson. It has been widely broadcast on VisionTV, BRAVO! and national and regional CBC TV. Her writing (literary and non-fiction) has appeared in a variety of Canadian journals and anthologies. She was a contributor to and co-editor of *We're Rooted Here and They Can't Pull Us Up: Essays in African Canadian Women's History*, published by the University of Toronto Press in 1993.

COLIN HOWELL is an Atlantic Provinces historian with an interest in cultural production and borderland studies. He is a professor of history at Saint Mary's University and Executive Director of the Gorsebrook Research Institute. His most recent book is entitled *Blood, Sweat and Cheers: Sport and the Making of Modern Canada (University of Toronto Press, 2001)*.

MALEK KHOURI is an associate professor of film studies in the Faculty of Communication and Culture at the University of Calgary. He is the author of *Filming Politics: Communism and the Portrayal of the Working Class at the National Film Board of Canada, 1939–49* (University of Calgary Press, 2007), and co-editor with Darrell Varga of *Working on Screen: Representations of the Working Class in Canadian Cinema* (University of Toronto Press, 2006). Khouri's forthcoming book is titled *Liberation and Identity: Arab National Project in Youssef Chahine's Cinema*. He is currently studying aspects of queer representations in contemporary Arab cinemas.

JOHN MCCULLOUGH teaches in the Department of Film at York University. He has a PhD in Social and Political Thought and was the first coordinator of the graduate programs in Interdisciplinary Studies in Fine Arts at the University of Regina. His current research includes analysis of popular Hollywood films, Canadian regional television production, and contemporary indigenous and First Nations film and television.

SHANA MCGUIRE is a PhD candidate in French at Dalhousie University in Halifax, Nova Scotia. Her doctoral research, funded by both the Killam Foundation and the Social Sciences and Humanities Research Council, examines representations of the body in contemporary French cinema, namely in the films of Catherine Breillat, Claire Denis, and Bruno Dumont. She has taught Film Studies at Mount Saint Vincent University and at NSCAD University.

PETER L. TWOHIG is Canada Research Chair in Atlantic Canada Studies at Saint Mary's University. He is particularly interested in representations of region in various media and how they have changed over time. His most recent book is *Labour in the Laboratory* (McGill-Queen's University Press, 2005).

JEN VANDERBURGH is a postdoctoral fellow in the Film Department at Queen's University (Kingston), where she is researching television archives as forms of national heritage. Jen is also writing a book on how television technology has shaped cities, and how the representation and construction of national identity is explored in television content through urban shot locations.

DARRELL VARGA is Canada Research Chair in Contemporary Film and Media Studies at NSCAD University (Nova Scotia College of Art and Design), where he teaches film studies and is the chair of the Halifax inter-university film studies program. He is the editor, with Malek Khouri, of *Working on Screen: Representations of the Working Class in Canadian Cinema* (University of Toronto Press, 2006), and author of numerous essays on Canadian and other cinemas.

PIERRE VÉRONNEAU began working at the Cinémathèque québécoise in 1973 and has been the Curator of Quebecois and Canadian Cinema since November 2002. He is an associate professor at the University of Montreal and at the University of Quebec in Montreal and also lectures regularly at Concordia University. He is a member of GRAFICS (Groupe de recherche sur l'avènement et la formation des institutions cinématographique et scénique/Research Group on the Beginnings and the Formation of the Cinema and Theatrical Institutions) and sits on the editorial board of the journal *Cinémas* and other professional associations. He is the author of several books on Canadian film and television, including *David Cronenberg: la beauté du chaos* (2003), *Répertoire des séries, feuilletons et téléromans québécois de 1952 à 1992* (1993), *Résistance et affirmation : la production francophone à l'ONF 1939–1964* (1987), as well as numerous research articles.

JERRY WHITE is an associate professor and Director of Film Studies at the University of Alberta, and a member of the education staff of the Telluride Film Festival. He is co-editor of *North of Everything: English-Canadian Cinema Since 1980* (University of Alberta Press, 2002), editor of *The Cinema of Canada* (Wallflower Press, 2006), and author of *Of This Place and Elsewhere: The Films and Photography of Peter Mettler* (Toronto Film Festival/Indiana University Press, 2006) and *Jean-Luc Godard and Anne-Marie Miéville* (University of Illinois Press, forthcoming, 2009).

TRACY ZHANG is a PhD candidate in the School of Communication, Simon Fraser University, Canada. Her research interests include cultural economy, cultural policy, and cultural resistance. She received her MA in International Development Studies from Dalhousie University, where her thesis focused on the history of the Halifax grassroots film and video. Currently, her dissertation is concerned with the interplay of cultural production and globalization in the case of the Tibetan carpet industry.

INDEX

W

Wakeham, Bob, 67, 79
Walker, James W. St. G., 285n7
Wallace, Keith, 194n1
Waller, Gregory A., 47, 49, 50
Walsh, Mary, 157, 241
Warrendale, 105
Washington, DC, 266
Washington Post, 120
Waugh, Thomas, 110, 118, 222
Wedderburn, Gus, 12
A Wedding and a Party, 119, 121, 123, 124
Weiner, Lawrence, 199
Wells, William, "Billy," 114–16
west coast, xiv
Whale Hunting/Qilaluqaniatut, 129n45
Wheeler, Ann, 237
When I Go..., 111
White Hills, 241
White, Jerry, xv, xvii, 81n6, 180
White, Portia May, xix, xx, 259, 260–83
    Portia White Prize, 259
    Portia White Trust, 259
    William Andrew White (father), 264
White, Shirley A., 128n19
White Thunder, 72, 74–77, 80
Whitney, Sir James, 56
William Wells Talks About the Island, 114
Williams, Raymond, xx, 132, 155
Wind at My Back, 145
Winds of Fogo, 114–17, 121, 122
Winnipeg, 270, 280
Wollen, Peter, 122
A Woman's Place, 123

Wonderland, 55, 56
Wood, Robin, 243
working class, xviii, 1, 8, 86, 89, 97, 99, 134, 140, 226, 227
Working on Screen, 100n6
World Trade Organization (WTO), 153
World War I, 62, 70, 264
World War II, 4, 88
        post-war, 172, 185
A World Without Shadows, 12
Wormwood's Monkey Theatre, 51
Would You Like to Smell My... Pocket Crumbs, 236
Wright, Janet, 157
Writer's Guild of Canada, 15
Wurlitzer, Rudy, 235, 247
Wyse, Russell, 14

Y

Y'a du bois dans ma cour, 25
Yale Falls, 70
Yarmouth, 51
Yellowknife, 40
YMCA, 49, 54
Young Triffie's Been Made Away With, 157
Young Woman at her Toilette, 209
Yuill, Charles Frederick Harry, 60

Z

Zeats, Chief of Police, 56
Zhang, Tracy, xv, xviii
Zion African Baptist Church, 264